TOURISM AND DEVELOPMENT

Tourism and Development

A Case Study of the Commonwealth Caribbean

JOHN M. BRYDEN
Overseas Development Group, University of East Anglia

CAMBRIDGE : AT THE UNIVERSITY PRESS 1973

Published by the Syndics of the Cambridge University Press
Bentley House, 200 Euston Road, London NW1 2DB
American Branch: 32 East 57th Street, New York, N.Y. 10022

© Cambridge University Press 1973

Library of Congress Catalogue Card Number: L73−77260

ISBN: 0 521 20263 9

Set in cold type by E.W.C. Wilkins Ltd.,
London and Printed in Great Britain
by Redwood Press Limited, Trowbridge, Wiltshire

CONTENTS

TABLES AND APPENDICES

ACKNOWLEDGEMENTS

The text of this book is substantially the same as that of a thesis submitted in part-fulfilment of the requirements of a Ph.d degree at the University of East Anglia.

A list of all those who have, in one way or another, helped me in the production of this study would be too long to reproduce here and I can only attempt to mention by name a few persons and organisations without whose help and encouragement it would not have been possible to complete it. The accuracy of the facts presented, and the use made of them, of course remain my own responsibility.

The subject of the study would not, in all probability, have suggested itself to me as being important had it not been for the early influence of Professor George Houston of the University of Glasgow and Professor David Edwards of the University of the West Indies. Much of the factual information which is embodied in the study would not have been collected had not the then Ministry of Overseas Development (U.K.) financed me directly or indirectly in the West Indies for various periods during the years 1965 to 1970. Nor would the results have been written up without the help and encouragement of my supervisors, Professor Athole Mackintosh and Mr Michael Faber.

I am also much indebted to my friends and colleagues at the University of East Anglia, four of whom deserve particular mention. Dr Keith Hart, now at the University of Manchester, and his wife Nicky Hart, discussed many of the ideas developed in this study with me from its inception in 1970. Mr Christopher Edwards also made some valuable comments on an earlier draft of Chapter 5, which discusses some of the methodological issues inherent in this kind of study. Finally, Mr Ian Gillespie gave me valuable assistance in the computational problems which arose in Part IV.

The calculations, which were many, and the work connected with the preparation of data for computer analysis were largely done by Miss Jacquie Guymer, Miss Diane Wyatt and Mrs Janet Hooper, while the typing of the numerous drafts was expertly executed by Mrs Jennifer Robbie, Miss Anne Buck, Mrs Dorothy Browning and Mrs Diana Armour.

The notes and references in the text will make clear the extent of my indebtedness to other writers.

Finally, it goes without saying that the study could never have been completed without the tolerance of my wife, Elspeth.

J.M.B.
December 1972

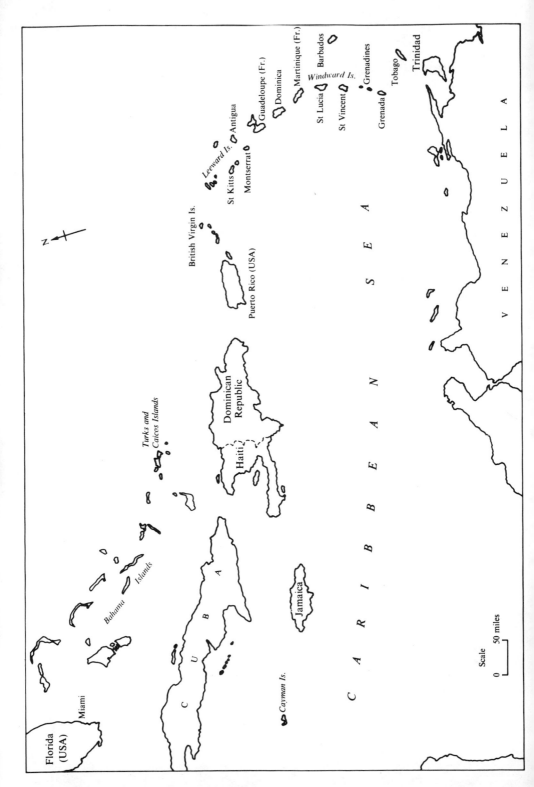

1 *Introduction*

Michael Peters, whose book on international tourism is the most comprehensive work recently published on the subject, wrote:

> The economic gap between rich and poor countries has widened over the past ten years. But to create new industries and to transform rural life in Asian, African and Latin American countries is a gigantic task. The relevance of tourism to this situation is that income from international travel can bring the foreign exchange essential for major investment. There is a widespread awareness of the potential benefits, but little has been done in practice to provide the means for expansion of tourism plant in most of the developing areas of the world.[1]

The 'potential benefits' to developing countries may be apparent to many, but discussion of them is invariably confused. Proponents of tourist expansion in developing countries point to the foreign exchange receipts generated by tourism, or at a more sophisticated level, to the impact of these foreign exchange receipts on gross domestic product either directly, or through the operation of the expenditure multiplier.[2] Critics of tourist expansion, on the other hand, point to the various social strains which are caused by tourist development, examples being the distortion of indigenous cultural expressions,[3] the conversion of small farmers into wage labourers due to the high land prices which tourism creates and associated alienation of land,[4] perpetuation of racial inequalities and the erosion of dignity.[5] The implication of this style of critism is that, whatever the economic benefits, these largely unquantifiable costs are of sufficient weight to argue against further expansion of tourism in the countries concerned.

However, it seems that these criticisms have had little impact on planners and politicians in developing countries, since many development plans contain explicit reference to the need to expand the tourist sectors. In some instances they have

---

1 Peters (1969), p. 10.

2 The expenditure multiplier is explained in Chapter 5.

3 Such an approach is to be found in Naipaul (1962), and Ban it Chiu in *Leisure-Tourism: Threat and Promise,* World Council of Churches, Geneva, 1970. See also Chapter 5.

4 Raymond, Monsieur, quoted in *Leisure-Tourism,* World Council of Churches (1970); Demas (1970), Watty (1970.

5 Howard (1971), Taylor (1970), Demas (1970).

influenced policy, nevertheless. President Nyerere of Tanzania, for example, has suggested that tourism is a necessary evil but that tourists must be isolated from the population.[6]

The Catholic Church, the International Union of Official Travel Organisations, Michael Peters, and most other western writers and consultants on the subject consider the social impact of tourism in ethnocentric terms. Social effects are normally discussed exclusively in terms of the *benefit to tourists* themselves, through seeing and meeting foreigners, through the favourable moral effect of:

> subjecting oneself, joyfully or sorrowfully, to the inconveniences great and small which can with difficulty be avoided, even on the best organised tours; making contact with habits, traditions, convictions and prejudices which are completely foreign to one's ordinary mentality.[7]

Whether such benefits for tourists exist is not our concern. It is no part of a developing country's responsibility to provide benefits to the wealthier inhabitants of developed countries who make up the bulk of the tourist market.

Economic costs associated with tourist development have received scant attention in the literature. Many have admitted the presence of such costs — but the general impression given is that they are negligible in comparison to the benefits. Still rarer are studies which attempt to measure the costs and benefits of tourist development in terms of social opportunity costs and returns. In fact, I know of no such study in any country.[8]

It is the purpose of this study to attempt such a reconciliation of costs and benefits, to examine the social aspects of tourism, and to consider the dynamic impact of the tourist sector. Emphasis will be placed on the likely impact of tourism in the existing institutional and political context, rather than on 'potential'. The distinction is important where the 'context' is such that a 'potential' is unlikely to be realised. This argument has its parallel in the controversy about the relevance of classical trade theory for developing countries and the distinction between actual and potential gains from trade.[9]

The particular context chosen is that of the smaller islands of the Commonwealth Caribbean. These are examples of developing countries which have already gone some considerable way in expanding their tourist sectors, which have invested public money in tourist infrastructure and promotion, which have passed laws governing incentives and other features of tourist development, and which have suffered in some degree the social and economic costs associated with tourism. It could be argued that the Caribbean countries may not provide an 'ideal' case study, if such a thing exists. They have a higher average per capita income than most developing countries. They are also extremely 'open' economies, with

---

6   Nyerere, Essay on Tourism in the House Magazine of the National Development Corporation, Dar es Salaam, Tanzania. I am indebted to Mr. David Feldman for this reference.

7   Pope Pius XII. Speech to the Directors of Italian Tourist Organisations, 30 March 1952.

8   Frank Mitchell has published a report called *The Costs and Benefits of Tourism in Kenya* for the Kenya Tourist Development Corporation. However, this does not contain a cost–benefit analysis in the accepted sense of the term (Mitchell, 1968).

9   See, for example, Singer (1950); Meir (1958); and Myint (1954–5).

exports (inclusive of tourist receipts) and imports forming a very high proportion of gross domestic product. Their population is small by any standard, even in the aggregate and individual islands often have fewer than 100,000 inhabitants. Finally, the history of slavery in the region may influence the nature of the social problems.

But there are many features which these islands do have in common with other developing countries. The reliance on export markets in industrial countries is not confined to small developing countries.[10] The small internal market and limitations regarding import substitution possibilities again are hard facts of life for many countries far larger than those in the Caribbean.[11] Population growth is fairly rapid in most Caribbean islands, and in some instances there appears to be growing unemployment in spite of relatively high rates of growth of gross domestic product.[12] This has been suggested as a fairly common situation in many developing countries, though there is a good deal of controversy surrounding such assertions.[13] Property, land and incomes are unevenly distributed to a degree noticed by the most casual observer. Agriculture is still an important source of income and occupation, though food production for domestic consumption has shown little sign of growth. Finally, there are common strands of history: colonial rule by a metropolitan power, racial conflict, and the division of economic and political power. It is therefore suggested that the information presented and the method of investigation used here may have some relevance for other developing countries which have embarked, or are proposing to embark, upon a tourist development programme.

The context of the study — the Commonwealth Caribbean — is the concern of Part I, since it is necessary to consider any activity in the light of the political and economic framework within which it takes place. What is socially profitable (or socially acceptable) in one country need not be in another. The readiness of the Caribbean governments to develop their tourist sectors can only be understood in turns of the political background of dependence and isolation from one another, and in terms of the very limited economic possibilities with which they are faced.

If tourism cannot be considered out of context, it is also true that Caribbean tourism cannot be viewed without some attention being given to the general phenomenon of tourism in the context of the developing world as a whole. Conventional theory, which appears to be at the root of much recent interest in the

---

10 Indeed, in most general text books on the subject it is cited as a general feature of developing countries.

11 In many very much larger countries the limits to import-substitution appear to be very close. See, for example, Little, Scitovsky and Scott (1970).

12 See, for example, Seers (1969).

13 Singer (1971) and Reynolds (1969: esp. pp. 95—7 and p. 101) suggest that growing unemployment is a common feature in developing countries. However this assertion has been challenged by Weeks (1971). Weeks correctly points out the difficulties of measuring and defining unemployment in developing countries.

possibilities offered by tourist development, runs approximately as follows.[14] Developing countries are faced with marketing problems in traditional exports and with secular declines in their terms of trade. These features arise because of the slow growth in demand,[15] the shift in the 'centre' of industrial production from Europe to the USA and the USSR,[16] competition from domestic protection of agriculture in industrial countries or synthetic substitutes,[17] and attempts by developing countries to increase export earnings by increasing their share of the slowly-growing market,[18] or because of structural differences between the developing and already industrialised nations which cause productivity increases in the latter to be captured by higher wages, whereas in the former productivity increases are followed only by lower prices.[19] Furthermore, attempts to diversify out of traditional agricultural exports into exports of manufactures are very largely frustrated because of the tariff policies of the industrial countries and limited domestic markets of developing countries. Tourism, on the other hand, appears to be subject to very different demand conditions. It is a rapidly growing industry, having a high income-elasticity of demand.[20] It seems to be less amenable to the operation of restrictions by industrial countries, although restrictions are not unknown.[21] The vested interests in industrial countries who might lose by an expansion of international tourism are perhaps less entrenched, less vocal, than is the case with agricultural producers or manufacturers. Perhaps also there are considerable vested interests in industrial countries who stand to gain from an expansion of international tourism.[22] Finally, the limitation of tourism, by currency restriction or passport control, is perhaps a more obvious restriction of individual 'freedom' than a restriction of the availability of developing countries' exports.

It is thus of some interest to examine the flows of international tourists and tourist expenditures, and in particular the flows to developing countries. The growth in Caribbean tourism may then be seen in the context of a phenomenon

14 Most international aid agencies, together with the World Bank, have recently become increasingly interested in tourism, while there are few development plans which do not refer to it in some form.

15 Engel's law and the effect of raw-material-saving technical progress.

16 Nurkse (1959).

17 Johnson (1967).

18 This result is possible under certain conditions regarding initial market shares and elasticities of demand and supply, at least in the short run.

19 The 'Prebisch thesis'. See, for example, Prebisch (1963).

20 The IUOTO has suggested a general income elasticity of demand for foreign travel of 1·5 although this 'would not, by itself, be enough to explain the growth of world tourism over the past thirteen years', IUOTO, 'Study of the Economic Impact of Tourism', 1966, p. 15.

21 For example restricted availability of foreign currency and traveller's cheques — a method used from time to time by the UK.

22 Especially international airlines, tour operators and travel agents.

which is of increasing importance and significance for many developing countries. Part II examines the global pattern of tourism, and views development in the Caribbean as part of this pattern. But the growth in tourist receipts tells us nothing about the economic and social benefits of tourism. The analysis of the apparent significance of tourism for developing countries is therefore followed by a discussion of the appropriate methodology for attempting to measure the economic and social impact of tourism in the context of developing countries, especially in the light of the paucity of previous approaches to this problem.

In Part III we move from the general context to the particular. The growth and structure of the tourist industry in the Commonwealth Caribbean over the last decade is examined, and the methods and sources for the statistical data used are discussed. Although tourism in all its aspects is considered at this stage, it is the hotel industry which has been responsible for most of the recent growth in tourist numbers and foreign exchange receipts from tourism in the smaller islands of the Commonwealth Caribbean. It is to this sector that most government policies concerned with the development of tourism have been directed. Subsequent analysis therefore concentrates on the impact of this sector, on the short term 'multiplier' effects of the outputs and on the longer term social costs and benefits of the allocation of resources implied by a commitment to its expansion. Some care is taken therefore to examine the hotels sector in terms of an input—output framework and the factors affecting the input—output coefficients of this sector in the Caribbean context.

Part IV turns to the analysis of the data presented in Part III; first by an examination of the concept and likely magnitude of the expenditure multiplier, then through an analysis of the factors affecting the size of this multiplier. But in the discussion of methodology it is argued that the multiplier cannot be used as a reliable indicator of the benefits to be derived from tourism except under very restrictive assumptions which are unlikely to be met in the real world.

An alternative framework of analysis is therefore required in order to assess the impact of tourism. Following the arguments on methodology the framework adopted is that of social cost—benefit analysis. Taking into account private and public costs associated with hotel development, and the adjustments to market prices which require to be made to reflect the use and availability of real resources, it is suggested that, on the information available, an adequate analysis of the benefits from tourism indicates rather low net social benefits in the present situation of the smaller Caribbean islands. These rather low net social benefits contrast with fairly reasonable rates of private benefit to hotel investors.

The framework proposed has a number of uses which should enable a more reasoned and consistent approach to be made to the problem of tourist development in the Caribbean, and is possibly not without potential for application in other developing countries. One use lies in the appraisal of the various proposals which have been published recently regarding future resource allocation in the field of tourism. Two such proposals are contained in the *Tripartite Economic Survey of the Eastern Caribbean,* and the *Zinder Report.*[23] The recommendations

23 *Tripartite Economic Survey of the Eastern Caribbean,* HMSO, 1966. Henceforward
referred to as the *Tripartite Survey* (1966). *The Future of Tourism in the Eastern Caribbean,*
H. Zinder and Associates, Inc., under contract with US AID and sponsored by the Regional
Development Agency, May 1969. Henceforward referred to as the *Zinder Report.*

of these reports are subjected to a cost—benefit analysis which indicates that even on their own assumptions, they were rather over-optimistic regarding the benefits to be derived from future tourism development in the Caribbean.

A second use of the analytical framework presented lies in its capacity to generate policy conclusions. For example, the variation of assumptions allows one to trace the principal features of Caribbean tourism which lie behind the low social rate of return, and hence suggests various policy measures which could, if implemented, serve to raise the net social benefits of tourism. This is further explored in Part V, which also contains a summary of the study and an attempt to draw together some ideas on the nature of the inter-relationships between the 'economic' and 'social' impact of tourism.

An understanding of these inter-relationships is, in the view of the present writer, essential to an understanding of the effects of tourism on people, and some preliminary comments would seem to be in order. It is useful to make the distinction between 'pecuniary' and 'non-pecuniary' costs and benefits,[24] so long as these are not regarded as being wholly independent phenomena, the study of which properly 'belongs' to quite separate disciplines. The purpose of such a distinction is to avoid the confusion between what economists normally call 'social costs', meaning in general the opportunity cost to society at large, and what other disciplines usually understand by the term 'social costs', meaning in general those costs (or benefits) not normally measured or analysed by economists! In most of the discussion of tourism to date, the benefits are usually described (albeit inadequately) in pecuniary terms while the costs are commonly expressed in non-pecuniary or transcendental terms. As an analytical framework for the examination of the impact of tourism on society, it is argued that this is inadequate and leads to confusion.

24 Another dichotomy could be between 'transcendental' and 'material' costs and benefits.

PART I

The context: the Commonwealth Caribbean*

* As pointed out in the Introduction, this study is largely based on the smaller
islands of the Commonwealth Caribbean – Grenada, St. Vincent, St Lucia, Dominica
(The Windward Islands), Antigua, Montserrat and St Kitts (The Leeward Islands);
The British Virgin Islands, Cayman Islands, Turks and Caicos (which will be referred
to as the 'Northern Group'); and Barbados. However, wherever possible, reference
will be made in the statistical tables to Jamaica, Trinidad and the Bahamas, which
together with the smaller islands described make up what will be termed as the
'Commonwealth Caribbean'.

2   *Political structure and resources*

The purpose of this chapter is to examine the political and resource framework of the Commonwealth Caribbean, and the changes which have taken place in recent years, with particular reference to the smaller territories of the region. Although the general picture which emerges differs little from that given by other studies of the region, in particular those by Demas and O'Loughlin, the introduction of additional hitherto unpublished information enables a somewhat more quantitative approach to be taken so far as the smaller islands are concerned.[1] The period covered by this information is by and large the period over which the growth of the tourist industry will be analysed, and consequently permits the examination of relationships between growth and structural change in the economy at large and the growth of the tourist sector. Finally, an important part of the subsequent argument of this study depends on an acceptance of the general picture presented in this chapter, and in Chapter 3.

There is general agreement that the economies of the Commonwealth Caribbean are both very small and extremely 'open' in their relationships with the rest of the world. The openness — which has been described in both structural and functional terms[2] — is mainly a consequence of size and location, but is partly also the result of historical and political factors, particularly the colonial relationship and the political fragmentation of the region. Before turning to the effects of openness *per se*, the recent political changes which have taken place in the region will be discussed.

The political context

Although by 1970 all the territories of the Commonwealth Caribbean were separate political and administrative entities, at the beginning of the decade there was an almost united federal structure. The West Indian Federation, as it was known, included all of the islands in the region with the exception of the Cayman Islands, the British Virgin Islands and the Bahamas, and was established following the Federal elections in 1958. Fraught from the start with political difficulties, and unable to reach agreement on vital economic issues such as customs union, the zoning of industrial development, and the financing of the regional government, the Federation had no long term basis for survival. Jamaica left the Federation after a referendum in 1961, and Trinidad and Tobago announced its intention of

1   Demas (1965), O'Loughlin (1968).

2   Demas (1965), p. 62.

seeking independence alone, outside the Federal structure. The smaller islands of the Windwards, the Leewards and Barbados prepared to form another federation (the 'Little Eight' as it became known).[3] However, Grenada withdrew from the discussions surrounding this proposal after the 1962 elections in which the main issue of the victorious party was statehood with Trinidad.[4] Eventually, and again mainly because of conflicts over economic issues in particular, arrangements for financing the new Federation and the unwillingness of the British Government to underwrite a capital programme which was suggested as being necessary in order to achieve internal economic and 'financial viability',[5] negotiations ceased in 1965 when the conference of the Regional Council of Ministers broke up, and Barbados resolved to seek constitutional advance alone.[6]

By the middle of the decade, then, Jamaica and Trinidad had become independent states within the Commonwealth, with Barbados following in 1966. The remaining territories in the region were still Crown colonies with Administrators acting as Chairmen of Executive Councils (Cabinets) and normally having overall responsibility for the civil service, finance, external affairs and defence, and the police.[7]

At the end of 1965 yet another White Paper was prepared which laid the foundation for the constitutional advance of Antigua, St Kitts—Nevis, Anguilla, Dominica, St Lucia, St Vincent and Grenada.[8] The constitutional status was termed 'associated statehood', and was adopted by Antigua, St Kitts, Dominica, St Lucia and Grenada in 1966, and by St Vincent in 1969. Associated statehood is widely regarded as a compromise solution to the constitutional problems of the small islands, involving as it does full internal self-government with the exception of foreign affairs and defence which remain the responsibility of the United Kingdom government.

More recently, two notable regional associations have been formed, despite the legacy of bitterness following the break up of the Federation, so passionately described by Lewis.[9] These are the Caribbean Free Trade Area (CARIFTA) and the

3 Details of these proposals were given in a White Paper, Cmnd. 1746, HMSO, 1962.

4 Mr Herbert Blaize led the winning party which narrowly defeated that led by Mr Gairy. The statehood was not forthcoming, however, and Mr Gairy was returned to power in 1967.

5 'Viability' was mainly conceived in terms of independence from recurrent grants-in-aid from the UK Government, control over which gave the UK substantial powers of interference in financial policies. The size of the proposed programme was very largely confirmed by the later *Tripartite Economic Survey of the Eastern Caribbean*, 1966.

6 The reasons for the collapse of the federal idea have been analysed by scholars such as Lewis (1965), O'Loughlin (1968), and Mordecai (1968), all of whom were closely involved at the time. It would be impertinence — and beyond the scope of this study — to attempt to do more than present a very brief summary of what appear to the author to be the key issues.

7 For a further discussion see Mills (1970A) and Urias Forbes (1970).

8 Constitutional Proposals for Antigua, St Kitts—Nevis—Anguilla, Dominica, St Lucia, St Vincent and Grenada. Cmnd. 2865, HMSO, 1965, later embodied in the West Indies Act of 1967 and the various Constitution Orders.

9 Lewis (1965).

Regional Development Bank.[10]

The functioning and impact of these associations affect the arguments of this study very little, and there is in any case little evidence to date of their impact on the smaller islands. The general feeling of economists in the region seems to be that CARIFTA offers very little — if anything — to the smaller islands and is heavily biased in favour of the larger territories, particularly in respect of manufacturing.[11] Indeed, the most recent move towards unity in the Caribbean — the Declaration of Grenada — was thought by some observers to be partly the result of the failure of the smaller islands to achieve any substantial gain from CARIFTA.[12] The Regional Bank had not yet started to function properly at the time of writing.

The political context, then, is still one of fragmented independent or quasi-independent nation states, in spite of several important and significant moves towards greater regionalism, and it is within this context that the problems of the smaller territories must be viewed.

Size, population and natural resources

Many, if not most, of these problems arise from considerations of size. Table 2.1 below gives some indication of the natural resource base and the size and growth of population in the various territories.

Four territories in the group have populations of less than 20,000. A further five have populations between 50,000 and 100,000, four have between 100,000 and 1,000,000, and only one, Jamaica, has over 1,000,000 inhabitants.

At the same time, population density is high in most territories, all but four having densities in excess of 250 persons per square mile.[13] Natural rates of population increase range from just under 2 per cent to as high as 3·3 per cent annually[14] in the group, while actual rates of increase have historically tended to be lower than this in most of the territories owing to net emigration from the region. Net immigration has occurred in the British Virgin Islands and the Cayman Islands in the latter half of the decade, but this is a recent phenomenon due to the existence of labour shortages and relatively high wage rates. Migration outlets from the region as a whole have been severely curtailed during the decade owing to restrictions imposed by the UK government, and this implies that actual rates of population increase have tended to be much closer to natural rates than was previously the case.

10 The CARIFTA Agreement was originally signed on 15 December 1965 by Antigua, Barbados and Guyana. A Supplementary Agreement was signed during March 1968. Subsequently the original signatories were joined by Trinidad and Tobago, Jamaica, and the remaining Windwards and Leewards.

11 See, for example, Yankey and Watty (1969).

12 The Declaration of Grenada was signed on 1 November 1971 by Dominica, Grenada, St Lucia, St Vincent, St Kitts–Nevis and Guyana. St Lucia has since withdrawn support; Trinidad decided not to participate. *Financial Times,* 2 December 1971.

13 See also Smith, (1967).

14 On St Vincent, see also Bryne (1969).

Table 2.1 *Population, land area, population density and population growth rates in the Commonwealth Caribbean*

	Population estimates 1965[a] 000	Land area in square miles	Population density per square mile	Historic rate of growth of population % per annum[b]
Grenada	102·3	133	780	2·9
St Vincent	99·4	150	635	3·0
St Lucia	97·8	238	410	2·6
Dominica	67·7	305	222	2·5
Antigua	53·9[c]	171	315	0·0
Montserrat	13·2	32	412	1·7
St Kitts	64·2	152	423	2·5
Barbados	244·2[c]	166	1,472	2.5[e]
British Virgin Is.	9·3	59	158	
Cayman Islands	9·0	100	90	
Turks and Caicos	7·0			
Jamaica	1,630·0[d]	4,411	370	3.3[e]
Trinidad and Tobago	859·0[d]	1,980	418	3.1[e]
Bahamas	134·0	4,400	34	n.a.

Notes and sources:

[a] Sources for population data, *Economic Surveys and Projections* (various territories), British Development Division in the Caribbean. Demas (1965) p. 97. *Tripartite Economic Survey of the Eastern Caribbean.*

[b] Except where noted, estimated rates of increase 1961–5, *de facto* population.

[c] End of 1964, data from *Tripartite Economic Survey.*

[d] 1961 data from Demas (1965).

[e] Natural rate of increase for 1960 excluding net migration. Actual rates not available.

Land resources in the region are limited in absolute terms as well as in relation to population. In terms of cultivable land, resources are generally even more limited since many of the smaller coral islands[15] lack both an adequate topsoil and rainfall, while many of the volcanic islands (e.g. Dominica and the other Windward Islands) suffer from extremes of rainfall in their interiors (up to 350 inches per annum in Dominica) together with a steep terrain and severe problems of erosion from surface run-off where cover has been removed. Figures relating to 'cultivable land' are not generally available in the region, but according to O'Loughlin, the area of land in farms at the 1961 census gives a fair guide to the area of cultivable land with the exception of Dominica and possibly St Lucia where much of the interior is inaccessible.[16] As Table 2.2 shows, a fairly high proportion of the total land area in the islands was farmed in 1961, the main exceptions being the Windward Islands with their rugged volcanic terrain.

In Montserrat and Barbados a very high proportion of land was in farms, while in St Vincent, Dominica and Antigua the proportion was much lower. In St Vincent and Dominica, physical factors are important in preventing access and use of land while in Antigua low rainfall has been one of the factors affecting agricultural potential — the area of land in farms fell from 49,000 acres in 1946 to

15 For example, those of the Bahamas, the Cayman Islands, Anegada in the British Virgin Islands, and Barbuda in the Leewards.

16 O'Loughlin (1968).

Table 2.2 *Population in relation to total land area and area of land in farms at 1961 census E. Caribbean*

	Area of land in farms, acres 1961	Area of farmed land as a proportion of total land area 1961 %	Population per '000 acres total land area	Population per 100 acres of farmed land 1964
Grenada	60,197	71	110·72	155·57
St Vincent	39,475	41	83·22	224·72
St Lucia	87,375	58	62·36	106·44
Dominica	76,163	39	33·76	86·53
Antigua	34,089	31	54·57	174·19
St Kitts	50,504	52	60·57	117·42
Montserrat	17,418	85	65·91	77·50
Barbados	84,458	79	229·80	289·10

Source:
Derived from O'Loughlin (1968), Table 7, p. 66.

34,000 acres in 1961, and continued to decline during the 1960s.[17]

A further aspect of the limited land area in the region is the absence and uneven distribution of mineral and sub-surface resources which might serve as inputs to manufacturing industry. Bauxite occurs in Jamaica in commercially exploitable quantities, while oil, natural gas and pitch are mined in Trinidad. Barbados has same natural gas but elsewhere in the region minerals are either in quantities or of types which do not yet justify commercial exploitation, or, as with pumice in Dominica, are in minor deposits the life of which is limited and which would not justify the establishment of further processing plant. Oil exploration concessions relating to continental shelves in the Bahamas, the British Virgin Islands, the Cayman Islands and Jamaica have been granted or are under consideration, but most of these operations are yet to proceed. Copper and molybdenite occur in the British Virgin Islands where they were mined in the eighteenth century, but although several small organisations have been given exploration concessions, little firm information on prospects is available, and it is unlikely that the resources will be extensive if commercially workable at all. Forestry resources are also limited in the islands, with the possible exception of Dominica where commercial exploitation of natural forest cover has recently commenced.[18] However, in most of the islands of the region deforestation has been taken too far with adverse consequences on both climate and soil cover.[19]

Not only is land limited absolutely, and unevenly distributed regionally; it is also unevenly distributed within the individual islands. In the Eastern Caribbean region as a whole[20] just over 60 per cent of the total area of land in farms was in

17 See also Campbell and Edwards (1965) and Chapter 3 below.

18 The concession was granted to a Canadian concern, and operations commenced in 1968.

19 For an excellent discussion of resources, including timber, in the region, see Lowenthal (1960).

20 The Windwards, Leewards and Barbados are referred to collectively as the Eastern Caribbean.

rms of over 100 acres, while these farms represented under 1 per cent of the total number of farms. Conversely, 89 per cent of the farms were in the size group 0 to 5 acres, and these accounted for only 17 per cent of the land area in farms.[21]

Although this does not give a true picture of land ownership, owing to multiple ownership of farms, and the prevalence of tenant farming in some islands, it is indicative of the general situation. There is a sharp dichotomy between the plantation agriculture, mainly on farms above 100 acres, and the peasant agriculture which is mainly on farms below 20 acres. Generally speaking, the former specialise almost exclusively in export crops while the latter usually produce foodstuffs for domestic consumption as well as export crops. Small farmers are extremely important in banana production in the Windward Islands, and much of the spectacular growth in banana output since the middle fifties has been due to the rapid acceptance of this crop by small farmers.[22]

Population, the labour force and employment

Any discussion of resources would be incomplete without consideration of the characteristics of the labour force in the Commonwealth Caribbean. Like other groups of resources used by economists, 'labour' is not a homogeneous category. Different sectors and different technologies within sectors use different categories of labour. Different categories of labour, in turn, have different opportunity costs. Thus at the 'macro' level if a new sector or industry competes directly with an existing sector or industry for categories of labour with positive opportunity costs, one would expect expansion of the new sector to be achieved only at some cost in terms of the output of the existing sector with given states of technique. In the later evaluation of the impact of tourism, it will be necessary to consider the extent to which the growth of this sector has involved declines in other sectors, and the extent to which this may be ascribed to competition for labour resources. At the 'micro' level, this relates to any discussion of what the appropriate 'shadow' wage should be in the evaluation of tourism and other projects.

The relation between the population as a whole and the size of the labour force is a complex one. In general, the population of working age is determined by the age structure of the population which, in turn, is a function of demographic characteristics and migration patterns. The population of working age is normally defined as the age group 15 to 64, but there is some argument for using 15 plus or even 10 plus in so far as age groups 10 to 15 and over 64 provide a significant proportion of the labour force.[23] The 'economically active' population consists of

---

21 *Tripartite Economic Survey,* Statistical Table No. 19.

22 Imports of bananas (including plantain) from the Windward Islands by the UK rose from just under 20,000 long tons in 1954 to about 90,000 long tons in 1960 and some 194,000 long tons in 1969, by which time they had secured about 55 per cent of the total UK market.
Source: *Annual Statements of the Trade of the United Kingdom,* HMSO.

23 Harewood uses 10 plus in his study of Trinidad, Harewood (1963); O'Loughlin suggests that about 1/5 of the school-age population were not enrolled in schools in Dominica and St Vincent, O'Loughlin (1968) p. 72. School-age children, enrolled or not, do provide assistance with crop harvests etc. but this is not generally recorded in census material.

14

the working population (those working for the whole or part of the year) together with those persons actively seeking employment.[24] The measure is thus designed to give some idea of the size of the available work force. That part of the population of working age which is economically inactive thus consists of housewives and single women or men who perform unremunerated domestic tasks; schoolchildren and students over 15 years of age; the sick, infirm and handicapped who are unable to work; certain categories of visitor included in the *de facto* population; and others who for one reason or another do not require 'work' as defined.[25]

The relationship between the economically active population and the total population is determined by demographic, social and economic factors. The principal demographic factors are the sex distribution and the age distribution of the working age population. As is common elsewhere, the participation rates of women are lower than for men,[26] while for both sexes they vary with age, being generally highest between the ages of 25 and 55. Female participation rates vary widely in the Commonwealth Caribbean — from below 20 per cent to nearly 50 per cent of the female working age population. The prevalence of marriage, common law unions,[27] and fertility rates are important social determinants of the female participation rates, while the availibility of suitable job opportunities for women is an important economic factor. Male participation rates are much more stable in the region as a whole, and generally vary only between 80 and 90 per cent. Variations in the overall participation rate are thus mainly 'explained' by variations in the female rate, which in turn are the result of a complex of demographic, social and economic factors.

Tables 2.3 and 2.4 below show some of these key relationships, and are mainly based on the West Indies Population census for 1960.

The principal sources of employment opportunities for women in the region are agriculture, commerce, services and light manufacturing where this is a significant activity. Hotels, guest houses and restaurants are important sources of employment for women within the services sector, and it would be surprising if the rapid growth in this sector in the region had not tended to reverse the trend towards lower female participation rates noted after the 1960 census. This has certainly occured in the Cayman Islands and the British Virgin Islands, for which

24 Harewood gives details of definitions and concepts employed in the West Indies Population Census of 1960. Harewood (1963) pp. 3–5.

25 According to Harewood, the 1960 census did not include 'subsistence' farmers with the economically active population, at any rate in Trinidad. Harewood (1963) p. 3.

26 Participation rates relate the economically active population to the population of working age.

27 Cumper notes higher participation rates for women in common law unions in 1946 (Cumper in Cumper (ed.) 1960 p. 161). This may be due to lower fertility rates in common law unions which were noted by Joycelin Bryne in St Vincent (Bryne 1969). Another reason for varying participation rates may be problems of enumeration — especially in agriculture, distribution and services where participation by women is often in non-wage or 'informal' activities, the enumeration of which presents considerable problems.

Table 2.3 *Population and the labour force: selected Commonwealth Caribbean Islands*

Islands and date	Total pop. (000)	Pop. 15 plus (000)	Economically active (000)	Working pop. (000)	Est. long-term unemployment (000)
Grenada (1960)	88·7	46·4	27·3	25·2	2·1
St Vincent (1960)	79·9	40·2	24·9	23·3E	1·6
St Lucia (1960	86·1	n.a.	31·4	n.a.	n.a.
Dominica (1960)	88·7	n.a.	23·4	n.a.	n.a.
Antigua (1960)	54·2	29·3[a]	18·2	17·5	2·3[b]
Montserrat (1960)	12·2	7·3[c]	4·3	n.a.	n.a.
St Kitts (1960)	56·7	32·0[c]	19·6	n.a.	n.a.
Barbados (1960)	232·3	n.a.	92·2	n.a.	n.a.
British Virgin Islands (1970)	10·5	n.a.	4·1	3·8	0·3[d]
Cayman Is. (1970)[f]	8·9	4·8[e]	3·2	3·1	0·1[d]
Jamaica (1960)	1,613·9	947·3	651·4	606·9	37·1
Trinidad and Tobago (1960)	828·0	467·9	278·1	262·6	15·5

E: Estimated
Notes:
[a] Age groups 15–69
[b] Total unemployment
[c] Age groups 14-plus
[d] Approximate
[e] Age groups 15–64
[f] Grand Cayman only
Sources:
Jamaica: Cumper (1964).
Trinidad: Harewood (1963).
Grenada: Harewood (1966).
St Vincent: Bryne (1969) and *Caribbean Statistical Yearbook* 1967, CODECA, Puerto Rico.
Antigua: Campbell and Edwards (1965).
British Virgin Islands: Elkan and Morley (1971).
Cayman Islands: Hart and Hart (1971).
All others: Caribbean Statistical Yearbook 1967. All figures for economically active population, with the exception of the Cayman Islands and the British Virgin Islands were also taken from this source.

manpower surveys were carried out in 1970 and 1971.[28]

If it is true that a major part of the employment created by tourism is for women who would not otherwise have found employment outside the home, then the problem of valuing the opportunity cost of this labour has to be faced. The fact that unremunerated domestic tasks do not feature in national income accounts is not a sufficient reason for treating such labour as 'costless'.[29]

For the economically active population as a whole, the structure of employment in the region is shown in table 2.5 below. The major sources of employment are thus agriculture and fishing, together with mining in Jamaica and Trinidad (20 to 45 per cent of the labour force in 1960), services (15 to 24 per cent).

28 The employment effects of tourism are discussed below in Chapter 7.

29 The problem of the appropriate shadow wage rate in these circumstances is considered in Chapter 5.

Table 2.4 *Participation rates in the Commonwealth Caribbean: selected territories*

Islands and date	Prop. of total pop. employed %	Prop. of pop. 15 plus %	Overall participation rate[a] %	Male participation rate[b] %	Female participation rate[c] %
Grenada (1960)	28·4	52·3	54·4	77·4	37·0
St Vincent (1960)	29·2	50·4	58·0	n.a.	n.a.
Antigua (1960)	32·3	54·0[d]	59·5[d]	83·0[d]	40·0[d]
Montserrat (1960)	32·8E	59·9[e]	59·5[e]	82·2[e]	44·0[e]
St Kitts (1960)	33·0E	56·5[e]	61·3[e]	84·2[e]	43·5[e]
British Virgin Islands (1970)	36·3	n.a.	n.a.	n.a.	n.a.
Cayman Is. (1970)	34·8	54·0	64·3	84·0[f]	44·5[f]
Jamaica (1960)	37·6	58·6	64·1	86·6	44·5
Trinidad and Tobago (1960)	31·8	57·6	55·2	81·9	28·4

E: Estimated

Notes:
[a] Unless otherwise stated, working population divided by population aged 15 plus.
[b] Unless otherwise stated, male working population divided by male population aged 15 plus.
[c] Unless otherwise stated, female working population divided by female population aged 15 plus.
[d] Datum is population (total, male, female respectively) aged 15 to 69.
[e] Datum is population aged 14 plus. Participation rates are calculated on the basis of the economically active population.
[f] Datum is the population aged 15 to 64. Figures refer to Grand Cayman only..
Sources: As for Table 2.3.

Table 2.5. *Economically active population by main industry: Commonwealth Caribbean.*

Sector	Windward Islands (1960) %	Leeward Islands (1960) %	Barbados (1960) %	Northern Group[d] (1960) %	Northern Group[d] (1970)[e] %	Jamaica (1960) %	Trinidad (1960) %
Primary[a]	44·7	42·0	24·9	19·8	5·9	39·8	24·6
Manufacturing[b]	11·4	12·4	14·9	7·7	3·6	15·3	16·5
Construction	10·1	10·4	9·7	13·3	30·0[f]	8·2	10·8
Commerce	9·5	8·8	16·0	5·9	18·8	9·9	12·6
Transport[c]	2·8	5·0	4·8	28·7	18·1	3·2	5·8
Services	14·5	21·2	21·8	21·9	22·4	21·8	24·0
Other n.e.s.	7·0	0·1	7·9	2·7	1·2	1·8	5·7
	100	100	100	100	100	100	100

Notes:
[a] Agriculture, forestry, fishing, hunting, mining and quarrying.
[b] Including utilities
[c] Including storage and communications.
[d] British Virgin Islands and Grand Cayman only.
[e] 1970 sectoral definitions not strictly comparable with those of the 1960 census, especially for commerce and transport.
[f] 1970 was the year of an abnormal building boom in the British Virgin Islands, which has since tailed off.
Sources:
1960 data from the *Caribbean Statistical Yearbook* 1967. *1970 data* for the Northern Group from Elkan and Morley (1971) and Hart and Hart (1971).

commerce (9 to 19 per cent), manufacturing (8 to 17 per cent), and construction (8 to 13 per cent in 1960). The largest islands in the region, Jamaica, Trinidad and Barbados, tend to have relatively larger manufacturing sectors and relatively smaller primary sectors than the smaller islands, Jamaica being something of an exception on account of bauxite mining. Otherwise, there are striking similarities in employment structure in spite of the large differences in size. These similarities do not, however, extend to the Northern Group, which are notable for their small primary sectors and large construction sectors, particularly in 1970. The transport sector, which in the Cayman Islands seems to include Caymanian seamen in 1960, is also relatively important in these very small islands owing to the extremely high import content of expenditures.

Very little can be said with certainty prior to the publication of the 1970 census about the changes in the structure and level of employment over the decade 1960 to 1970. Some changes can, however, be inferred from the movements in economic structure discussed in Chapter 3. For the smaller islands, the major changes suggested are a declining proportion of the labour force in agriculture, and an increasing proportion in construction, services and, possibly, commerce. Little reliable factual evidence exists in the region to support the contention that levels — or rates — of long term unemployment have increased during the decade, but many scholars feel that this has been, and is, a major problem.[30]

Certainly with the curtailment of emigration opportunities during the 1960s and rapid rates of population growth since the war, it seems probable that the smaller islands have had to absorb a larger annual net addition to the population of working age than was the case in the 1950s. On the other hand, there seems little doubt that migration had its negative effects, and growth rates appear to have been somewhat higher in the 1960s than in the 1950s. Even if levels of unemployment have not increased, however, it seems likely that the vulnerability of the economy to unemployment has. This is particularly because of the increased importance of the construction industry in many islands and the significance of capital inflows for the level of activity in this sector. That apart, it is not always clear how much official unemployment statistics tell us in differing economic and social settings.[31]

If the absolute size of the labour force seems at times a somewhat nebulous concept, the quality of the labour force is even more so. Some guidance is given by levels of educational attainment, or classification of the economically active

---

30 For example, Demas (1965) pp. 133–4, O'Loughlin (1968) p. 73, Seers (1969) pp. 218–9, Bryne (1969), McFarlane (1970), Jefferson (1970) among others. In the Bahamas, the British Virgin Islands and the Cayman Islands, recent evidence suggests a shortage of labour, but these are almost certainly special cases, See Mills, D. (1970), Hart and Hart (1971) and Elkan and Morley (1971). However, the larger islands do have deficit 'sectors' of the labour market existing alongside surplus 'sectors'; 'sectors' in this sense applying to skill-levels.

31 The problems of interpreting figures of unemployment in any meaningful way in developing countries have been discussed by Hart. In the Caribbean it is difficult to see how they give any reliable indication of 'excess supply of labour' given the wide variation in female participation rates. Hart criticises the failure to recognise 'informal non-wage income opportunities – which, legal or not, have income-generating effects and therefore an opportunity cost, Hart (1972).

population by broad occupational group. But 'primary education' means something very different in the West Indies than in other parts of the world. Similarly, occupational groups generally serve to conceal very wide differences within each group. Nevertheless, some general points can be made with respect to the Commonwealth Caribbean.

O'Loughlin discusses the levels of educational attainment in the Windwards, Leewards and Barbados.[32] In 1960, between 83·5 per cent (in Barbados) and 96·4 per cent (in St Lucia) of the population aged 15 or over had only primary education or less. Those with school certificate or a university education accounted for 5·1 per cent of the adult population in Barbados, but less than 3 per cent in the other islands. Vocational training is almost non-existent in the smaller islands, so that skills are either acquired overseas or through 'on the job' training. The general picture is one of a small elite with a high level of educational attainment, and the bulk of the adult population having only a very inadequate primary education and little formal training of any sort beyond that level.

This picture also emerges, though less clearly, from an examination of the occupational structure of the economically active population given in Table 2.6 below.

Table 2.6 *Occupational structure of the economically active population in the Commonwealth Caribbean*[a]

Occupational category		Windward Islands %	Barbados %	Jamaica %	Trinidad %	Bahamas %
I	Professional, technical etc.	4·2	4·7	3·0	6·7	9·8
II	Administrative, exec and managerial	2·5	2·9	1·2	2·5	8·8
III	Clerical	2·7	4·1	4·4	7·2	15·6
IV	Sales	4·2	9·0	9·9	7·2	5·7
V	Farmers, fishers, hunters etc.	44·2	23·2		19·6	2·8
VI	Miners, quarrymen etc.	0·3	0·7	42·1	1·9	0·1
VII	Transport and communications	5·0	8·4		8·7	5·9
VIII	Craftsmen and production process workers	20·0	22·4	22·8	25·4	25·4
IX	Service, sport and recreation	9·7	16·6	15·2	14·6	25·9
X	Others n.e.s.	7·2	8·0	1·3	6·1	0·0
		100	100	100	100	100

Note:
[a] 1960 except for Bahamas, which is 1968 (first quarter).
Sources:
Except Bahamas, *Caribbean Statistical Yearbook* 1967. Bahamas: Mills, D. (1970), Table 7.

32 O'Loughlin (1968) Chapter 5.

Although the occupational categories used were different, the results of the manpower surveys in the Cayman Islands and the British Virgin Islands in 1970—1 tend to confirm an occupational structure very similar to that of the Bahamas. This is to be expected given the similarity in economic structure, with a high degree of dependence on tourism, tax haven activities and construction, and the minimal importance of agriculture. This type of economic structure is associated with higher proportions of the economically active population in the first three occupational categories — professional, technical, administrative, executive, managerial and clerical, and in the last two categories, especially service workers.

The occupational categories used by the Cayman Islands manpower survey are in many ways more instructive and for this reason are given below in Table 2.7.

Table 2.7 *Occupational structure of the working population: Cayman Islands, 1970*

Occupational category		Percentage distribution of the labour force	Percentage of females in each category	Percentage of expatriates in each category
I	Higher and lower professional managerial and administrative	16·5	29·7	64·4
II	Clerical and allied grades	19·2	80·6	27·5
III	Skilled (mainly manual)	21·5	14·2	36·9
IV	Semi-skilled (mainly manual)	19·6	37·3	18·0
V	Unskilled manual	23·1	25·1	20·4
		100	36·6	32·1

Source: Hart and Hart (1971), Tables 6.3 and 1.7.

The concentration of expatriates in the highest three occupational grades is a feature common to the Bahamas[33] and the British Virgin Islands[34] as well as the Cayman Islands. Of a total of 344 professional, administrative, executive and managerial employees in the British Virgin Islands in 1970, only 75 were British Virgin Islanders by birth. In the Bahamas, over half of those employed in many professions were expatriates in 1968. The significance of this is that, though the economic structure of these largely tourist economies seems at first sight to offer a 'superior' opportunity structure in the sense that a higher proportion of trained and skilled labour appears to be required, the benefits of this have to a significant extent escaped the indigenous population which tends to be concentrated in the more menial and lower level jobs.[35]

33 Mills, D (1970) Table 8.

34 Elkan and Morley (1971) Tables 2.14 and 2.15.

35 Hart and Hart (1971). It could be argued that this is a short-term 'deficit' situation in the skilled labour market. On the other hand the fiscal framework, the nature of the economic system, and the heavy demands on government resources which rapid growth in tourism gives rise to, mean that the investments necessary to cure these 'deficits' are not in fact made.

In so far as the other territories of the region have moved towards the type of economic structure exhibited by those three rather extreme cases — and this is discussed in Chapter 3 — it seems likely that similar sorts of trends will be emerging elsewhere, particularly in the smaller islands where facilities for formal training are scanty or even non-existent, except at the university level where a regional institution — the University of the West Indies — exists. Moreover, in the larger islands of Jamaica, Trinidad and Barbados, which are more usually characterised as 'surplus' labour economies, there are 'surplus' and deficit' sections of the labour market, with expatriates tending to fill jobs in the 'deficit' sections.

Summary

This chapter has been concerned with the political structure and resources of the Commonwealth Caribbean. Political fragmentation, geographical isolation, similarity of resource structure, and corresponding absence of complementary production structures mean that each territory has to be considered on its own to a very large extent. Separately, they must be considered very small countries indeed in terms of population and land area.[36] The density of population is generally high, especially by reference to farmed land, which is itself unevenly distributed. Mineral resources outside the larger islands of Trinidad and Jamaica are largely absent.

The labour force is related to the population through a complex of social, demographic and economic factors. The rapid population growth rates and consequent age structure mean a relatively low population of working age. Participation rates for men of working age are generally high, and fairly consistent throughout the region. Those for women on the other hand vary considerably and this largely accounts for variations in overall participation rates. The large majority of this labour force have primary education only, and especially in the smaller islands, lack formal training in vocational skills. There is, however, a small and highly educated elite with university education or its equivalent. Little factual evidence exists regarding the change in the structure and level of employment in the region during the 1960s, though some inferences can be drawn from the changes in economic structure discussed in Chapter 3, and recent evidence from the Bahamas, the British Virgin Islands and the Cayman Islands. These suggest a declining proportion of the labour force in agriculture, and increases in construction, services and possibly commerce. As these are important sources of opportunities for women, it seems possible that the trend towards lower female participation rates (at least in 'formal' or wage employment) noted after the 1960 census may have been reversed or at least arrested. It seems likely also that the vulnerability of the economy to unemployment has increased owing mainly to the increased importance of the construction sector.

Evidence from the islands most highly dependent on tourism and related activities suggests a higher requirement for trained and skilled labour. On the other hand, the absence of training facilities and the low general level of formal education have

36 Demas considers a 'small' country to be one with less than 5 million people and 10,000 to 20,000 square miles of useable land. This definition would imply that all the countries of the Commonwealth Caribbean including the Bahamas would be thus classified — by a considerable margin. Demas (1965) p. 22. See also Table 2.1.

meant better jobs tend to be filled by expatriates, so that the benefits of this have largely escaped the indigenous population.[37] Similar trends can be inferred for the other smaller islands whose tourist sectors have grown rapidly.

37 Another factor which could be relevant is the bias in the US immigration laws in favour of skilled and trained personnel – compounded in 1967. This actively encourages the 'brain drain' from developing countries.

3   *Economic structure and change*

This chapter is devoted to an examination of structural changes which have taken place recently in the region. The main concern will be to highlight those changes in the economy which serve as a background to the subsequent analysis of the impact of tourism on economic growth and structural change. It was suggested in Chapter 2 that competition for resources may imply growth in one sector at the expense of others. The evidence presented below tends to support the argument that this has happened in the case of the recent growth of tourism, at least in the smaller islands where growth of tourism has been most rapid.

The method of analysis employed is based on an open-economy 'model' which shares certain similarities with other open-economy models in the literature.[1] Basically, income is generated by exports of goods and services, and, important in this context, capital inflows which influence levels of activity in the construction sector directly. Domestic sectors consist of domestic agricultural production, government, distribution and finance, transport, manufacturing and other services. The domestic sectors, with the possible exception of domestic agriculture, are highly dependent on income generated by the export sectors and construction. The analysis thus starts with an examination of the export sectors — export agriculture and tourism — followed by an examination of the construction sector and investment, and finally the remaining domestic sectors including government. An attempt will be made throughout to establish the nature of the inter-relationships between the export and the domestic sectors.

Before proceeding with the sectoral analysis, some general points can be made regarding overall domestic product and trade in the region. Detailed figures for gross domestic product by sector, including growth rates, for the individual islands are given in Appendix Tables 3A.1 to 3A.3. The principal aggregates are summarised in Table 3.1 below.

These broad aggregates suggest a rising income per capita, a rising import coefficient and a rising visible trade deficit in the smaller islands of the region. If constant price series were available, the rise in per capita income would be less marked than it appears, since price increases seem to have been fairly rapid throughout the decade.[2] Too much significance should not be read into the

1   For example that of Seers (1964).

2   Most of the islands do not have — or do not publish — cost-of-living indices. The price
    rises were, of course, most noticeable after the sterling (and EC$) devaluation in 1967.

Table 3.1 *Domestic product and trade: Principal aggregates for the Windward Islands, Leeward Islands and the Northern Group.*

	Windwards 1962	Windwards 1966	Leewards 1962	Leewards 1966	Northern Group 1966	Northern Group 1968
GDP $m EC[a]	103	132	46	71	19	32
Est. population '000	323	352	127	139	25	28
GDP per capita $EC	319	375	352	510	760	875
Imports $m EC[b]	55	83	38	64	15	30
Exports $m EC[c]	28	37	13	10	< 1	< 1
Visible trade deficit	(27)	(46)	(25)	(54)	(15)	(29)
Imports/GDP (%)	53·5	62·9	82·5	90·1	79·0	93·8

Notes:
[a] Factor cost, current prices.
[b] C.i.f. values.
[c] Domestic exports f.o.b.
Sources: Appendix Table 3A.1; *Trade Returns* (individual islands); Population data from *Economic Surveys and Projections.*

differences in per capita GDP between the Windwards, Leewards and, especially, the Northern Group because of differences in the level of prices. In the Northern Group most imports come from the USA, mainly for locational reasons, but also because of the closer links which these islands tend to have with America and the effect of this on consumption patterns.[3]

The rising import coefficient is rather difficult to interpret since it occurred during a period of increased construction activity. Nevertheless, it provides little *prima facie* evidence of improvements in the economic structure of the smaller islands.

The visible trade deficit has also increased over the period in all cases. This has been financed by aid flows, net receipts on travel account, and net capital inflows. However, since gross tourist receipts nowhere matched the increase in the trade deficit, it must be concluded that there has been an increased dependence on aid and capital inflows during the period. Once again, the indications suggest increasing rather than decreasing 'openness', and in the following discussion of the individual sectors, some emphasis will be placed on this aspect of the development process.

The principal export sectors

These are 'export agriculture', defined to include agricultural commodities grown mainly for export, and 'hotels and services', which is the largest single recipient of tourist receipts. Table 3.2 below summarises the contribution of these two sectors to GDP and their respective growth between 1962 and 1966.

Export agriculture

The principal agricultural exports from the region are sugar and bananas. Sugar is subject to preferential trading arrangements with the UK under the terms of the Commonwealth Sugar Agreement (CSA), which has given some degree of protection to West Indian producers, and has ensured a stable market for prices and

---

3 The currency of the British Virgin Islands is the US dollar, so that 1968 data expressed in $ EC were affected by the sterling (and EC $) devaluation in 1967.

Table 3.2 Value added and growth in the principal export sectors: Windwards and Leewards only.

	Windwards 1962	1966	Leewards 1962	1966
Export Agriculture				
Value added	19·3	27·1	9·2	7·8
Proportionate contribution to GDP	18·7%	20·5%	19·7%	10·9%
Growth rate 1962–6	8·9% p.a.		−4·0% p.a.	
Hotels and services				
Value added $m	7·4	10·4	4·2	8·1
Proportionate contribution to GDP	7·2%	7·9%	9·0%	11·4%
Growth rate 1962–6	8·9% p.a.		18·1% p.a.	

Sources: Appendix Tables 3A.1 to 3A.3.

quantities known in advance. Banana producers receive a different form of protection in the UK market; in this case non-Commonwealth producers pay a tariff of £7·50 per ton, while a quantitative restriction of 4,000 tons (about 1 per cent of the UK market) applied to the important banana producing countries in the 'dollar' area, where yields are higher and costs of production reputed to be substantially lower than in the Caribbean.[4] Sugar is exported from Jamaica, Trinidad, Barbados, St Kitts and (negligibly) Antigua. The principal banana exporters in the region are Jamaica and all of the Windward Islands. Other agricultural exports from the region include cocoa (Trinidad and Grenada), coffee (Jamaica), copra, arrowroot, nutmeg and other spices, citrus fruits, cotton, and ginger. Agricultural exports from Antigua, the Northern Group, and the Bahamas are now almost non-existent.

The growth performance of this sector over the period has been varied. In the Windwards, the growth in banana exports already mentioned has been mainly responsible for the steady growth in GDP from this sector noted in Table 3.2. This growth has been achieved by a steady increase in the share of the UK market, largely at the expense of Jamaica.[5] In the Leewards, where agricultural exports consist of sugar and sea-island (extra-long staple) cotton, the value added in export agriculture declined by about 4 per cent per annum. Sugar production has consistently fallen below CSA quotes in Antigua and St Kitts, while cotton production also declined. The decline in sugar and cotton production seems to be due to supply factors in the main.[6] In respect of Antigua, Campbell and Edwards commented:

> Although the population continued to grow, migration to the United Kingdom, and the development in tourism and associated industries both

4 See also Beckford (1967) pp. 2–3.

5 See Chapter 2.

6 Cotton experienced some marketing difficulties, but these were not new to the industry and cannot explain the rapid decline in production.

reduced the pool of unemployed *and drew labour away from agriculture* ... The peasant farmers also experienced a labour shortage which led to a significant reduction in the acreage of sugar cane and an even more marked fall in the area of cotton when these crops *could not compete with the tourist industry for the services of women who had hitherto served as cotton pickers.* Some of the farmers themselves gave up agricultural work in favour of more lucrative non-agricultural employment.[7]

The competitive demand for labour could have been overcome by changing production functions, and Campbell and Edwards made a number of recommen-dations to this effect. But this would have required other resources, notably skilled staff and public expenditure on research and extension. Given the expansion of tourism in Antigua, the government's resources were fully utilised and, in the event, budgetary allocations to agriculture declined between 1960 and 1968. The result was a continuation of the trends noted by Campbell and Edwards for the remainder of the decade.[8]

The relative importance of the various agricultural exports in the region as a whole is shown in Table 3.3 below. In total, agricultural exports accounted for some 23 per cent of all exports of commodities in 1962, though in the smaller islands they constituted virtually the whole of domestic exports. Oil and bauxite exported from Trinidad and Jamaica account for the major part of the difference.[9]

The value of these exports grew by just under $21 million EC, or by about 10 per cent, between 1955 and 1962 and most of this rise seems to be due to the rise in the CSA price for sugar. Throughout the decade the prospects for growth of agricultural exports have seemed dim, and this pessimism has recently been com-pounded by the renewed efforts of the UK government to join the EEC.[10] In the circumstances, governments in the region can hardly be blamed for not devoting more of their own resources to increasing exports of agricultural products and changing the nature of the production function in the sector as a whole.

Hotels and services

Activities included in this sector are hotels and guest houses, bars and restaurants, professions other than those in government service, domestic, entertainment and sport, clubs, religious organisations, beauty solons, hairdressers, broadcasting and telecommunications (except where run by government, when they are treated as a public utility), and similar (legal) service activities.[11] In its aggregated form, therefore, it contains a mixture of 'export' and 'domestic' activities. Although Table 3.2 shows quite rapid growth for the sector as a whole, it is the hotel and

7 Campbell and Edwards (1965) page 5. (Emphasis supplied.)

8 Expenditures related to 'agriculture' fell from $645,151 in 1960 to $389,307 in 1966 and $423,576 was approved for the 1968 estimates. See Appendix Table 3A.4 and notes.

9 According to Demas, bauxite and alumina plus sugar and sugar products account for 76 per cent of Jamaican domestic exports, while petroleum, sugar and sugar products account for 90 per cent of Trinidad's domestic exports. Demas (1965) p. 103.

10 The prospects for export crops have been discussed by Frank Barsotti (1966).

11 The detailed composition of this sector is given in O'Loughlin (1966) and Bryden (1970).

Table 3.3 *Exports of principal agricultural commodities: Commonwealth Caribbean, 1962*[a]

Commodity	Value of exports 1962, $000 EC	Proportion of total exports, %
Sugar	142,754	14·3
Molasses	10,797	1·1
Bananas	36,519	3·7
Cocoa	13,473	1·4
Citrus fruit	4,255	0·4
Citrus juices	9,004	0·9
Coffee	2,573	0·3
Nutmeg and nutmeg prods.[b]	2,403	0·2
Cotton lint	718	0·07
Copra	3,472	0·35
Arrowroot	1,708	0·17
Essential oils	1,342	0·13
Coconut oil	653	0·07
Total	229,671	23·1

Notes:
[a] Excludes Northern Group and Bahamas.
[b] Excludes Trinidad and Tobago.
Source: Bryden (1967).

guest house element that has shown the most rapid growth. Disaggregation of hotels and guest houses was carried out for many islands from 1964 onwards, and Table 3.4 below shows the growth of this sector between 1964 and 1966.

Hotels and guest houses contributed 6·2 per cent of GDP in the Cayman Islands and 14·6 per cent in the British Virgin Islands in 1967.[12] No separate figures for this sector exist for the Turks and Caicos, but the contribution is known to be small in these islands.[13]

In relation to the hotels and services sector as a whole, the value added in hotels and guest houses accounted for 40 per cent of value added in the entire sector in the Windwards, and over 60 per cent in the Leewards where agriculture is less significant.

In the smaller islands the receipts of hotels and guest houses can, for all practical purposes, be taken as their foreign exchange earnings.[14] Some other services also derive a significant proportion of their services from tourists or other overseas sources, these being relatively more important where tourism and tax haven facilities are more advanced. Anything from under 1 to over 7 per cent of tourist receipts may accrue to 'services' other than hotels.[15]

In the Cayman Islands, some 30 per cent of the gross receipts of services came from overseas in 1968,[16] while in Antigua around 13 per cent of the gross receipts

12 *Economic Surveys and Projections* (1969).

13 *Ibid.*

14 See also Chapter 7.

15 See below, Chapter 6.

16 *Economic Survey and Projections:* a significant proportion of this derives from tax haven services.

Table 3.4 *Absolute and proportionate contribution of hotels and guest houses to GDP in 1964 and 1966, showing growth rates.*

| | Absolute contribution | | Proportionate contribution | | Average annual growth rate |
	1964 $000	1966 $000	1964 %	1966 %	1964–6 % p.a.
Grenada	805	1,431	2·8	4·0	33·3
St Vincent	380	567	1·5	2·0	22·1
St Lucia	758	1,943	2·7	4·7	60·1
Dominica	143	234	0·7	0·9	27·9
Windwards	2,086	4,175	2·0	3·2	41·5
Antigua	2,431	4,100	10·7	9·8[a]	29·9
St Kitts	n.a.	490	n.a.	2·2	n.a.
Montserrat	n.a.	357	n.a.	5·6	n.a.
Leewards	n.a.	4,947	n.a.	6·9	n.a.

Notes:
[a] As noted in the Appendix tables, there was an exceptional rise in GDP in 1966 in Antigua, due to various construction activities. The proportionate contribution of this sector rose again in 1967 to 13·1%.
Sources: As for Appendix Table 3A.1.

of services came from non-residents, mainly tourists.[17]

The rapid growth rates in Table 3.4, and confirmed over a longer period in Chapters 6 and 7, are partly the result of favourable government policies towards tourism and a willingness to invest in infrastructure and utilities associated with tourist development.[18] Given the uncertainties surrounding export crops, the absence of mineral resources, and the apparently limited potential for import substitution, it is not surprising that such favourable attitudes evolved among politicians, merchants and civil servants.

By 1967, tourist receipts in the region excluding the Bahamas amounted to roughly $300 millions EC. It seems unlikely on the evidence available that these had exceeded $110 millions EC in 1961. Thus, during the decade, tourist receipts rose from roughly half the value of agricultural exports to a figure in excess of the value of agricultural exports by 1967–8.[19]

Such direct comparisons of foreign exchange receipts tell us relatively little, however, since the different exporting sectors have different direct and indirect requirements of primary inputs per dollar of final demand. As will be demonstrated later, tourist receipts in the Caribbean have a high import content and a correspondingly lower value added per unit of foreign exchange earned, especially when adjustments are made to take account of remitted profits and income accruing to employees who are non-nationals.[20]

17 O'Loughlin (1965).

18 See Chapter 8.

19 Detailed estimates of tourist receipts are given in Chapter 6.

20 See Chapters 5 and 9.

The contrast with export agriculture can be seen from a cursory examination of the national accounts data, and is particularly marked in the case of the banana industry where foreign ownership of assets is relatively lower and production units relatively smaller than is the case with sugar, and, *a fortiori*, tourism.[21] The growth in the import coefficient noted earlier is therefore in part the consequence of the increasing importance of the tourist sectors in the smaller islands. But this elementary structural change is not by itself sufficient to explain the rapid increase in imports over the period, since these increases have everywhere exceeded the increase in tourist receipts by a substantial margin.

Construction and investment

The construction sector is the accounting vehicle for all recorded private capital formation and an important part of public capital formation.[22] It achieves greatest prominence in those islands where the growth of tourism has been of major significance. Thus the proportionate contribution was as high as 32 per cent in the Cayman Islands in 1967, 27·5 per cent in Antigua in 1966 and 23·2 per cent in the British Virgin Islands in 1967. The Windwards tended to have the smallest construction sectors — generally under 10 per cent of GDP — between 1962 and 1966, partly because of the smaller absolute growth in tourism and smaller volume of capital formation in the public sector. Another reason may be inadequate treatment of investment in the banana industry.[23]

A major difficulty, however, is the weakness of the data relating to capital formation in the smaller islands, these being compiled by various direct and indirect methods none of which is completely satisfactory. Figures for public capital formation are relatively good, but even here definitional problems arise. Some items in the recurrent budget are more properly capital expenditure, while others in the capital budget ought to be treated as recurrent items.[24] Figures for private sector capital formation must be treated with considerable caution.

The estimates in Table 3.5 allow some tentative explorations into the sources of finance for capital formation in the Eastern Caribbean over this period.

O'Loughlin estimates total net capital inflow for the Windwards and Leewards at $25·0 m. in 1962, of which $6·5 m. was to the public sector.[25] The average

21 Beckford (1967) p. 8 shows the distribution of growers, acreage and production by farm size in the West Indian banana industry.

22 The sector includes private capital formation, private maintenance expenditures, and public sector capital formation and maintenance in so far as it is carried out by the private sector and not by government agencies (mainly public works departments). In the figures up to 1964, all government capital formation was usually included in the construction sector irrespective of which agency carried it out. In more recent work it has been considered preferable to make a distinction between that part of public capital formation actually carried out by the public sector agencies and that part which was contracted out. To this end a new sector — government capital account — was compiled which was the public sector analogue of the construction sector. Unfortunately, this makes comparisons with earlier years difficult, but adjustments have been made to the data so far as has been possible. See also Bryden (1970).

23 This is speculative, but reasonable given the general weakness of agricultural statistics.

24 See also Bryden (1970) for further comments on this point.

25 O'Loughlin (1968) pp. 130, 131.

Table 3.5 *Estimates of gross domestic fixed capital formation at current prices: 1964–7 inclusive, Windward and Leeward Islands.*

	Private GDFCF $m EC	Public GDFCF $m EC	Total GDFCF $m EC
Grenada	24·2	6·0	30·2
St Vincent	13·1	4·9	18·0
St Lucia	19·8	8·0	27·8
Dominica	12·5	6·7	19·2
Windwards	69·6	25·6	95·2
Antigua	44·7	18·7	63·4
St Kitts	17·8	8·0	25·8
Montserrat	6·6	4·1	10·7
Leewards	69·1	30·8	99·9

Sources: Economic Surveys and Projections. For methods see O'Loughlin (1966) and Bryden (1970).

Table 3.6 *Capital formation, GDP, and sources of finance, 1964–7 inclusive: Eastern Caribbean*

	Windwards $m EC	Leewards $m EC	Total $m EC	Per cent of GDP
GDP 1964–7	503·6	248·5	752·1	100·0
GDFCF	95·2	99·0	194·2	26·0
Local savings[a]	25·2	12·4	37·6	·5·0
Net capital inflow[b]	70·0	87·5	157·5	21·0
Public inflow[c]	25·6	30·8	56·4	7·5
Net private inflow[d]	44·4	56·7	101·1	13·5
Hotel investment[e]	12·2	12·4	24·6	3·3
Other private i.[f]	57·4	55·8	113·2	15·2

Notes:
[a] 5% of GDP assumed. See O'Loughlin (1968) p. 86.
[b] Total capital formation less local savings. Gross capital inflow will be larger to the extent that local savings are held overseas. See later discussion of the finance sector.
[c] Assuming all public investment to be financed by aid, or external loans in one form or another. This is reasonable since all but three of the islands were receiving grants-in-aid of recurrent budget during most of the period. See also discussion of the government sector below.
[d] Net capital inflow less public capital inflow.
[e] Based on a uniform cost of $25,000 per room; See Chapter 7.
[f] Residual item.
Source: Economic Surveys and Projections.

annual net capital inflow for the four years 1964 to 1967 was $39·4 m., of which $14·1 m. was to the public sector. Over this short period, then, inflows of public capital more than doubled, while net inflows of private capital increased by some 35 per cent. Table 3.1 indicated an increase in the visible trade deficit of $48 m between 1962 and 1966; the figures above suggest that a substantial part of this was financed by capital inflows.

The public sector accounted for some 29 per cent of all capital formation, the proportion being higher in the Leewards than in the Windwards. Of all private investment, about 18 per cent was accounted for by direct investment in hotels, the proportion being slightly higher in the Leewards. But this understates total investment in *tourism* by a substantial margin. For one thing, a considerable proportion of public sector investment was in infrastructure or utilities directly or indirectly related to tourism. For another, given that somewhere between 20 and 50 per cent of all tourist receipts accrue to sectors other than hotels and guest houses — to transport, distribution, finance and other services — considerable investments must have been made in these sectors providing boutiques, beauty salons, tourist shopping centres, yacht slips and marinas, taxis and so on.[26]

Much of the private sector investment has received benefits under the fiscal incentives offered by all of the smaller islands.[27] These apply to almost all hotels, some guest houses, and many of the newer manufacturing firms. A further part has been in real estate and housing for foreigners retiring to the sun or wanting a holiday home. While not subject to the fiscal incentives mentioned above, the absence of adequate property taxes means that little government revenue is obtained directly from such investments.

These factors, together with the dominance of foreign capital, have several important implications. First, taxes derived from much of the new investment are a very much smaller proportion of profits than is the case in the economy as a whole. Second, the control of a high proportion of incremental profits, and therefore potential 'domestic' savings, lies in the hands of non-nationals. To the extent that these profits are remitted overseas the gap between GDP and national income is widened, and the dependence on foreign capital is further increased since this potential source of savings is not in fact reinvested locally. Third, the dependence on a continued flow of foreign capital necessitates the continuance and even strengthening of concessions, and forces the government to pursue even more 'open' policies which receive the approval of foreign investors, but which may not be in the long run interests of the indigenous population.[28] Severe as these problems are for Jamaica, Trinidad and Barbados, they are much more so in the smaller islands of the Windwards, the Leewards and the Northern Group.

The point to be stressed is the tenuous nature of the increases in GDP from this source. Much of the public capital inflow in the 1960s arose from using up 'slack' debt capacity which was the legacy of stringent financial accounting and control. The inflows of private capital, which also increased substantially, were doubtless attracted by the favourable policies mentioned above. These policies are under increasing attack from intellectuals, opposition, and other groups who doubt their long-term benefits. Yet the increasing dependence syndrome makes the reversal of these policies an increasingly difficult task.

26 An attempt is made in Chapter 8 to gauge the size of government investment in tourist-related infrastructure and utilities.

27 These fiscal incentives are described in Chapter 8.

28 Demas (1965), pp. 62 *et seq.* It should be noted that these flows of capital become increasingly important in the *current* sense as the significance of the construction sector increases.

The principal domestic sectors

The sectors which remain for discussion, and their proportionate contribution to GDP, are shown in Table 3.7 below.

Table 3.7 *Proportionate contribution to GDP of the principal domestic sectors; Windwards, Leewards and Northern Group, showing changes during the decade.*

	Windwards 1962 %	Windwards 1966 %	Leewards 1962 %	Leewards 1966 %	Brit. Virgin Is. 1964 %	Brit. Virgin Is. 1968 %	Cayman Is. 1967 %
Domestic agriculture	17·8	12·3	9·7	6·4	21·9	6·2	10·5
Manufacturing	4·1	4·7	1·9	2·2	a	3·2	4·1
Distribution and finance	14·8	16·8	16·4	15·7	8·3	14·2	17·2
Transport	2·7	3·2	2·6	3·2	1·9	6·2	3·9
Rent-of-dwellings	9·2	8·6	6·8	5·2	3·4	5·9	7·9
Government	17·2	17·9	18·8	16·8	21·8[b]	14·5[b]	11·2[b]
	65·8	63·5	56·2	49·5	57·3	50·2	54·8

Notes:
[a] Negligible: included in other sectors.
[b] Excluding capital account: sources include capital account in the government sector, but permit adjustment.
Sources:
Windwards and Leewards: Appendix Tables 3A.1 to 3A.3. British Virgin Islands: Phillips (1966), for 1964 estimates; 1968 date from *Economic Surveys and Projections.* Cayman Islands: *Economic Surveys and Projections.*

The most significant point to note about the domestic sectors in general is the decline in their proportionate contribution to GDP in all the smaller islands for which data are available. The most consistent and important declines occur in domestic agriculture, which is the one domestic sector with any significant element of autonomy, the others being highly dependent on the performance of the export sectors and the construction sector. The reasons for these declines are therefore worthy of further investigation.

Domestic agriculture

So far, only relative declines in this sector have been discussed. In fact, the output of domestic agriculture, forestry and fishing declined absolutely over the period in all of the smaller islands except Dominica, St Kitts and Montserrat, and relatively in all cases. But statistics for domestic agricultural production and value added are notoriously unreliable and the Caribbean is no exception.[29] In view of the importance of this issue, therefore, it is necessary to seek some further indicative evidence of the failure of domestic agriculture to provide for increases in food demand during the decade. Such evidence may be obtained from food import data, which are fairly reliable.

Assuming that value added in domestic agriculture is normally between 80 and

29 O'Loughlin (1966) pp. 35 and 36.

Table 3.8 *Value and growth of food import: Eastern Caribbean*

| | Value of food imports[a] | | Average annual growth rate 1962–6 % p.a. |
	1962 $000 EC	1966 $000 EC	
Grenada	4,529	6,269	8·5
St Vincent	3,258	4,610p	9·1
St Lucia	3,904	6,989	15·7
Dominica	3,532	4,725p	7·6
Windwards	15,223	22,593	10·4
Antigua	5,657	7,406	7·0
St Kitts	3,727	4,510	4·9
Montserrat	672	1,129p	13·9
Leewards	10,056	13,045	6·7

p: provisional, usually based on 10 months' data
Notes:
[a] SITC Section O.
Sources: Trade Returns. Provisional data from *Economic Surveys and Projections.*

90 per cent of gross output of domestic agricultural products,[30] that duties on food imports amount to between 5 and 9·5 per cent of the c.i.f. values,[31] and that distributive margins are broadly similar for imported and domestically produced supplies, it is possible to make some estimates of the degree of self-sufficiency in food supplies, and the changes during the period under discussion.

The broad picture given by Table 3.9 tends to confirm the direction of change in domestic agricultural production, and the consequent decline in self-sufficiency in food supplies in all the islands. Total food supplies per capita generally rose between 1962 and 1966, but normally by less than the increases in GDP per capita, which is what one would expect in the Caribbean. Further, if allowance is made for distributive margins, total food supplies would be between 30 and 40 per cent of GDP in 1962, which compares reasonably closely with the estimates reported by Cumper for Trinidad and Guyana a decade earlier when per capita product was similar to that obtaining in the Windwards and Leewards in 1962.[32]

The position in the still smaller islands of the Northern Group is even more acute in respect of domestic agricultural production. Only negligible amounts of agricultural produce are exported, and value added in agriculture and fishing is estimated at under 5 per cent of GDP in the Turks and Caicos for 1967, around 6 per cent of GDP in the British Virgin Islands in 1968, and 7 per cent of GDP in the Cayman Islands. Moreover, similar downward trends in this sector were noticed in all of these islands during the decade. Although figures for the Bahamas are not available, the employment data for 1968 show only 2·8 per cent of employees included in the occupational group farmers, fishermen, hunters, loggers and related

30 O'Loughlin (1966) pp. 35 and 36.

31 The *Economic Survey and Projections* of the various islands give the breakdown of duties by commodity.

32 Cumper in Cumper (ed.) (1960) p. 133.

Table 3.9 *Estimated self-sufficiency in food supplies in 1962 and 1966: Windwards and Leewards*

	Est. gross output of domestic agric. farm gate value[a]		Est. gross value of food imports after duty[b]		Est. self-sufficiency in food supplies[c]	
	1962 $000	1966 $000	1962 $000	1966 $000	1962 %	1966 %
Grenada	6,860	6,220	4,890	6,770	58·5	48·0
St Vincent	6,250	4,150	3,510	4,990	64·0	45·4
St Lucia	4,080	3,780	4,220	7,550	49·1	33·3
Dominica	4,300	5,050	3,810	5,100	53·0	49·8
Windwards	21,600	19,200	16,430	24,410	56·8	44·0
Antigua	1,350	1,090	6,120	8,000	18·1	12·0
St Kitts	2,620	2,910	4,025	4,875	39·5	37·4
Montserrat	1,300	1,410	726	1,219	64·1	53·6
Leewards	5,270	5,400	10,871	14,094	32·7	27·8

Notes:
[a] Value added assumed to be 85% (approx.) of farm gate sales.
[b] Average duty on food imports assumed to be 8% of c.i.f. value.
[c] Ratio of domestic to total estimated food supplies.
Sources: Value added in domestic agriculture from Appendix Table 3A.1. Food imports from Table 3.8.

workers.[33]

In examining the reasons for the trends noted above, it is necessary to distinguish between supply and demand factors. On the supply side, competition for resources must be considered as a major factor. In the Windward Islands, the principal competitor was banana production, the increase in which has been due to an expansion in the area under production rather than yield increases.[34] Banana production is relatively attractive to small farmers who might otherwise produce domestic crops, because cash receipts continue fairly regularly throughout the year and prices are known in advance of production within fairly narrow limits, under the contractual arrangements between Geest Industries Ltd. and the Windward Islands Banana Growers Association (WINBAN). Furthermore some central services, such as leaf spot control and insurance against wind damage, are provided, and, from time to time, free or subsidised fertiliser has been distributed to growers.[35] These marketing and production conditions contrast markedly with those existing for domestic agricultural products. Private and public resources were, in the Windwards, directed towards increasing the output of bananas to take advantage of the market situation. Even so, in 1966 the *Tripartite Survey* commented as follows:

The need has been established for various measures to be introduced in

33 Mills, D. (1970) Table 7.

34 For example, in Dominica the acreage under bananas increased from 5,913 in 1955 to 24,771 in 1965, while yields declined from 232 stems per acre to 162 stems per acre. Bryden (1967) p. 14.

35 *Tripartite Survey* p. 42.

cultural practice and in the infrastructure (such as better roads). These measures require the support of services, a strengthened extension service to help bring about the improvement in methods being one of the most obvious and important. No less important is a substantial investment in research directed towards solving the many problems confronting the grower. The present research undertaken under the auspices of Winban (*sic*) has too little resources to be able to solve the problems fast enough to meet the industry's pressing needs in the areas of nutrition and fertilisers, pests and diseases, fruit quality, timing for increased summer production, and other agronomic problems.[36]

There were other competing demands in the economy, notably tourism and construction, which were growing rapidly, especially in St Lucia and Grenada.

But it was in the Leewards and the Northern Group that competition for resources from tourism and construction had its most serious effect on agricultural production. In Antigua, the effects of this competition for labour and government resources have been noted already in respect of export crops. In Montserrat, real estate development competed for agricultural land as well as for other resources.[37] Similarly, in the Northern Group, there was competition for land from real estate developments, and for labour and government resources from the rapid growth in tourism and related construction activities.

On the demand side, there is reason to suppose that the pattern of demand changes away from the more traditional domestic crops as incomes in the rest of the economy rise. Income-elasticities of demand are low for cereals and cereal products, starchy vegetables and sugar. Moreover, as Cumper has suggested, at higher income levels some items in these categories may become inferior goods, with a negative elasticity.[38] Casual empiricism and the trends in food imports suggest a high income elasticity of demand for packaged, processed and imported goods. No doubt the strength of the merchant classes has had something to do with this trend; the form in which many traditional domestic crops are produced and offered for sale — in small ungraded lots from small production units — does not suit the supermarkets which have grown up in the better-off residential areas of the larger islands, and increasingly in the smaller islands also. The threat of competition from domestic producers made planning of imports, particularly of perishables, a difficult task for traders. The lack of refrigeration facilities in most households may also partly explain the preference for powdered over fresh milk, salt over fresh butter, and salt meat and fish, though historical factors have no doubt played their part. Finally, one may postulate a demonstration effect on consumption from the nature of tourist development in the region. It will be shown later that the bulk of tourist expenditures are generated by tourists from the upper income groups in North America and Europe, particularly the former. Unless these groups change their consumption patterns radically when they are on holiday, and there is no evidence that they do so, then the consumption element of their expenditure is

36 *Ibid.* p. 44.

37 Over 500 acres of good agricultural alnd had been alienated for this purpose by 1966. *Tripartite Survey* p. 131.

38 Cumper in Cumper (ed.) (1960) p. 138.

bound to have a high import content. To those for whom tourists become an important 'reference group' it seems highly plausible to suggest some impact on consumption patterns which has adverse effects on the demand for locally produced commodities including food.[39] There may also be some adverse effect on savings behaviour given the gap between the expenditure of tourists and the income of nationals.[40]

A distinction can be made between 'static' and dynamic' factors affecting domestic agricultural production. At the level of static analysis, we have competitive demands by different sectors for scarce resources. There is some evidence for the smaller islands that this kind of competition has been important in the structural changes which have taken place during the decade. In Antigua, Montserrat and the Northern Group, the main competitor with domestic agriculture has been tourism, including real estate in some cases, and construction, while in the Windwards, the main competitor has been banana production, but possibly also tourism and construction.

At the level of dynamic analysis one has competition for those resources which would serve to *change* the production functions in domestic agriculture to meet changing demand structures and changing resource availabilities. In this respect, one may contrast the institutional support given to export crops and tourism with that provided for domestic crops. As the Tripartite Survey noted '... the possibilities and problems of these local food crops and livestock ..., far more than the major export crops, require the introduction of widespread institutional changes for their growth to be made possible'.[41] To effect the necessary changes in institutions and production functions considerable resources are required in terms of skilled and professional manpower, and public investment in research, credit and specific infrastructure, such as irrigation, together with increased allocations of government current expenditures on extension and marketing facilities, including information services.[42] In the event there has been little change throughout the decade in the allocations of the various governments in the region to agriculture, either in recurrent or in capital expenditures. In some cases the allocations have declined significantly during the decade.[43] One of the major reasons for this has been the heavy demands of tourism for government resources, particularly in terms of infrastructure, but also on recurrent account. Yet, in spite of this, many of the islands ended the decade with what one report described as inadequate tourist infrastructures. The same report commented that in some cases, growth in tourism

---

39 See also Chapter 5, which examines the concept and relevance of 'reference groups' for analysis of the economic and social impact of tourism.

40 Weber emphasises the importance of consumption style as a determinant of status. c.f. Runciman (1969). This is intimately related with the concept of reference groups, which, it is argued, presents a more coherent framework for analysing such effects than the more normal idea of a 'demonstration effect'.

41 *Tripartite Survey* p. 33.

42 *Tripartite Survey, passim.*

43 See for example Appendix Table 3A.4.

had 'outstripped the ability of the islands to cope with the situation'.[44]

Manufacturing

The manufacturing sector in the smaller islands is the smallest of all domestic sectors, and it is here that the diseconomies of very small scale become most obvious. Domestic markets for individual manufactured commodities are very small indeed, even in the large islands, and in general the islands lack a cheap power source. So the manufacturing sectors of the islands tend to be composed of industries which are highly specific as to location, and therefore enjoy natural protection, together with a few processes based on agricultural raw materials. Trinidad and Jamaica are exceptions, having oil and bauxite/alumina respectively. Electricity is produced in every island, usually from imported fuel,[45] though in some islands it is produced by government agencies and is excluded from the manufacturing sector.[46] Bakeries exhibiting a wide range of techniques are also uniformly present. Other common manufacturing activities in the smaller islands include printing, concrete block manufacture, tailoring and dressmaking, souvenirs and a certain amount of straw work. Where copra is produced, so is coconut oil, and sometimes soap. Where sugar is produced, edible sugars, molasses and rum are also usually manufactured. Soft-drink manufacture on the basis of imported essence is common except in the Northern Group, while beer is occasionally brewed locally, normally under protection of a heavy tariff. Furniture and clothing manufacture, well established in Trinidad, Jamaica and Barbados, exists only on a small scale in the smaller islands.

The proportionate contribution of manufacturing to GDP is shown in Table 3.7 above. The reason for the rather higher contribution to GDP in the Windwards and the Cayman Islands is mainly the inclusion of electricity in the manufacturing sector of most of these islands, whereas in the Leewards and the British Virgin Islands it is a government operation. In the Windwards, agricultural-resource-based industries, such as the manufacture of lime juice and lime oil in Dominica, and coconut oil in Dominica and St Lucia, are included in manufacturing, whereas in Antigua and St Kitts, sugar processing is included within export agriculture. In the Caymans and the British Virgin Islands, the large construction sector had some impact on the growth of concrete block manufacture.

The contribution of manufacturing, though small, has tended to increase somewhat, especially in the Windwards where electricity and the agricultural processing industries tend to have expanded rather faster than overall GDP, the latter being based on export as well as internal markets. Export markets were particularly important for Dominica which had the largest manufacturing sector of all the smaller islands. It is estimated that some 38 per cent of the sales of manufacturing

---

44 *Zinder Report.*

45 In Dominica a limited amount of hydro-electricity is produced, and there has been talk of using geo-thermal power in St Lucia.

46 Since 1964 it has been customary in the smaller islands to distinguish a public utilities sector, which would include utilities run by the government.

in Dominica were exported in 1966.[47]

There is very little in the way of intermediate demand for the output of this sector, most of it being sold either directly or through the distribution sector to the final demand sectors. Without a deliberate regional policy for the location of industry within a protected and unified Caribbean, it is difficult to see this sector playing anything other than a minor role which is dependent on growing household incomes and based almost entirely on location-specific industries, at least in the smaller islands. Even some of the existing manufacturing industry, especially that part which is highly capital intensive, foreign owned and managed, and subject to fiscal incentives, is of questionable economic benefit to the small islands.[48]

Distribution and finance

This sector encompasses the distributive trades, banking, and insurance. With the exception of the 'tax havens' of the Bahamas and the Cayman Islands, the growth in this sector has been highly dependent on the growth of imports in the smaller islands. This follows from the fact that distributive trades are very largely concerned with the distribution of imports to households and other sectors, while banking and insurance services are geared towards the financing of imports and exports. Beyond the establishment of more tax havens, which have a heavy cost in terms of an inflexible and inequitable fiscal structure, there seems to be little scope for autonomous growth in the sector as a whole.

Recent work has tended to disaggregate 'distribution' from 'finance and insurance'; the sectors are treated here as a whole because of their aggregation in earlier national income accounts and because the treatment is still not uniform. This recent work indicates that, of the two, distribution is the more important in terms of contribution to GDP in the smaller islands.[49]

The close relationship between imports and value added in this sector is shown in Table 3.10 below. Although value added in distribution tends to be a smaller proportion of imports in the Leewards than in the Windwards, the proportionate contribution to GDP is similar for both groups. The reason for this is the greater significance of domestic agriculture in the Windwards. Some of the other variations between islands are more difficult to explain — for example the low proportion of both GDP and imports which this sector represents in both Dominica and Montserrat. The sudden drop in the value added by this sector in Antigua in 1966, however, was due to an abnormal rise in imports largely due to stockpiling (SITC Section 3) for the new oil refinery, which did not pass through the distribution sector.[50] But, by and large, the relationship shown in Table 3.10 seems

47 *Economic Survey and Projections.*

48 For example, beer brewing.

49 Distribution usually contributes between 2 and 3 times as much to GDP as finance and insurance. See also, *Economic Surveys and Projections.*

50 See also notes to Appendix Table 3A.1. Very little reliable information regarding this oil refinery is available; it seems to be a curious anomaly thrown up by the oddities of the oil market in general, and the advent of CARIFTA. At least until 1968, it appears to have had little impact on the Antiguan economy besides losing the government a considerable sum in import duties on fuels.

fairly clear.

Any discussion of the financial sector would not be complete without some consideration of its role in the mobilisation of savings. The territories of the Eastern Caribbean are members of the Eastern Caribbean Currency Authority, and their currency is completely convertible with sterling in unlimited amounts at a fixed exchange rate.[51] Under this system, balance-of-payments problems in the form of pressure on the exchange rate cannot arise. In theory, the growth of the money supply is tied to the balance-of-payments, so that balance-of-payments deficits would cause a reduction in the money supply, which would, in turn, reduce imports. In practice, the commercial banks, which are commonly branches of overseas banks, tend to operate indepentently and autonomously, and short-term balance-of-payments deficits are usually financed by increases in short-term bank lending.[52] The situation in the British Virgin Islands, which uses the US dollar as its currency, is exactly analogous, as is that in the Cayman Islands, which until recently used Jamaican currency.[53]

But loans by the commercial banks are usually short-term in nature, to finance imports and exports, for short-term overdraft requirements, hire purchase finance for consumer durables (almost always imported), or construction loans, generally of less than three years' duration. When surpluses of deposits over advances occur, as they do from time to time, these tend to be placed in short term investments overseas (usually, to avoid unnecessary exchange risk, in the UK), and this frequently occurs *pari passu* with an inflow of long-term capital. Demas terms this 'excess borrowing' and points out that it is generally an uneconomic procedure for the territories in question since 'funds invested abroad will usually be placed in short-term assets carrying lower rates of interest than those paid on long-term loans raised abroad'.[54] There are real problems in utilising local savings in small economies. The savings market may lack a 'long-term' end, because savings tend to be short term in nature, hedging against price changes or natural disasters beyond the control of the local economy and the individual. On the other hand, the absence of a structured capital market means that commercial banks have a problem in achieving a balanced portfolio for the funds at their disposal.[55]

In respect of the earlier comments on the agricultural sector, it seems likely that the banking sector has tended, if anything, to take funds out of this sector, particularly small farming. Savings are made by small farmers commonly engaged in the production of both export and domestic crops, although these are mainly short term in nature. On the other hand, it is generally the case that advances to the agricultural sector are but a small proportion of total advances of the commercial

---

51 The monetary mechanisms of the small Caribbean economies have been analysed by Demas (1965), Thomas (1963) and 'Analyst' (1953).

52 O'Loughlin (1968) p. 129.

53 But they receive no share of currency profits, and the currency outstanding represents a free loan to the USA and Jamaica respectively.

54 Demas (1965) p. 64.

55 These are among the reasons for the establishment of the Regional Development Bank.

Table 3.10 *Value added in distribution and finance as a percentage of total imports (c.i.f):
Windwards and Leewards, 1962 to 1966*

	1962 %	1963 %	1964 %	1966 %
Grenada	29·8	36·2	32·2	29·4
St Vincent	39·2	35·7	30·3	35·2
St Lucia	29·7	33·0	26·4	27·7
Dominica	11·8	15·1	14·5	14·5
Windwards	27·8	30·6	26·2	26·8
Antigua	20·4	21·2	21·3	15·6
St Kitts	20·8	24·5	23·4	24·8
Montserrat	16·0	15·2	15·2	15·0
Leewards	20·3	21·8	21·4	17·6

Source: National accounts and trade data, reported in *Economic Surveys and Projections.*

banks. Finally, although published banking statistics do not normally distinguish between small and large farmers, it seems likely that what advances are made are given to larger farmers and estates, concentrating on exports, since they are most likely to have access to the form of security recognised by the commercial banks.[56]

Transport[57]

Table 3.7 shows that the contribution of this sector to GDP is small in all of the islands of the Windwards, the Leewards, and the Northern Group. The largest contribution was recorded in Antigua, the British Virgin Islands, and the Cayman Islands. Antigua was the headquarters of the Leeward Islands Air Transport Company (LIAT), while the Cayman Islands had its own airline (Cayman Airways Ltd) which contributed 25 per cent of the gross earnings of the sector. The British Virgin Islands, on the other hand, had a large number of trading vessels as well as a small passenger aircraft operation.

Tourism has been of some importance for the growth of this sector. Tourist spending on transport facilities has been variously estimated at between 3 per cent and 12 per cent of total tourist receipts. Tourist receipts by the transport sector accounted for some 22 per cent of total sector sales in Antigua, 16·5 per cent in St Kitts, and 58 per cent in the British Virgin Islands in 1967.[58] In the Windwards, the banana industry has been a significant source of earnings in the transport sector; Bartell estimated that some 47 per cent of total sales of the transport sector derived from the trucking and shipping of bananas in Dominica in 1963.[59] Finally, both

56 This feature of commercial banking in developing countries is not confined to the Caribbean. See for example Maynard (1970).

57 The sector includes taxis, bases, road haulage, sloops and schooners, inter-island air transport by locally based firms, and similar activities.

58 *Economic Surveys and Projections.*

59 Bartell (1965).

the construction and the distribution sectors are significant users of transport facilities.

Enough has been said to demonstrate that this sector is now highly dependent on the growth of the export sectors and construction. However, it is worth mentioning the frequently forgotten role of the inter-islands schooner trade in moving domestically produced foodstuffs between islands. Again it has to be noted that this small and potentially valuable indigenous industry has had little moral or financial support in recent years. At the same time the two former Federal ships, owned jointly by the ten islands which formed the Federation, are subsidised to the tune of $1 million (EC) per annum.[60]

Rent-of-dwellings

This sector, a convention in national income accounting, reflects actual and imputed rents for housing in the different territories.[61] Generally speaking, net actual and imputed rents amount to below 10 per cent of GDP in the region. Too much should not be made of inter-island differences, and changes over the period in question, however, since the data relating to this sector are rather weak. Housing surveys are irregular, while records of new housing are not generally kept in the islands in question. Nevertheless, the declining contribution of this sector is consistent with an income elasticity of demand for housing which is below unity; this receives some support from data reported for Barbados, Kingston, Jamaica and British Guiana in the early 1960s.[62]

The renting of houses and flats to tourists, and the ownership of houses by non-residents and retirees, is an activity of varying significance in the different islands. Very little reliable information is available on this aspect of tourism, which is generally not as yet of great importance in the tourist industry of the region as a whole. According to O'Loughlin, rents from visitors accounted for 11·8 per cent of gross rents in Antigua in 1963, and 2 per cent of gross tourist receipts.[63]

The significance of tourism to this sector is related in part to the growth in real estate development, an activity which has received encouragement from some governments in the region during the decade. In some cases this type of development has competed with agriculture for land, for example in Montserrat where some 1,200 acres had been alienated for this purpose in 1966.[64]

Government

Two important features emerge from the data relating to the contribution of government to GDP. The first is that the proportionate contribution to GDP is

60 The figure is from Hawkins, I. (1971).

61 Value added is net rent, which equals gross actual and imputed rents less maintenance, insurance etc. See also O'Loughlin (1966) and Bryden (1970).

62 Cumper in Cumper (ed.) (1960) pp. 136–49.

63 O'Loughlin (1965) pp. 32 and 16 respectively.

64 *Tripartite Survey,* p. 131.

relatively high, generally above 15 per cent, and in some islands above 20 per cent.[65] The second is that this proportion has remained fairly static in general, and in some cases it has declined significantly, for example in Antigua and the British Virgin Islands.

The importance of the government sector is a reflection of the very high costs of administration per capita in small territories which are geographically and politically fragmented. Demas suggests that 'for a country with less than three million people, the full economies of scale of basic governmental administration services may not be realised. And apart from strictly administrative services, there may also be economies of scale in the operation of certain public utilities, in particular railways, telephones and water systems'.[66] On this criterion, severe diseconomies are bound to exist in the provision of governmental services and utilities in the territories of the region. In 1964, recurrent expenditures on services other than public utilities ranged from $66 per capita in St Vincent to $160 per capita in Antigua. The corresponding figure for Barbados, with a population approaching a quarter of a million, and a higher standard of public services and utilities, was $108·1 in 1964; this was lower than Antigua and Montserrat, and only a little above that in St Kitts.[67]

That the proportionate contribution of government to GDP has remained fairly static, or even declined, may be attributed to a number of factors. Firstly in many of the territories the limits of taxable capacity given the present revenue sources may well have been reached, and there has been little attempt at major fiscal reform in the region during the decade.[68] Secondly, much of the increase in GDP has come from tourism and construction. Imports for the construction of hotels are generally duty free, while most hotels in the region pay no direct taxes on profits.[69] Though of less importance, the same applies to much of the growth in manufacturing. Thirdly, food imports have sometimes increased more rapidly than total imports, and these are often subject to low rates of duty.[70] Finally, in some islands there has apparently been a tendency for the ratio of government sector GDP to government current expenditure to fall.[71]

The structure of government revenues in the smaller islands of the region is shown in Tables 3.11 and 3.12.

The dominance of import duties as a source of local revenues is to be expected in small 'open' economies. Export duties are of less importance, particularly in the

65 Government and Public Utilities accounted for 9 per cent of GDP in Jamaica in 1961, 12·8 per cent in Trinidad, 10·7 per cent in British Guiana in 1960. Demas (1965) p. 108.

66 Demas (1965) p. 57.

67 *Tripartite Survey,* Statistical Table No. 6.

68 The major untapped source of revenue is a land tax based on land valuations. Proposals for such a tax in the small islands have been made from time to time, but implementation has been frustrated by the absence of adequate records of land ownership, divergences between law and custom in the matter of transfer of rights, and fear of the unknown, e.g. discouragement of capital inflow etc. See also Chapter 8.

69 See Chapter 8.

70 See page 33 above.

71 For example, Antigua.

Table 3.11 *Sources of government recurrent revenues, 1964 and 1966 $000 EC*

	Windwards 1964	1966	Leewards 1964	1966	N. Group 1964[c]	1966[d]
Import duty	10,482	12,799	5,151	7,055	1,285	1,328
Export duty	1,754	2,186	480	350	4	–
Excise duty	1,315	1,417	422	530	–	–
Income tax	3,619	4,895	2,487	2,721	–	–
Hotel tax[a]	–	–	120	193	12	23
Other taxes and licences	1,542	1,816	969	1,269	58	65
Other revenue raised[b]	2,796	3,015	2,834	2,408	254	623
Public utilities	2,219	2,936	3,297	4,745	77	111
Total local rev.	23,727	29,064	15,760	19,116	1,609	2,150
Recurrent aid	5,440	6,282	2,600	2,736	730	53
Total recurrent revenue	29,167	35,346	18,360	22,016	2,420	2,203

Notes:
[a] i.e. taxes levied on a bed-night or percentage of sales basis.
[b] Includes fees, fines, sales of produce and stamps, rents, interest, currency profits and other miscellaneous small items.
[c] Turks and Caicos and Cayman Islands only.
[d] Cayman Islands only.
Sources: Economic Surveys and Projections; government estimates.

Table 3.12 *Percentage distribution of recurrent revenue by source, 1964 and 1966*

Source	Windwards 1964	1966	Leewards 1964	1966	N. Group 1964[a]	1966[b]
Import duty	36·0	36·2	28·0	32·0	53·1	60·3
Export duty	6·0	6·2	2·6	1·6	0·2	–
Excise duty	4·5	4·1	2·3	2·4	–	–
Income tax	12·4	13·8	13·6	12·4	–	–
Hotel tax	–	–	0·7	0·9	0·5	1·0
Other taxes and licences	5·3	5·1	5·3	5·8	2·4	3·0
Other revenue raised	9·6	8·5	15·4	10·9	10·5	28·2
Public utilities	7·6	8·3	17·9	21·6	3·2	5·0
Total local rev.	81·4	82·2	85·8	87·6	69·9	97·5
Recurrent aid	18·6	17·8	14·2	12·4	30·1	2·5
Total recurrent	100·0	100·0	100·0	100·0	100·0	100·0

Notes:
[a] Turks and Caicos and Caymans only.
[b] Caymans only.
Sources: Table 3.11

Leewards and the Northern Group. Hotel tax, which is sometimes levied on the basis of the number of bed-nights and sometimes on the basis of hotel bills for accommodation and meals, is a form of 'export duty' although in this case it may be argued that part of the burden falls on tourists.[72] This tax has statistical as well as fiscal utility, though its contribution to revenue is, as yet, small. Income taxes, including taxes on corporate profits, are important in the Leewards and Windwards where they are quite steeply progressive.[73] However, there are no income taxes in the Turks and Caicos or the Cayman Islands, and rates of income tax in the British Virgin Islands are very low. Taxes on property, included in 'other taxes and licences', are as yet unimportant in all of the smaller islands.

Other revenue raised includes the sale of stamps, which tends to become relatively more important the smaller the island. The main reason for this is the demand by foreign philatelists, which tends to be fairly stable *between* islands irrespective of their size. Sales of stamps to this market were estimated at some $164,000 EC in the British Virgin Islands in 1968, and some $230,000 in the Cayman Islands in 1967. The comparable figure for Antigua in 1967 was $202,500 EC.[74]

The other major source of current revenue is receipts of public utilities, of rather greater importance in the Leewards where electricity generation is commonly a government activity.[75] However, the significance of this source is largely illusory, since many public utilities make losses. Furthermore, a large proportion of the capital costs of some public utilities — notably airports, harbours and water supplies — were met by grants from aid donors. Consequently, debt charges which do exist seriously understate the true economic costs of capital employed in utilities. It is notable in this respect that airports and harbours are usually the only utilities to show a current surplus. Bearing this point in mind, some idea of the operating position of public utilities in the Eastern Caribbean may be obtained from Table 3.13 below.

In order that these figures may be seen in perspective, it is worth noting that, between 1966 and 1969, one island in the above group budgeted for capital projects in utilities amounting to some $25·6 millions. The breakdown of these capital projects was as follows:[76]

Deep water harbour	$12 millions EC[77]
Airport rehabilitation etc.	$3·9 millions EC
Electricity projects	$4·9 millions EC
Water projects	$2·8 millions EC
Telephone system	$2.0 millions EC

72 It is doubtful whether this argument would hold true in the longer run. In the short run its validity probably depends more on the high proportion of 'new' visitors who are *ex ante* unaware of the existence of the new tax, rather than on the relevant elasticities.

73 At least in theory. In practice there are severe problems of administration, and evasion tends to be widespread. Partly because of these problems, and partly to encourage real estate development, Montserrat reduced its rates of income tax substantially in 1967.

74 *Economic Surveys and Projections.*

75 See Table 3.13. In Dominica, government was only responsible for a minor part of the total operation of electricity.

76 *Estimates of Revenue and Expenditure of Antigua,* 1966, 1967, 1968, 1969, Government Printing Office, Antigua.

77 For some reason expenditure on the harbour has never appeared overtly in the Estimates. The figure is from *Economic Survey and Projections,* Antigua (1969).

Table 3.13 *Operating position of public utilities: E. Caribbean 1965*

| | Operating profits (losses) $000 EC | | | | |
	Airports	Harbours	Electricity	Water	Telephones
Grenada	(5)	99	nil[a]	(4)	nil[a]
St Vincent	23	191	nil[a]	(15)	(37)
St Lucia	29	226	(28)	n.a.	(66)
Dominica	(26)	273	(7)	n.a.	(99)
Antigua	445	64	188	(210)	17[b]
St Kitts	30	120	(118)	(45)	(61)
Montserrat	1	25	13	(35)	(11)
Totals	497[c]	998[d]	46[e]	(309)[f]	(257)[g]

Notes:
[a] Operated privately.
[b] The surplus on telephones is ironic. The country telephone system has been described as one 'through which often whispering of cane on the wires is the only voice that can be heard'. O'Loughlin (1963)
[c] Loan charges of $10,800 in Antigua. Antigua was at that time the only island in the group with an international airport.
[d] Loan charges of $1,000 in Montserrat.
[e] Loan charges of $426,150 included.
[f] Loan charges of $80,000 included.
[g] Loan charges of $18,060 in Antigua.

The declining dependence on recurrent budgetary aid (mainly grants in aid provided by the UK government) is of some significance in view of the substantial powers which this form of aid gave to the UK government in matters of financial policy.[78] It is not surprising that a major objective of governments in the region has been to reduce this dependence as rapidly as possible, and the achievement of this objective has been assisted by the fairly buoyant local revenues. By the end of the decade seven islands in the Commonwealth Caribbean were dependent on this source.[79]

While recurrent aid in money terms remained almost static at around $9 millions between 1961 and 1966 for the Leewards and Windwards as a whole, capital grants increased markedly from some $6·5 millions EC in 1961 to some $12 millions EC in 1966.[80] In addition, as islands have 'come out of grant-in-aid' of recurrent budget, they have tended to utilise slack debt capacity which existed as a result of stringent control of debt policy under the grants-in-aid system.[81] The net result has been an increased dependence on aid and loan funds for capital expenditures during the decade. Table 3.14 below shows the sources of capital account revenues of the various governments between 1964 and 1967.

It will be argued in Chapter 8 that a very substantial proportion of government capital expenditures was in infrastructure and utilities directly or indirectly serving

78 See O'Loughlin (1968) pp. 172–3.

79 These were Grenada, St Vincent, Dominica, Montserrat, St Kitts, Turks and Caicos and the British Virgin Islands. However, Grenada, St Vincent, Dominica and the British Virgin Islands had made very substantial progress towards ending dependence on grants-in-aid.

80 1961 figures are from O'Loughlin (1963) Table 15, p. 135. 1966 figures are from *Economic Surveys and Projections.* Total aid in 1953 was some $3·0 millions: Prest (1957).

81 O'Loughlin (1963).

Table 3.14 *Capital revenue sources, 1964–7 inclusive: E. Caribbean ($000 EC)*

	Local sources[a]	Loan funds	Capital grants[b]	Other sources	Total capital rev.
Grenada	67	1,612	5,738	486	7,903
St Vincent	265	–	5,067	–	5,332
St Lucia	3,465	473[c]	3,796	–	7,734
Dominica	52	115	4,837	–	5,004
Antigua	2,361	12,651	4,661	–	19,673
St Kitts	224	4,419	3,902	–	8,545
Montserrat	103	2,551	6,409	127	9,190
Total	6,547	21,821	34,410	613	63,381

Notes:
[a] Includes transfers from recurrent budget, sales of assets including crown lands, and other miscellaneous items.
[b] Mainly CD and W.
[c] Includes a 'deficit' of $333,000 budgeted in 1966, presumably financed by overdraft borrowing.
Sources: Economic Surveys and Projections. Figures are mostly *actuals* for 1964–6 and revised estimates for 1967. This explains the slight inconsistency with the totals for public capital formation in Tables 3.5 and 3.6.

the tourist industry. Although some of the funds involved have been obtained in the form of capital grants, it is suggested that this does not constitute adequate grounds for presuming such funds to have a low or even zero opportunity cost. Consequently, any evaluation of the costs and benefits of tourism will have to take into account the costs involved in diverting these resources to the encouragement of tourism.

The trend towards increasing dependency on aid and loan funds adds urgency to this point, since it is difficult to see this trend continuing even if it were desirable. Slack debt capacity has, at least in some islands, been virtually used up, and the burden of debt servicing has increased. Inevitably, the rate of increase in new debt will slow down unless substantial new revenue sources can be found, or the rate of growth of revenue substantially increased. But the prospects for this depend ultimately on the prospects for the economy as a whole, which in turn depend on the export sectors, construction, and domestic agriculture.

Summary and conclusions

This chapter has been concerned with the changes in economic structure of the smaller Commonwealth Caribbean islands which have occurred during the past decade. In particular, an attempt has been made to identify those changes which seem, on an inter-temporal and inter-island comparison, to be particularly associated with growth in tourism.

The principal aggregates relating to domestic product, population and trade suggest a rising income per capita (probably in real as well as money terms), a rising import coefficient, and a rising deficit of visible trade in the smaller islands as a whole. The increasing trade deficit has been financed by increasing tourist receipts and increasing capital inflows on private and public account.

For analytical purposes, it is convenient to distinguish between the export sectors, the construction sector, and the domestic sectors. The principal 'export' sectors are export agriculture and 'hotels and services'. Export agriculture is insignificant in the Northern Group and the Bahamas, but relatively important in the Windwards and Leewards. The Windwards have expanded banana production rapidly during the decade, mainly expanding their share of the UK market at the expense of Jamaica. This expansion has been responsible for a sector growth rate of nearly 9 per cent per annum. In the Leewards, whose main agricultural exports are sugar and, to a minor extent, cotton, the value of agricultural exports, and the value added in export agriculture have declined absolutely as well as relatively.

Hotels and services, which grew at a modest rate in the Windwards, grew rapidly in the Leewards and the Northern Group. In the region as a whole, gross tourist receipts had overtaken receipts from agricultural exports by the end of the decade, whereas at the beginning of the decade tourist receipts were roughly half the value of agricultural exports. However, such direct comparisons of foreign exchange receipts are of little relevance in view of the different input structure as between the different export sectors. In particular, tourism has a higher import content and a lower value added per unit of foreign exchange earned *vis-à-vis* export agriculture,

The level of capital formation in both private and public sectors has been high during the decade, due largely to increased capital inflows. This is particularly true of the Leewards and the Northern Group, suggesting some positive association with the growth and relative importance of tourism in the islands. Construction activity provided a substantial part of GDP in these islands, but this contribution is especially vulnerable in view of its critical dependence on capital inflows.

So far as the domestic sectors are concerned, their relative importance has declined in all islands during the decade. The most important 'domestic' sector from the point of view of autonomous income generation capacity is domestic agriculture, and it is in this sector that the most important and significant declines occurred. According to the data available, the output of this sector declined absolutely during the decade in all of the smaller islands except Dominica, Montserrat and St Kitts, which, significantly, are the islands with the smallest hotel sectors. These trends tend to be confirmed by an examination of food import data and a check on overall self-sufficiency and total food supplies. In the Cayman Islands, the British Virgin Islands and the Bahamas, agriculture has dwindled to the status of an almost peripheral activity.

It is argued that the declines in domestic agriculture — and in some cases export agriculture as well — are mainly the result of competition for resources, for which the rapid growth in tourism and related investments has been primarily responsible, and possibly also (but more tentatively) of the effects of tourism on consumption patterns. These effects are most noticeable in the Leewards and the Northern Group, where tourism has grown most rapidly and is of greater relative importance. In the Windwards, the evidence is not so clear in view of the rapid growth of the banana industry which has also competed for resources with domestic agriculture. This competition for resources occurs in two related ways. First there is competition for labour, and, to a lesser extent, land and domestic capital resources. Second, there is competition for public resources which could bring about changes in the agricultural production functions in the face of changing resource availabilities.

This argument depends on two basic assumptions. First, that the relevant resources are limiting, and second, that public resources are increasingly necessary to change the agricultural production functions. Both of these assumptions are supported by the evidence of expert observers in the region, and by the evidence in Chapter 2. In many islands this constitutes the only rational explanation for the structural changes that have taken place.

But to establish the validity of this argument is not to prove that it would have been more socially beneficial to devote the available resources in other directions. All it suggests is that some or all of the resources used have positive opportunity costs. It is this conclusion that serves as the starting point for the later analysis of the impact of tourism.

Appendix Table 3A.1 *Estimates of gross domestic product by main sectors at current factor cost*, Eastern Caribbean territories, 1962 and 1966 ($000 EC)*

A 1962	Grenada	St Vincent	St Lucia	Dominica	Windward Islands total	Antigua	Montserrat	St Kitts–Nevis–Anguilla	Leeward Islands total
Main exporting sectors:									
Export agriculture	5,200	4,500	5,991	3,618	19,309	2,449	280	5,425	9,154
Hotels and services	2,111	2,100[a]	1,987	1,192	7,390	2,806	122	1,247	4,175
Main domestic sectors:									
Domestic agriculture	5,851	5,310	3,569	3,651	18,361	1,147	1,106	2,230	4,483
Manufacturing	651[b]	260[c]	1,514[d]	1,816[e]	4,241	607[f]	70[g]	200[h]	877
Construction	2,961	1,428	2,186	1,919	8,494	4,546	430	1,909	6,885
Government	5,450	3,964	5,161	3,189	17,764	4,229	1,010	3,499	8,738
Other sectors:									
Distribution/finance	3,970	4,891	4,973	1,506	15,340	4,424	405	2,800	7,629
Transportation	824	648	763	562	2,797	841	43	333	1,217
Rent-of-dwellings	2,170	2,575	1,998	2,730	9,473	1,621	260	1,263	3,144
Total GDP	29,168	25,676	28,142	20,183	103,169	22,669	3,826	19,906	46,401
B 1966									
Main exporting sectors:									
Export agriculture	7,100	4,990	10,540	4,508	27,148	1,090	271	6,420	7,781
Hotels and services	3,195	1,853	3,834	1,542	10,424	5,967	471	1,697	8,135
Main domestic sectors:									
Domestic agriculture	5,280	3,520	3,209	4,283	16,292	927	1,193	2,460	4,580
Manufacturing	1,140[b]	1,161[c]	1,814[d]	2,095[e]	6,210	980[f]	100[g]	486[h]	1,566
Construction	2,850	1,880	3,398	2,580	10,708	17,508[i]	1,335	1,625	20,368
Government	5,870	5,639	7,247	4,946	23,702	5,225	1,661	5,079	11,965

Other sectors:									
Distribution/finance	6,382	5,403	7,856	2,580	22,221	6,842	908	3,434	11,184
Transportation	1,230	842	1,195	1,036	4,303	1,689	91	482	2,262
Rent-of-dwellings	2,674	2,976	2,323	3,384	11,357	2,021	345	1,350	3,716
Total GDP	35,731	28,264	41,416	26,954	132,365	42,158	6,375	22,673	71,206

Sources:

1962 data *National Accounts* of Antigua, Dominica, St Kitts prepared by the ISER (E. Caribbean) at UWI. For methods and sources see O'Loughlin (1966).

1966 data *Economic Surveys and Projections* for the various territories prepared by the British Development Division in the Caribbean. These followed the O'Loughlin methodology as closely as was possible. See also Bryden (1969) for a detailed account of methodology employed.

Notes:

a The estimate for this sector was reduced to 1,381·0 in 1963 by O'Loughlin.

b Includes electricity which accounted for 25·6% of total sector sales in 1966.

c Includes electricity.

d Excludes electricity which is a government utility. Coconut oil manufacture accounts for 23·6% of total sector sales in 1966.

e Includes electricity which was responsible for 10·8% of sector sales in 1966. Lime juice and lime oil were 41% of total sector sales in 1961, but only 24·7% in 1966 due partly to growth in other manufactures and partly to decline in prices of lime products.

f Excludes electricity which is a government utility. An oil refinery which commenced production in 1967 will boost the sales of this sector considerably. As is the convention in sugar islands, sugar manufacture has been included in export agriculture.

g Excludes electricity which is a government utility.

h Excludes electricity which is a government utility, and, as in Antigua, sugar processing.

i 1966 was an abnormal year for construction and investment in Antigua, and it is now thought that, in spite of this, the estimates for that year may have been too high in view of the high proportion of capital equipment in relation to construction work and the unreliability of the investment figures for the oil refinery, the chief cause of the abnormal rise. In 1967, the proportional contribution had dropped to 27·5 per cent in spite of a relatively large government capital programme in that year financed mainly by loans.

Appendix Table 3A.2 *Proportionate contribution to GDP by sectors, Eastern Caribbean 1962 and 1966 (%)*

	Grenada %	St Vincent %	St Lucia %	Dominica %	Windward Islands total %	Antigua %	Montserrat %	St Kitts–Nevis–Anguilla %	Leeward Islands total %
A 1962									
Export agriculture	17·9	17·5	21·3	18·0	18·7	10·8	7·3	32·3	19·7
Hotels and services	7·3	8·2	7·1	5·9	7·2	12·4	3·2	6·3	9·0
Domestic agriculture	20·0	20·7	12·7	18·1	17·8	5·0	28·9	11·2	9·7
Manufacturing	2·2	1·0	5·4	8·7	4·1	2·7	1·8	1·0	1·9
Construction	10·2	8·6	7·8	9·5	8·2	20·1	11·2	9·6	14·9
Government	18·7	15·4	18·4	15·8	7·2	18·7	26·4	17·6	18·8
Distribution/finance	13·6	19·0	17·7	7·5	14·8	19·6	10·6	14·1	16·4
Transportation	2·8	2·5	2·7	2·8	2·7	3·7	1·1	1·7	2·6
Rent-of-dwellings	7·5	10·0	7·1	13·5	9·2	7·2	6·8	6·4	6·8
Total all sectors	100	100	100	100	100	100	100	100	100
B 1966									
Export agriculture	19·9	17·6	27·9	16·8	20·5	2·6	4·2	28·3	10·9
Hotels and services	8·9	6·6	9·3	5·7	7·9	14·1	7·4	7·5	11·4
Domestic agriculture	14·8	12·5	7·8	15·9	12·3	2·2	18·8	10·9	6·4
Manufacturing[a]	3·2	4·1	4·4	7·8	4·7	2·3	1·6	2·1	2·2
Construction	7·7	6·6	8·2	9·6	8·1	41·5[b]	21·0	7·2	28·6
Government	16·4	19·9	17·5	18·3	17·9	12·4	26·1	22·4	16·8
Distribution/finance	17·8	19·1	19·0	9·6	16·8	16·2	14·2	15·1	15·7
Transportation	3·4	3·0	2·9	3·8	3·2	4·0	1·4	2·1	3·2
Rent-of-dwellings	7·5	10·5	5·6	12·6	8·6	4·8	5·4	6·0	5·2
Total all sectors	100	100	100	100	100	100	100	100	100

Source: Computed from Table 3A.1

Notes:

[a] See notes on manufacturing sector in Table 3A.1.

[b] See note i. in Table 3A.1.

51

Appendix Table 3A.3 *Average annual growth rates of GDP by sectors, Eastern Caribbean, 1962–6 in per cent per annum*

	Grenada	St Vincent	St Lucia	Dominica	Windward Islands total	Antigua	Montserrat	St Kitts–Nevis–Anguilla	Leeward Islands total
	% p.a.	% p.a.	% p.a.	% p.a.	% p.a.	% p.a.	% p.a.	% p.a.	% p.a.
Export agriculture	8·1	2·6	14·9	5·6	8·9	–18·3	–0·8	4·3	–4·0
Hotels and services	10·9	–3·0[a]	17·9	6·6	8·9	20·8	40·2	8·0	18·1
Domestic agriculture	–2·4	–9·8	–2·6	4·1	–2·9	–5·2	1·9	2·5	0·5
Manufacturing[b]	15·0	45·4	4·6	3·6	10·0	12·7	9·3	24·8	15·6
Construction	–0·9	7·1	11·7	7·7	6·0	40·1	32·7	–3·9	31·1
Government	1·9	9·2	8·9	11·6	7·5	5·4	13·2	9·8	8·2
Distribution/finance	12·6	2·5	12·1	14·4	9·7	11·5	22·4	5·2	10·0
Transportation	10·5	6·8	11·9	16·5	11·4	19·0	20·6	9·7	16·8
Rent-of-dwellings	5·4	3·7	3·8	5·5	4·6	5·7	7·3	1·7	4·3
Total all sectors	5·4	2·5	11·5	7·5	6·0	17	13·5	4·8	12

Source: Derived from Table 3A.1

Notes:

a The estimated contribution of this sector was reduced considerably in 1963 to $1,381,000. Based on this figure the growth rate for 1963–6 would be 10·4 per cent per annum for St Vincent.

b See notes to Table 3A.1.

Appendix Table 3A.4 *Antigua – Government current expenditures on and related to agriculture 1960–8*

	1960 (actual) $	1962 (actual) $	1964 (actual) $	1966 (actual) $	1968 (estimated) $
1 Administration	134,240	145,076	155,416	164,818	156,966
2 Peasant development	129,982	1,294,514	1,291,083	195,745	226,659
3 Fisheries	47,593	97,890	80,884	50,623	48,886
4 Botanic gardens	6,971	6,455	6,287	6,301	6,627
5 Veterinary	–	–	22,099	17,474	58,006
sub total	*312,154*	*1,543,935*	*1,555,769*	*434,961*	*497,144*
6 'Self-balancing' exp	1,431,890	–[a]	–[a]	–[b]	–
less Revenue items	*1,098,893*	*986,164*	*764,479*	*45,654*[b]	*73,568*
Net expenditures	*645,151*	*557,771*	*791,290*	*389,307*	*423,576*

Source: Antigua government estimates, 1962, 1964, 1966 and 1968 giving actual expenditures for 1960, 1962, 1964 and 1966 together with estimated expenditure for 1968.
Notes:
[a] Moved to peasant development in 1962.
[b] Peasant development services reorganised in 1965–6 so that self-balancing items did not appear in the estimates from that date.

The context: international tourism and developing countries

Introduction to Part II

The purpose of this section is twofold. In Chapter 4, the role of tourism in the international economy, especially in relation to developing countries, is examined. Statistical data relating to tourist numbers and tourist receipts are analysed, and the place of the Caribbean in this overall picture identified.

Recognising that simple analysis of tourist receipts tells us very little indeed about the economic and social impact of tourism, Chapter 5 is concerned with the general question of *how* one would seek to measure this impact. Special emphasis is placed on a methodology for small 'open' developing countries. It is here, against the background of previous approaches to this question, and a discussion of the theoretical issues involved, that the method to be used in Part IV for measuring the economic and social impact of tourism in the Caribbean is outlined.

4　Tourism in the world economy

Studies of the role of tourism in the international economy are only now beginning to appear in published sources, although 'scientific' approaches to the study of tourism in individual countries date back to perhaps the beginning of the century. The leaders in this field appear to have been the Italians, and an early work by Bodio[1] was followed by further studies in Italy, Germany, the United States and Czechoslovakia.[2] Works of reference in English are few and far between, and that of Ogilvie[3] written in 1933 was probably the first to examine the economic significance of tourism on a cross-country basis. These early works were largely concerned with the problems of statistical measurement which arise in any quantitative study of tourism, and made valuable contributions in this field. The feasibility of studies of world tourist movements and international flows of resources consequent upon tourist development was clearly limited by an extreme paucity of information.

More recent studies have attempted to examine tourism on an international scale, and these rely heavily on data collected by the International Union of Official Travel Organisations (IUOTO) in Geneva. These data, it is freely admitted, are still far from complete.[4]

The most recent published work of this kind is that of Michael Peters,[5] who obtained most of his information from IUOTO sources. According to Peters, world tourist expenditure — both domestic and foreign — now comprises about five per cent of total world consumer expenditure. Between the years 1950 and 1966 total international tourist expenditures are estimated in the same source to have grown at twelve per cent per annum, or almost twice the annual rate of growth of national incomes over the same period.[6] Some reservations must be expressed about the quality of the data used in arriving at these estimates, but if the order of magnitude can be taken as broadly correct, tourism must now be recognised as an important activity both nationally and internationally.

The high growth rates are the result of continued rapid expansion in national

1　Bodio, L. 'Sul Movimento dei Forestieri in Italia e sul Denaro che vi Spendono', *Giornale degli Economisti,* 1899.

2　For details see the bibliographical note at the end of this chapter.

3　Ogilvie (1933).

4　IUOTO, *International Travel Statistics,* published annually since 1953.

5　Peters (1969).

6　Peters (1969) p. 21.

incomes in the developed countries combined with increasing leisure time for significant numbers of people. These features mean that the income elasticity of demand for travel services in the developed countries tends to be very high.[7] In addition, there has been a general downward trend in air fares since 1950, particularly on routes between Europe and North America.[8] IATA studies have indicated that the price elasticity of demand for vacational travel is relatively high – an elasticity of 2·0 having been calculated for US vacationers to Europe.[9]

Finally, there has been a rapid expansion of charter-inclusive tour traffic, which multiplied nearly ten fold between 1960 and 1966 on intra-European routes and showed substantial growth on other routes as well.[10]

Although the majority of expenditures on tourism are still made within national boundaries, some 22 per cent of total tourist expenditures are estimated as being spent on foreign travel, and, as Table 4.1 indicates, international tourism has also expanded rapidly during the 1960s.[11]

There is no doubt that this expansion of international tourism and the demand conditions associated with it have suggested considerable potential for foreign exchange earnings to developing countries in general, particularly those who are located in a favourable position *vis-à-vis* the main tourist markets in Europe and North America. The growth in Caribbean tourism is thus only one aspect of a more general phenomenon, and it is significant that many developing countries outside the Caribbean have recently introduced legislation to promote and facilitate foreign investment in the tourism industry of the country.[12]

Tourism has seemed more attractive in view of the problems faced by many countries in expanding exports of 'traditional' commodities and the high tariffs facing exports of manufactures. In addition, the future potential for protectionist policies of import substitution has been seriously questioned by some writers.[13]

It is not clear from Peters' study to what extent the figures given in Table 3.1 are complete. However, an examination of his source material, the IUOTO annual statistics, suggests that there are some gaps, particularly in the case of developing countries. And greater gaps exist in data for tourist receipts than in data for tourist arrivals. Consequently, in the analysis that follows, data have only been used

7 Certainly above unity. A cross-section analysis by the IUOTO suggests an income elasticity of 1·5 over all countries, this coefficient tending to rise with income level. IUOTO *Study of the Impact of Tourism*, Geneva 1966, p. 15.

8 This trend has not been uniform. Air fares from London to Nairobi, Accra, Delhi, Bangkok, Tokyo and Sydney went up between 1950 and 1968. Peters (1969), Exhibit 6, p. 273.

9 IUOTO, *Economic Review of World Tourism*, 1970 p. 51.

10 Peters (1969) pp. 84 to 88 and Table 38.

11 Peters (1969) p. 27, states 'In 1967 some £26,000 million were spent on tourism in the world, of which nearly one-quarter, £6,000 million, was spent on international tourism.'

12 IUOTO *Economic Review of World Tourism* (1970) p. 44. The review mentions Ceylon, India, Iran and Thailand, but many African countries have also introduced favourable legislation for tourism during the 1960s.

13 For example Little, Scitovsky and Scott (1970). These features are discussed at greater length in Chapter 1.

Table 4.1 *International tourist receipts and arrivals, 1960–7*

Year	Receipts, £ m[a]	Total arrivals, millions[b]
1960	2,444	71·0
1961	2,601	75·3
1962	2,900	81·4
1963	3,147	92·8
1964	3,623	106·4
1965	4,163	117·8
1966	4,644	128·2
1967	5,050	138·0
Average growth rate p.a. 1960–7	10·9%	10·0%

Source: Peters (1969) Exhibit 2 p. 269; Exhibit 3, p. 270.
Notes:
[a] Excludes expenditure on international transportation.
[b] Recorded tourist arrivals summed by country. To the extent that many tourists visit a number of countries this overstates the actual number of individuals involved.

where *both* receipts and arrivals figures are available. This procedure is different from that used by the IUOTO and, presumably, by Peters, which means that the figures will not be strictly comparable with those reported by these studies. In addition, greater coverage of the Commonwealth Caribbean is possible as a result of information produced during the past few years and reported in Chapters 6 and 7. IUOTO coverage of this region is still incomplete.

A distinction has also been made between 'developed' and 'developing' countries for the purposes of the present study. This distinction is not made by either the IUOTO or by Peters. For convenience, the OECD definition of 'developing' countries is used with the addition of some rather notable exclusions.[14] Table 4.2 below shows the consequent distribution of tourist arrivals and tourist receipts by developing and developed regions.

These figures reveal the dominant position of Europe and North America in the international tourist business. In terms of developing countries, those of Europe and the Mediterranean have the major share, as might be expected from their general proximity to the more prosperous countries of Europe and their relative proximity to North America.[15] Although the Commonwealth Caribbean has a rather minor share of total receipts and arrivals, its position among developing countries outside Europe and the Mediterranean is quite significant, especially when considered against the relatively small population and land area of the region.[16]

If one is interested in where the tourists come from in the different regions, it is necessary to distinguish between arrivals who come from *within* the region and

14 Notably Portugal, Bulgaria, Albania. In theory China, Tibet, N. Korea, N. Vietnam and Mongolia ought also to be included, but in practice data are not yet available for these countries.

15 This is especially true, if one considers economic rather than geographic proximity – because of the lower air fares per mile on North Atlantic routes, and the greater importance on non-scheduled charter traffic across the N. Atlantic and within Europe itself.

16 The relative 'density' of tourism, expressed in terms of population or land area, in tourist countries is discussed in Chapter 5.

Table 4.2 *International tourist receipts and arrivals in 1965 by developing and developed regions*[a]

Region	Tourist arrivals '000	% of total	Tourist receipts[b] $ m	% of total
Developing				
Africa	1,459·7	1·3	147·4	1·3
Asia	3,143·8	2·9	387·2	3·5
America, S and C	2,713·5	2·5	1,079·6	9·8
Commonwealth Caribbean[c]	947·8	0·9	150·7	1·4
Europe and Mediterranean	18,738·2	17·2	1,569·8	14·3
Sub totals	27,003·0	24·8	3,334·7	30·4
Developed				
Europe	16,456·0	56·5	5,514·5	50·2
N. America	19,393·8	17·8	1,906·7	17·4
S. Africa	226·9	0·2	49·0	0·4
Asia and Oceania[d]	633·2	0·6	178·5	1·6
Sub totals	81,709·8	75·2	7,648·7	69·6
Total world[a]	108,712·8	100·0	10,983·4	100·0

Notes:
[a] See appendix A to this chapter for exclusions.
[b] Excluding transportation.
[c] Trinidad, Jamaica, Barbados, Windward Islands, Leeward Islands, British Virgin Islands, Cayman Islands, Turks and Caicos and the Bahamas.
[d] Japan, Australia and New Zealand.
Source: IUOTO *International Travel Statistics* 1965 *except* for Caribbean. For Caribbean sources see Tables 6.1 and 6.11 below.

those who are inter-regional, or come from outside the region as defined. Similarly if one is interested in *net* flows of tourists and tourist receipts in different regions, it is necessary to distinguish between arrivals in a region and arrivals generated by that region. Peters carries out such an analysis on his definition of 'regions' and his results are summarised in Table 4.3 below.

In so far as inter-regional tourism is taken as being synonomous with 'longhaul' tourism, it appears from Table 4.3 that North America is by far the most important net contributor to the longhaul tourist market, and Europe the most important net gainer.

But the results of this analysis are highly dependent on the choice of region and the degree of disaggregation. For present purposes, it is important to distinguish between developed and developing countries and Table 4.4 below gives the results of a similar analysis based on the previous classification of developed and developing regions.

This analysis reveals a different picture. From the point of view of the developing countries, the developed countries of Europe provide the greatest number of total inter-regional arrivals.

The developing countries themselves provide a substantial proportion of inter-regional arrivals, especially the developing countries of Europe and the Mediterranean.

Table 4.3 *Tourist arrivals and arrivals generated by region, 1965*

Region	Arrivals (thousands)		Arrivals generated (thousands)		'Net' inter-regional generation of arrivals[b] (thousands)
	From within region[a]	Inter-regional	In same region	Inter-regional	
Europe	66,581	9,113	66,580	2,292	− 6,821
N. America	19,208	1,073	19,208	8,632	+ 7,559
Latin America	526	1,134	527	750	− 384
Middle East	516	713	516	658	− 55
Africa	558	981	558	1,010	+ 29
Asia/Australasia	1,439	1,177	1,439	849	− 328
Total	88,828	14,191	88,828	14,191	0

Notes:
[a] These are equal to arrivals 'generated' in the same region, and thus balance out in any given region.
[b] Inter-regional arrivals generated *less* inter-regional arrivals, giving some idea of the relative contribution to the 'long haul' tourism market.
Source: Peters (1969) Tables 12 and 13.

Table 4.4 *Tourist arrivals and arrivals generated by developed and developing regions, 1965[a]*

Region	Arrivals (thousands)		Arrivals generated (thousands)	
	From same region	Inter-regional	In same region	Inter-regional
Developing				
Africa	481·3	764·3	481·3	738·3
Asia	2,066·7	1,705·1	2,066·7	617·5
S and C America	617·4	2,031·2	617·4	1,067·1
Commonwealth Caribbean	48·6	324·5	48·6	19·0
Europe and Mediterranean	3,414·6	14,589·3	3,414·6	3,932·8
Sub total	6,628·6	19,423·4	6,628·6	6,374·7
Developed				
Europe	54,620·5	11,924·1	54,620·5	14.908·5
N. America	39,638·4	1,363·7	39,638·4	10,978·8
S. Africa	nil	223·5	nil	276·9
Asia/Australasia	132·5	565·0	132·5	819·7
Sub total	94,391·4	14,076·3	94,391·4	26,983·9

Note:
[a] Includes *all* countries which give the necessary breakdown of tourists by nationality. see Appendix B to this chapter for exclusions.
Source: IUOTO *International Travel Statistics*, 1965.

The main reason for the difference is the division of Europe into 'developed' and 'developing' countries, surely a legitimate procedure, because as it can be just as far and just as expensive for residents of Northern European countries to travel to Southern Europe and the Mediterranean as it is for North Americans to visit parts of

Latin America and the Caribbean.

The totals in Table 4.4 differ from those in Table 4.2. This is partly due to the inclusion of all countries which have data on arrivals by nationality even if they have none on tourist receipts,[17] but mainly due to the number of tourists not classified by nationality in the individual country data; that is to say, they appear in the category 'other countries'. Observation of country data suggests that these 'other countries' are mainly developing countries, many of which, if taken individually, do not feature largely in the generation of tourist arrivals. North American countries and the larger developed countries of Europe appear individually in the statistics of nearly every country. The total number of arrivals under the category 'other countries' in 1965 was 5,638,100, of which 4,234,000 were arrivals in developed countries. It is probable, therefore, that Table 4.4 substantially understates the inter-regional generation of tourist arrivals by developing countries and, consequently, overstates the apparent net flow to developing countries from developed countries.

With this in mind, Table 4.5 indicates the regional balances of tourist arrivals and arrivals generated.

Peters' conclusions must therefore be somewhat modified. Although North America remains the principal region in terms of net generation of non-regional arrivals, the developed countries of Europe are also major contributors in this sense. However, bearing in mind the remarks made above about arrivals generated by 'other countries', it is probable that a complete picture would yield a smaller net balance from the point of view of developing countries, and a larger net balance from the point of view of the developed countries.

International data on tourist receipts and expenditures and net balances on travel account in the balance of payments are unfortunately even less complete than data on tourist arrivals. Moreover, because of the difficulties of estimation involved, much of the data is of doubtful reliability.[18]

However, according to IUOTO, the pattern of tourist receipts shown in Table 4.6 emerges between the developing and developed regions already defined.

In terms of aggregate world tourist receipts, developed countries received about 70 per cent of the total. This compares with about 75 per cent of total arrivals (see Table 4.2), the difference being apparently due to somewhat lower levels of receipts per arrival in the developed countries. In both the developed and developing regions as specified, it is clear that Europe and the Americas are the most important recipien Too much should not be made of the difference in average receipts per arrival between regions. All that can be said is that the figures for South and Central America look very high and, although international transportation receipts are not officially included, it is possible that this may explain the difference. Practices vary widely in the matter of compiling data on tourist receipts, and a great deal may depend on the

17 And exclusion of some countries which have data on total arrivals and total receipts but no breakdown of tourists by nationality. See Appendix B to this chapter.

18 This is apparently as true in the UK as anywhere else — *Britain's Invisible Earnings: Report of the Committee on Invisible Exports,* British National Export Council (BNEC) 1967, Chapter X.

Table 4.5 *Balance of tourist arrivals and arrivals generated by developed and developing regions, 1965*

Region	Inter-regional arrivals generated *less* inter-regional arrivals (thousands)
Developing	
Africa	+ 26·0
Asia	+ 1,087·6
S and C America	+ 964·1
Commonwealth Caribbean	+ 305·5
Europe and Mediterranean	+ 10,665·5
Developed	
Europe	− 2984·4
N. America	− 9,615·1
S. Africa	− 53·4
Asia/Oceania	− 254·7

Source: Derived from Table 4.4.

Table 4.6 *International tourist receipts and receipts per arrival by region, 1965*[a]

Region	Tourist receipts $ m US	Average receipts per arrival, $ US
Developing		
Africa	147·4	101·1
Asia	387·2	123·2
S and C America	1,079·6	397·9
Commonwealth Caribbean	150·7	159·0
Europe and Mediterranean	1,569·8	83·8
Sub total	3,334·7	123·5
Europe	5,514·5	89·7
N. America	1,906·7	98·3
S. Africa	49·0	215·9
Oceania and Australia	178·5	281·9
Sub total	7,648·7	93·6
Total	10,983·4	101·0

Note:
[a] See Appendix A for exclusions.
Source: International Travel Statistics, IUOTO, 1965.

motivation of the body responsible for compiling data.[19] It may be noted, however, that the figures for the Caribbean look reasonable by comparison with other regions – slightly higher than average, which is what one would expect given the structure

9 For example, the Tourist Board in the Cayman Islands persistently included land sales to foreigners in 'tourist receipts'. The error may be due to a lack of qualified staff and, possibly, an anxiety to 'push' the case of tourism.

of the Caribbean tourist industry.[20]

The net balance of tourist receipts and expenditures between developed and developing regions is of greater significance. Although there are considerable gaps in the data, particularly for developing countries, some indication of these flows can be obtained from Table 4.7 below.

Table 4.7 *Net balance of travel accounts by region, 1965*

Region	Tourist receipts $ m	Tourist expenditures[a] $ m	Balance, surplus (+) deficit (−) $ m
Developed			
N. America	1,906·7	3,198·3	− 1,291·6
Europe	5,690·1	5,125·1	+ 565·0
Asia/Australia	178·5	276·5	− 98·0
S. Africa	49·0	72·8	− 23·8
Total	7,824·3[b]	8,672·7	− 848·4
Developing[c]			
Africa	82·1	55·6	+ 26·5
Asia	95·1	74·6	+ 20·5
S and C America	101·7	153·4	− 51·7
Commonwealth Caribbean[d]	12·5	14·5	− 2·0
Europe and Mediterranean	1,435·7	216·5	+ 1,219·2
Total	1,727·1[e]	514·6	+ 1,212·5

Notes:
[a] i.e. Expenditures by residents on foreign travel.
[b] Differs from the total in Table 4.2 by $175·6 millions due to exclusion of Belgium and inclusion of Iceland in Table 4.2 totals for Europe. Sample for developed countries is therefore fairly complete.
[c] Sample is very incomplete; see note e.
[d] Trinidad only.
[e] Comprises only 51·8% of total receipts given in Table 2 due to absence of data on tourist expenditures for most developing countries.
Source: IUOTO *International Travel Statistics, 1965.*

The general conclusion which seems to emerge from an examination of Table 4.7 is that, although the developed countries as a whole were in deficit to the tune of $848·4 millions in 1965, most, if not all, of this net flow of foreign exchange accrued to the less developed countries of Europe, and in particular to Spain. Unless the statistics of tourist expenditures used in the balance-of-payments statistics of the developed countries are substantially in error,[21] it seems likely that the developing countries outside Europe and the Mediterranean are, in aggregate, in significant *deficit* on their travel accounts, indicating a net flow of resources from the developing countries to the developed through the tourism market. This feature of

20 See also Chapter 7 below.

21 This is not to be ruled out. See p. 62 fn. 18.

international tourism has so far received little comment.[22]

Such situations presumably arise mainly as a result of the very uneven distribution of income in many developing countries.

On the face of it this conclusion, taken together with the evidence of Table 4.6 which suggests rather higher average receipts per arrival in developing countries, appears inconsistent with the figures presented in Table 4.5 which show a substantial surplus of 'arrivals' over 'arrivals generated' in developing regions. Some possible explanations of this inconsistency are given below:

(a) Errors in tourist expenditure estimates of developed countries;[23]
(b) Errors in tourist receipts estimates of developed and developing countries;[24]
(c) The problem of 'other arrivals', raised in comments following Table 4.4;
(d) The possibility that developed country visitors to developing countries may spend less per capita than developing country visitors to developed countries;
(e) The treatment of developing countries in Europe and the Mediterranean;
(f) The incomplete coverage of the balance of travel account data, though the relatively complete coverage of developed countries and developing countries in Europe and the Mediterranean suggests that this cannot be of major importance.

Whatever the reasons, it must be held on this evidence that, at best, tourism at present involves only minimal net flows of foreign exchange from developed countries to developing countries outside Europe, and at worst a net flow of foreign exchange to the developed countries. From the point of view of the Commonwealth Caribbean, the figures in Table 4.7 include data for Trinidad alone, and these indicate a deficit on travel account. In view of the figures in Tables 4.4 and 4.5, however, it seems likely that the region as a whole has an overall surplus on travel account. O'Loughlin, for example, estimates a net surplus of $12·3 million (EC) in 1962 for the Windwards and Leewards as a whole.[25]

The figures for international tourist receipts and expenditures exclude receipts and expenditures on transportation. If these were included it seems likely that the

22 Peters (1969), p. 10, comments as follows: 'Many of the less-developed countries of the world — surprisingly at first sight — have travel deficits'. He shows (Table 1) Argentina, Bolivia, Ceylon, Colombia, Cyprus, Iran, Ivory Coast, Nigeria, the Philippines and Sudan as having deficits on travel account.
    Seers notes that in pre-revolutionary Cuba 'Payments by Cubans for tourism exceeded receipts until 1955 and even thereafter continued to represent a high fraction of gross receipts on the tourist account.' Seers (ed.) (1964), p. 19.

23 It seems quite probable that expenditures by nationals of these countries abroad is underestimated.

24 OECD countries use two principal methods of estimating tourist receipts — the bank reporting or 'ticket' system, and the 'estimation' method. The latter may involve sample surveys collection of data from hotel associations, travel agencies etc. For a discussion of the errors involved in these methods see the BNEC report (1967) Ch. X.

25 O'Loughlin (1968) Table 19.

above conclusion would be reinforced, since the majority of international transportation is undertaken by carriers based in the developed countries. For example, according to the IATA statistics for 1968, of a total of 114,000 million passenger kilometers flown on international scheduled services, at least 84,200 million, or some 74 per cent, were flown on airlines registered and based in developed countries as defined earlier.[26] Even where developing countries have their own carriers, it seems that a substantial part of the capital may be in the form of loans from various organisations in developed countries, and the equity capital which is owned by nationals or their governments may earn little or no return.[27] There are also institutional features of the air transport industry which make it difficult for the airlines of all but the largest developing countries to compete with those of developed countries.[28]

The overall growth in international tourism was given in Table 4.1. This showed an annual average growth in tourist receipts of 10·9 per cent as compared with 10·0 per cent for tourist arrivals between 1960 and 1967. It is not clear how complete the aggregate figures used in these calculations are, but an examination of IUOTO statistics reveals large gaps in the data, particularly for earlier years, and especially in developing countries. From the data that are available, the aggregates reveal quite large regional variations in growth rates, as Table 4.8 shows.

The Commonwealth Caribbean has had below average growth in arrivals, but above average growth in receipts over both periods chosen. The data for other developing regions are too incomplete to permit further analysis, particularly in the case of Africa.

Even in the Caribbean, if Trinidad were excluded the growth in tourist arrivals would be very much closer to the growth in tourist receipts — probably indicating compensating movements between the variables 'proportion of visitors from developed countries' and 'average length of stay'.

What, then, is the place of the Commonwealth Caribbean in the total tourist market? According to Table 4.2 it received 0·9 per cent of aggregate world arrivals and 1·4 per cent of aggregate world receipts from international tourism in 1965. Taking only the developing world, the Commonwealth Caribbean received about 3·5 per cent of arrivals and 4·6 per cent of total receipts in developing countries. According to Table 4.5, the region received many more arrivals than it generated, indicating a substantial inter-regional inflow of visitors. Finally, the growth of tourism in the Commonwealth Caribbean during the 1960s has been very rapid.[29]

The conclusions to be drawn from this chapter may be summarised as follows:

(a) Quantitative data on financial and human flows due to tourism are only now becoming available in spite of early work on definitions. Indications

26 International Air Transportation Association (IATA) World Air Transport Statistics, 1968.

27 The Commonwealth Caribbean has four national airlines: British West Indian Airways (Trinidad), Air Jamaica, Air Barbados and Bahamas Airways. The former Leeward Islands Air Transport Company (LIAT) which was privately owned but publicly subsidised, was recently taken over by Court Line of the UK.

28 See, for example, De Castro (1967).

29 The growth in Caribbean tourism is anlaysed at greater length in Chapters 6 and 7.

Table 4.8 *Tourism – growth rates by regions 1961–7 and 1962–8*

	Tourist arrivals		Tourist receipts	
	1961–7	1962–8	1961–7	1962–8
Developing Regions	Growth rates in % per annum			
Africa	11·83[a]	21·35[b]	5·64[c]	9·47[d]
Asia	15·14[e]	16·90[f]	14·74[g]	15·06[h]
C and S America	9·81[i]	12·21[j]	−4·70[k]	−10·17[l]
Commonwealth Caribbean	9·73[m]	12·02[n]	14·79[o]	16·53[o]
Europe and Mediterranean	20·66[p]	18·7[p]	22·61[q]	16·60[q]
Total Developing	18·11	17·85	10·53	8·15
Developed Regions				
Europe	20·53[r]	11·53[s]	9·73[t]	8·55[u]
N. America[v]	30·21	26·59	13·08	10·92
Oceanias and[w] Australia	10·95	11·98	0·80	4·27
Total developed	17·08	15·30	10·41	9·07

Notes: Data include the countries noted:
[a] UAR, Morocco, Tunisia, Rhodesia, Mauritius.
[b] Morocco, Tunisia.
[c] UAR, Ethiopoa, Morocco, Tunisia, Rhodesia, Libya, Mauritius.
[d] Ethopia, Morocco, Tunisia.
[e] India, Pakistan, Philippines, S. Korea, S. Vietnam, China (Taiwan), Hong Kong, Israel Lebanon, Jordan, Singapore.
[f] India, Pakistan, S. Korea, S. Vietnam, China (Taiwan), Hong Kong, Israel, Lebanon, Jordan, Singapore.
[g] India, Pakistan, Philippines, S. Korea, Iran, S. Vietnam, China (Taiwan), Ceylon, Nepal, Hong Kong, Isrcal, Lebanon, Jordan.
[h] Countries in Note f except Philippines.
[i] Mexico, Guatemala, Puerto Rico, Curacao, Colombia, Bolivia.
[j] Data available only for Mexico.
[k] Data available only for Mexico, Haiti, Guatemala, Puerto Rico, Brazil, Colombia, Peru, Venezuela, Bolivia.
[l] Data available only for Mexico.
[m] Complete, but growth rate would be in region of 16%–17% if Trinidad excluded. Trinidad shows negative growth rate over period probably due to data deficiencies.
[n] Excluding Leeward Islands. Again growth rate would be higher if Trinidad excluded. See Note m.
[o] Excluding Bahamas and Trinidad and Tobago.
[p] Cyprus, Malta, Greece, Spain, Turkey, Yugoslavia, Portugal and Bulgaria only.
[q] As in Note p, excluding Bulgaria.
[r] Excluding Sweden, Denmark, Finland, Norway.
[s] Excluding Sweden, Denmark, Finland, Norway, Iceland.
[t] Excluding USSR, Poland, Rumania, Czechoslovakia, Hungary.
[u] Excluding countries in Note t *plus* Denmark, Finland, Norway, Luxemburg, Iceland.
[v] Complete, USA and Canada.
[w] Complete, Japan, Australia and New Zealand.
Source: IUOTO *International Travel Statistics,* 1961, 1962, 1967, 1968.

are, however, that the financial flows involved form a significant portion of world trade in goods and services.

(b) Unlike many traditional exports of developing countries, tourism appears to have a high income elasticity of demand. It would therefore appear at first sight to offer many advantages as a source of foreign exchange for such countries.

(c) However, from the partial data available, there is little, if any, evidence that there is a *net* flow of resources from 'developed' to 'developing' countries via the tourism market — indeed if we can trust the data, quite the reverse seems to be indicated for most of the developing world.

(d) The Commonwealth Caribbean accounts for some 3·5 per cent of arrivals and 4·6 per cent of tourist receipts in the developing world as a whole. Unlike some other developing regions, there was a substantial *net* inflow of visitors in the Caribbean.

BIBLIOGRAPHICAL NOTES TO CHAPTER 4

Early works on tourism

The following works are noted in Ogilvie:[30]

Bodio, L., 'Sul movimento dei forestieri in Italia e sul denaro che vi spendono', *Giornale degli Economisti* 1899, pp. 54–61.

Nicefero, A., *Il movimento dei forestieri in Italia,* 1923.

Benni, R., 'Sulla reforma dei metodi di calcolo del movimento turistico', in *Statistica del movimento turistico,* 1926–7.

Morgenroth, W., 'Fremdenverkehr', in the *Handwörterbuch der Staatswissenschaften,* Bd. IV, 1923.

Morgenroth, W., *Die Quellen des Münchener Wirteschaftslebens,* Abschnitt IV.

German Forschungsinstitut für den Fremdenverkehr, monthly bulletins *Monatliche Mitteilungen:* quarterly journal, *Archiv für den Fremdenverkehr.*

Glückman, R., *Das Gaststättenwesen,* 1927 (Economics of the Hotel industry).

Grünthal, A., *Fremdenverkehrsanalyse der provinz Oberschlesion* 1932. Monog. published by Forschungsinstitut für den Fremdenverkehr.

Viner, J., *Canada's Balance of International Indebtedness 1900–1913,* 1924, pp. 83ff.

Taussig, F.W., *International Trade,* 1927, index vs. Tourist Expenses.

Trade Information Bulletin of U.S. Department of Commerce, No. 761 of 1931.

Xenophon, *Public Finance* (De Vectigalibus) III (Xenophon argues that the State should build hotels from public funds).

U.S. Department of Commerce, *The promotion of tourist travel by foreign countries,* 1931. Trade Promotion Series no. 113.

APPENDIX A: COUNTRIES EXCLUDED FROM TABLES 4.2 AND 4.6 ON ACCOUNT OF LACK OF DATA

A Developing Countries

Africa

Excludes Nigeria, UAR, Congo Republic, Tanzania, Uganda, Malagasy Republic, Cameroon, Angola, Upper Volta, Mali, Malawi, Ivory Coast, Guinea, Senegal, Chad, Niger, Rwanda, Burundi, Dahomey, Somali Republic, Sierra Leone, Togo, Central African Republic, Liberia, Mauritania, Congo (Brazzaville), Lesotho, Mauritius, Botswana, Gabon, Gambia, Swaziland

30 Ogilvie (1933) pp. 8–10.

Asia
Excludes Mainland China, India, Thailand, Burma, Iran, North Vietnam, Afghanistan, North Korea, Ceylon, Saudi Arabia, Yemen, Laos, Singapore, Mongolia, Kuwait

South and Central America
Excludes Cuba, Guatemala, El Salvador, Honduras, Nicaragua, Costa Rica, Curacao and Dutch West Indies, French West Indies, Uraguay, Paraguay, Panama, Guyana, Surinam, French Guyana, Falkland Islands

Europe and Mediterranean
Excludes Albania and Gibraltar

B Developed Countries
Excludes USSR, Romania, East Germany, Hungary, Belgium

APPENDIX B: COUNTRIES EXCLUDED FROM TABLE 4.4 ON ACCOUNT OF LACK OF DATA

A Developing Countries

Africa
Ethiopia, Congo Republic, Sudan, Morocco, Kenya, Uganda, Malagasy Republic, Cameroon, Angola, Upper Volta, Mali, Malawi, Ivory Coast, Guinea, Senegal, Chad, Niger, Rwanda, Burundi, Dahomey, Somali Republic, Sierra Leone, Togo, Central African Republic, Liberia, Mauritania, Congo (Brazzaville), Lesotho, Mauritius, Botswana, Gabon, Gambia, Swaziland

Asia
Mainland China, Thailand, Burma, North Vietnam, North Korea, Nepal, Saudi Arabia, Yemen, Laos, Mongolia

Central and South America
Cuba, Dominican Republic, El Salvador, Honduras, Nicaragua, Costa Rica, Colombia, Uruguay, Paraguay, Panama, Surinam, French Guyana, Falkland Islands, French West Indies

Commonwealth Caribbean
Bahamas, St Vincent, St Lucia, Montserrat, St Kitts—Nevis, Northern Group [31]

Europe and Mediterranean
Albania, Gibraltar

B Developed Countries

Europe
East Germany

APPENDIX C: COUNTRIES FOR WHICH A TRAVEL ACCOUNT BALANCE WAS AVAILABLE IN 1965

The following countries are included in Table 4.7:

A Developing Countries

Africa
Algeria, Morocco, Rhodesia, Sudan, Zambia

31 IUOTO data. See also Chapter 6.

Asia
Israel, Jordon, Syria, Malaysia

Central and South America
Argentina, Chile, Venezuela

Commonwealth Caribbean
Trinidad

B Developed Countries

Europe
Austria, Belgium, Luxembourg, Czechoslovakia, Denmark, Finland, France, West Germany, Ireland, Italy, Netherlands, Norway, Poland, Sweden, Switzerland, UK

North America
Canada, USA

South Africa

Asia, Oceania
Japan, Australia, New Zealand

5 Measuring the economic and social impact of tourism in developing countries

In Chapter 4, the growing significance of international tourism to many developing countries was examined in terms of flows of tourists, tourist receipts and tourist expenditures. In addition, the hypothesis that, unlike many 'traditional' exports of the developing countries, the demand for international tourism is highly income-elastic receives support from the available data. But an examination of tourist movements and foreign exchange receipts generated by tourists tells us nothing about the economic and social impact of this growth of international tourism in developing countries. This chapter is therefore concerned with the general problem of providing a theoretical framework for an analysis of this impact in the context of developing countries.

One of the first questions a policy maker would wish to ask concerns the relationship between the foreign exchange receipts and the income generated for nationals by these receipts. Assuming that all assets in the economy are owned by nationals and, further, that all employees in the economy are nationals, then there will be no distinction between value added and income to nationals. In these circumstances, the relationship between the generation of a unit of foreign exchange and the consequential generation of value added by any exporting industry depends principally upon the input structure of the industry (determining 'direct' effects), the input structure of other productive sectors in the economy including government (determining 'indirect' effects), the structure of consumption (determining 'induced' effects), and the opportunity cost of resources utilised at all stages in the creation of direct, indirect and induced income effects. This general statement applies to any industry, and it is obvious that the foreign exchange generated (or saved) by different industries will normally tend to have different effects on value added, and *a fortiori* where input structures are very significantly different.[1] But even in cases where input structures are similar, a relaxation of the assumptions regarding employment of nationals and the ownership of assets by nationals can lead to important differences between industries as regards the relationship between export receipts and the income of nationals.[2] Finally, there may be important areas of interdependence which cannot be ignored. For example, the pattern of

1. This has been explicitly recognised by staple theories, though these usually assume complete local ownership of all factors of production and are primarily concerned with the potential exploitation of 'linkages' through differential rates of profit (and reinvestment) and different input structures, c.f. Watkins (1963), Thoburn (1971).

2 c.f. Mamalakis and Reynolds (1965), especially on the 'Returned Value Terms-of-Trade' concept.

consumption may be affected in different ways by different industries through differential effects on the distribution of income and the social determinants of the consumption function.[3] Such interdependence can lead not only to differences in value added per unit of foreign exchange earned in different industries, but also within industries where techniques of production differ. The analysis contained in Chapters 2 and 3 above suggests that, in the case of tourism, all of these considerations are likely to be important.

With these general comments in mind, we may turn to examine the particular case of tourism. According to Peters, there are at least five potential benefits from tourism for any developing country.[4] These are:

(1) A contribution to the balance-of-payments as an earner of hard currency;
(2) The dispersion of development to non-industrial regions;
(3) The creation of employment opportunities;
(4) The effect on general economic development through the multiplier effects;
(5) The social benefits arising from a 'widening of people's interest generally in world affairs and to a new understanding of "foreigners and foreign tastes",'

The first of these is a perfectly general point which can be applied to any export-generating or import-substituting activity. It is, as we have seen, true that the income elasticity of demand for tourism appears to be high in developed countries. But, as in the case of other industries, the contribution to the balance-of-payments is not a sufficient criterion for establishing whether or not there is a potential gain from the allocation of resources to the tourist industry. In any event, any positive balance-of-payments effects may be dissipated by foreign ownership.

The second point concerns the effects of tourism on the development of non-industrial regions in a developing country. While it is not disputed that the bulk of tourist development takes place in non-industrial locations – normally rural, mountain areas, or coastal areas – the question is whether this leads to a dispersion of development 'generally' in a way which an alternative allocation of resources would be unable to achieve except at higher real cost. It is difficult to see why this should be the case. If the region in question is both non-agricultural and non-industrial, then there is unlikely to be either the requisite infrastructure or the requisite labour force, and the development of tourism in that region is likely to require both heavy infrastructure costs and relocation of labour. In addition, there is unlikely to be significant secondary income generation in the immediate location. Finally, much of the infrastructure required by tourism has few alternative uses, and hence the 'externalities' argument seems unlikely to be of great significance. If, however, the region is agricultural then there will be competition for land between recreational uses and agricultural uses, and for labour, at least in the planting and harvesting seasons. In addition the point regarding infrastructure will still hold, though perhaps with less force. Consequently, it is difficult to accept that tourism has special advantages in this respect for developing countries.

Peters' third potential benefit concerns the creation of employment

3 See also below, p. 92.

4 Peters (1969) pp. 10–12. The ordering of these points is my own.

opportunities. It is true that hotels and other tourism services require employees, and possibly acceptable that the ratio of employees to hotel beds or rooms is likely to be higher in developing countries than in developed countries.[5] What is less acceptable is the inference that tourism has special advantages in this respect, especially when the whole gamut of investments required to establish a tourism sector are taken into account, including relatively capital-intensive and tourist-specific infrastructure. Furthermore, one must be aware of the possibility that at least certain categories of labour used in the tourist industry will tend to have a high opportunity cost.

The first three points, commented on above, are really parts of the fourth point which concerns the effect on development via the 'multiplier' effects of tourism. It is upon these alleged multiplier effects that most studies of tourism in developing countries to date have concentrated, and the argument is therefore worthy of more detailed attention.[6]

The tourist multiplier

Peters develops what appears at first sight to be a rather curious brand of aggregate multiplier.[7] The derivation of this multiplier is shown below.

If K_t is the tourist multiplier

s is the propensity to save

e_a is the marginal propensity to spend on tourism *abroad* by nationals.

Then

$$K_t = \frac{1}{s - e_a} .$$

However, further reading suggests that the coefficient e_a is intended to represent the marginal propensity to import (goods and services) which, of course, embraces foreign travel by nationals. In effect, then we are left with the familiar Keynesian expenditure multiplier,

$$k = \frac{1}{s + m} = \frac{1}{1 - c + m} ,$$

where m is the marginal propensity to import, and c the marginal propensity to consume.

Strictly speaking, Peters' multiplier is an aggregate multiplier in a tourist economy, rather than an expression of the multiplier effects of tourist expenditure. At the heart of this distinction lies the general problem of aggregative Keynesian multipliers, notably that they fail to take account of the different input structures in different industries, and because of this suggest that *any* increase in autonomous demand will have the same multiplier effects throughout the economy. In general, the structural characteristics of the tourist industry are such that a disaggregated approach is essential, and this requires the use of a rather more sophisticated 'tool', notably

---

5 The labour–capital ratio in hotels may however be low in developing countries because of higher capital costs. See also Chapter 7 below.

6 Peters (1969), Checchi (1961), *Zinder Report* (1969), *Tripartite Survey* (1966) being examples. An exception is Mitchell's work in East Africa (1968A) and (1969). Mitchell calculates only 'first round' expenditure effects.

7 Peters (1969) pp. 236–8.

the inter-industry transactions matrix.

A more proper statement of the tourist multiplier is

$$K_t = \frac{\Delta Y}{\Delta T},$$

where ΔT is the change in tourist receipts (exports) and ΔY is the consequential change in domestic incomes which results from the change in tourist receipts given fixed coefficients within the transactions matrix and a fixed pattern of tourist receipts accruing to the different sectors.[8] The meaning of this multiplier is quite precise in terms of inter-industry analysis providing we are willing to accept the assumptions of this analysis. Thus, if $(I - A)^{-1}$ is the Leontief inverse, where I is the identity matrix and A is the matrix of technical coefficients, then

$\Delta Y = \Delta T (I - A)^{-1}$ where T is the column vector of sectoral tourist receipts. Including consumption within the matrix makes a closed Leontief system, in which case $K_t = (I - A)^{-1}$. The Keynesian multiplier for the economy as a whole will be weighted averages of the individual sector multipliers. Since tourist receipts accrue to a number of sectors, the tourist multiplier will be the multiplier for each sector as described by the Leontief inverse weighted by the distribution of tourist receipts between the various sectors.

Some estimates of tourist multipliers for various countries and regions are given in Table 5.1 below.

These estimates show wide variations in the estimated value of the tourist multiplier between different regions, though without careful study of each individual estimate it is not possible to be certain of the extent to which this variation is due to faulty methods and/or inadequate data rather than genuine structural differences. In the case of Zinder's estimates, which refer to the Eastern Caribbean, the major problem was a faulty methodology which led to a 'multiplication' of the multiplier.[9] Although some variation between countries is to be expected on *a priori* grounds, one would expect this variation to be due principally to variations in the structure of the economy and the structure of consumption rather than differences in the pattern of tourist receipts or the structure of the tourist industry itself, especially in the case of variations between developing countries. It is hard to believe that the structural characteristics of Pakistan, or the Pacific and the Far East, are such as to explain the very high estimates made for these areas as compared with the other countries and regions cited.

Apart from problems of basic data, misplaced aggregation, and methodological errors of a more obvious nature, a number of criticisms can be made regarding the concept of the tourist multiplier and the use to which it is put. The first of these concerns the content of the income (Y) which is multiplied. Normally this relates to gross domestic product derived by summing the gross profits, gross wages and salaries, and rent and interest received in each sector. Partly because of data

8 Feedback from abroad is ignored as this is unlikely to be significant in the circumstances.

9 For detailed criticism of Zinder's multiplier see Bryden and Faber (1971) and Levitt and Gulati (1970). Checchi's multiplier for the Pacific and the Far East has also been criticised by Mitchell (1968B). I have been told, informally, that Zinder's estimates were compiled by the same person who compiled Checchi's estimates for the Far East.

Table 5.1 *Estimates of uncorrected 'tourist multiplier': various countries and regions*

Country or region	Tourist multiplier
Pacific and Far East[a]	3·2 to 4·3
New Hampshire[b]	1·6 to 1·7
Hawaii[c]	0·9 to 1·3
Greece[d]	1·2 to 1·4
Pakistan[e]	3·3
Ireland[f]	2·7
Lebanon[g]	1·2 to 1·4
Caribbean A[h]	2·3
Caribbean B[i]	0·58 to 0·88

Notes:
[a] Checchi and Co. (1961).
[b] *Economic Impact of Recreation, Vacation and Travel on New Hampshire,* 1962.
[c] Craig, P.G., *Future Growth of Hawaiian Tourism,* 1963.
[d] Suits, D.B., *An Econometric Model of the Greek Economy,* 1964.
[e] *Master Plan for the Development of Tourism in Pakistan,* 1965.
[f] *Study of the Economics of Tourism in Ireland,* 1966.
[g] Gorra, P., *Nouvelle étude prospective sur l'apport du tourisme au développement économique du Liban,* 1967.
[h] Zinder, H. and Associates, *The Future of Tourism in the Eastern Caribbean,* May 1969.
[i] own estimates; see Chapter 9.
Sources: Except for the Caribbean, Peters (1969) Table 80, p. 240. For Caribbean, sources as stated above.

inadequacies, partly because such concepts have often been borrowed wholesale from a different economic context, it has not been normal practice to calculate income to nationals (ITN), which is the most relevant aggregate from the point of view of developing countries.[10] Differences between GDP and ITN arise because of foreign ownership of factors of production and because of employment of non-nationals in the economy, both of which are likely to be important in certain sectors of developing countries. Two separate points may be made. First, incomes accruing to non-nationals who are also non-resident together with directly remitted incomes of non-nationals who *are* resident need to be distinguished in each sector, since such incomes will not be re-spent in the economy, and can have no 'multiplier' effects.[11] They are tantamount to an import of services, and must be treated as part of the cost of employing non-nationals. The exclusion of these elements of GDP from the matrix could have a significant impact on induced income effects, and hence on the size of the multiplier, for different sectors and for the economy as a whole. Second, it can be argued that after the process has worked itself out, income accruing to non-nationals resident in the economy is, for policy purposes, largely a matter of indifference to the government. In economist's shorthand, such incomes do not normally form a part of the 'welfare function' which the government is seeking to maximise. In view of the significance of foreign ownership in the tourist industry, and the employment of non-nationals in skilled positions, already noted in the case of the Caribbean, it seems likely that the ITN multiplier may be significantly lower

10 See also Bryden and Faber (1971).

11 Again it is assumed that feedback from abroad is negligible.

than the GDP multiplier.[12]

The second major criticism concerns the assumptions of multiplier analysis which, in the case of tourist multipliers, are usually left tacit. The basic Keynesian multiplier was designed for use in devising short-run policies in situations where all resources, but especially labour and the existing stock of capital, could be assumed to be generally underutilised. In the circumstances, real income and employment could be increased in a closed economy by an autonomous increase in any of the elements of final demand, and the amount of the increase in real incomes would be determined by the size of the multiplier. In an open economy, the income generation process is constrained by the size of the marginal propensity to import, but so long as $s + m < 1$, the multiplier will be greater than unity. The same assumptions, which are tantamount to treating all resources as having zero opportunity costs from the point of view of society, apply where a sector multiplier is utilised to show how real incomes are increased as a result of an increase in the final output of that sector. But significant underutilisation of the capital stock is not generally thought to be a feature of developing countries. Nor does the thesis that labour is 'costless' nowadays receive much theoretical and empirical support.[13] It must therefore be assumed that, in general, resources in developing countries will have positive opportunity costs. In these circumstances, an increase in final demand in the short run is likely to lead either to rising prices, or to replacement of certain domestic inputs by imports, or more probably to some combination of the two, and possibly to some increase in real output. However, rising prices will alter the distribution of income, and hence in all probability the propensity to consume and the pattern of consumption.[14] Given that higher income groups in these countries tend to have a higher propensity to import consumer goods, to the extent that these groups benefit from the redistribution of income there will again be a tendency for the import function to shift, such that the average propensity to import will rise. In addition, if exchange rates are fixed there will be a tendency for rising domestic prices to lead to even greater substitution by imports for domestic produce. In short, there is reason to suppose that the coefficients in the inter-industry transations matrix (including consumption within the matrix) will change in a *dependent* way, and further, that these changes are such as to *reduce* the multiplier through the effects on the import coefficient. Such a process would explain at least some of the structural changes which have taken place in Caribbean tourist economies over the past decade or so, and which were examined in Chapters 2 and 3 above. It is consequently incorrect to suggest as Peters does that if the *ex ante* tourist multiplier is four, a change in tourist expenditures 'will lead to a four-fold change in income' as a general rule in developing countries.[15] Furthermore, it is by no means clear just what the multiplier does tell us even when it is calculated from an inter-industry

12 See also Chapter 9.

13 Little and Mirrlees (1968) p. 51; Mishan (1971) pp. 73–5. Thirlwall (1972) pp. 212 *et seq.* contains a useful discussion of the planning wage.

14 C.f. Hasan (1960). However, the short-run price effects resulting from changes in the distribution of income may not be empirically significant.

15 Peters (1969) p. 238.

transactions matrix, unless there is considerable additional information regarding the utilisation of the relevant portions of the capital stock and the labour force.

However, even where portions of the capital stock and the labour force are underutilised, the tourist multiplier by itself tells us nothing about the most efficient way of alleviating this problem in the short run. If the excess capacity exists in other export industries, the expansion of tourism will do little to solve this problem since resources are unlikely to be mobile from these industries except in the long run, and the allocation of resources in the longer run poses different problems. If, on the other hand, the excess capacity is in domestic industries, then it seems likely that an increase in government expenditure via a budget deficit would be more effective in the short run, since the direction of government expenditure at least could be made more selective in its impact.[16]

But the over-riding criticism of tourist multipliers and the use to which they have been put concerns the inference that they measure either the benefit or the potential benefit from the expansion of tourism to the economy as a whole over the longer run.[17] The only circumstances in which this could be so are quite unreal, namely a zero opportunity cost for all the resources used directly and indirectly in tourism.

In general, therefore, any attempt to measure the benefits from particular economic activities requires some assessment of the real cost to society of devoting resources to that activity, and a comparison with the benefits to be obtained from the allocation of these resources to other activities. At the macro-level this could be handled by a programming approach provided that data on inter-industry transactions and resource use by industry together with resource availabilities and other constraints were available (or could conceivably be collected) in sufficient detail.[18] Providing we can accept both the basic data and the assumptions of linear programming, the solution to the programming model will show us the optimal levels of each activity in the economy given the constraint levels associated with the various commodities and resources.[19]

In addition the 'dual solution' to the programme gives the correct valuation of the various resources available to the economy, and hence enables computation of 'correct' prices (shadow or accounting prices) to be attached to inputs and outputs in any planned activity.[20]

In practice, the problems of programming for the entire economy in terms of data relating to existing activities are formidable in any economy, let alone in terms of data relating to all possible activities. In addition there is certainly scope for

16 In any case good reasons can be advanced for suggesting that the tourist multiplier will tend to be less than multipliers relating to other forms of expenditure.

17 It has never been explicitly suggested, to my knowledge, that the tourist industry should be expanded to cure short-run problems of excess capacity. Nevertheless this is the import of Keynesian multipliers.

18 The problem is formally stated in Chenery and Clark (1959) p. 86.

19 The assumptions are: (a) linear homogeneous production function for each activity; (b) lack of external economies and diseconomies; (c) non-negative activity levels; (d) any commodity can be produced by any number of activities; (e) each activity may have several outputs. Chenery and Clark (1959) p. 88.

20 Chenery and Clark (1959).

considerable argument regarding the empirical significance of external economies and diseconomies and non-linear and non-homogenous production functions for important activities.[21] Finally, there is the problem of time and the appropriate time discount. In the particular case of tourism in the Caribbean, while data problems are paramount, it is argued that non-homogeneity is important because hotel sectors are generally operating below capacity,[22] and that external diseconomies are likely to be important.[23] On the other hand there *may* be certain economies of scale which affect the linearity assumption, principally because of indivisibilities which arise in the provision of certain items of tourist infrastructure.[24] At this stage then, a programming approach to the evaluation of the economic impact of tourism in the Caribbean is not feasible, although the discussion of the approach itself is of interest as a further corrective to the normal conclusions which are explicitly or implicitly drawn from the tourist multiplier approach.

A reasonable compromise is suggested by cost−benefit analysis, although this has more normally been used for public investment projects.[25] But there seems no reason in principle why the techniques of social cost−benefit analysis should not be used to discover the social benefits arising from the expansion of different sectors where this expansion involves both private and public funds, so long as one thinks in terms of marginal projects in each sector.[26]

It is perhaps notable that neither Peters nor the other studies cited earlier suggest that the social justification for tourist development in developing countries is to be measured by private profitability in the industry. It is, however, self-evident that where private investment does take place in the tourist industry the investment decision will at least be highly dependent upon the expected private returns. And where there is little government control over the industry, its rate of growth will depend on the rate of profit as compared with alternatives. If the rate of private profit should, however, exceed the rate of social profit in the industry, there will be a tendency for the industry to grow too rapidly from the point of view of society, and resources will be bid away from other socially profitable uses. There will also be pressure on the government to keep up with the rate of growth of private investment in the industry in terms of its contribution to tourist infrastructure.

It is, however, generally recognised that private profitability is not an adequate guide for investment decisions, perhaps especially in the case of developing countries. The principal reasons which have been advanced for this are:

(a) The existence of external economies and diseconomies.[27]

21 Some tentative evidence on the empirical significance of external economies in industry in certain developing countries is offered by Little, Scitovsky and Scott (1970).

22 See Chapter 7.

23 See below p. 164.

24 See Chapter 8.

25 Little and Tipping however use, cost−benefit analysis in their study of the Kulai Palm Oil Estate. Little and Tipping (1970).

26 Marginal in the sense that they are relatively small projects in each sector which would be undertaken if more funds were available, *ceteris paribus*.

27 Rosenstein-Rodan (1943), Scitovsky (1954), Dosser (1962). See also (c).

78

(b) The existence of uncertainty.[28]

(c) The relative lack of technical knowledge and skills, so that the best techniques available may not be employed and the acquiring of skills may be undervalued.[29]

(d) The possibility of a low-level equilibrium trap.[30]

(e) The likelihood of imperfections in factor and product markets, especially the labour and capital markets.[31]

(f) The apparent sub-optimality of savings.[32] This is simply one aspect of (e).

(g) The possible existence of non-uniform inflation.[33]

(h) Currency overvaluation or undervaluation, especially the former.[34]

(i) Inequalities of income and wealth which mean that the private profitability criterion cannot be used when society is not indifferent as regards the distribution of costs and benefits.

In circumstances where some or all of these features seem likely to be important, either for *a priori* reasons, or because their importance has been empirically verified, it seems preferable to start with the assumption that significant differences are liable to arise between the private and social profitability of any project. And it is in such cases that the cost–benefit approach is held to be the most useful.[35]

In the particular case of tourist development, at least three other reasons exist for expecting significant divergences between social and private profitability,[36] namely:

(j) The foreign ownership of capital.

(k) The employment of non-nationals.

(l) The possibility of adverse effects of a more 'transcendental' nature, which can be treated as particular types of external diseconomy.[37]

Three principal decisions require to be faced in cost–benefit analysis. These concern, firstly, the welfare function to be maximised; second, the selection of an appropriate discount rate; third, the means of calculating surrogate prices.[38] Two

---

28 Thus if the profitability of A's investment is partly dependent on B undertaking his investment and *vice versa* then A may not invest at all if he is uncertain about B's plans. A demonstration of this proposition is given by game theory, c.f. 'The Prisoner's Dilemma' in Luce and Raffia (1957), p. 94 *et seq.*

29 The second is a type of external economy.

30 Leibenstein (1957), Nelson (1956).

31 Little and Mirrlees, pp. 33–4.

32 There are several reasons why this might be so. According to Pearce, Marglin emphasises the significance of 'schizophrenia', the argument being similar to that relating to uncertainty in n. (31) above. Pearce (1971), pp. 42–4. See also below.

33 Little and Mirrlees (1968), p. 32.

34 Little and Mirrlees (1968), p. 32.

35 Little and Mirrlees (1968), Chapter 2 *passim.*

36 These are also important for certain other key industries in many developing countries.

37 See below, pp. 90–6.

38 The term is used literally here, covering both non-marketed effects of a project and marketed inputs and outputs where market prices are rejected.

minor problems concern the discounting procedure itself,[39] and the incorporation of risk and uncertainty into the analysis.

The theoretical problems involved in arriving at the appropriate social welfare function have been widely discussed.[40] Recognising that the implementation of any policy (or project) generally creates both 'gainers' and 'losers', the debate has centered around three main issues:

(1) Can a change only be said to be worthwhile if at least one person gains while no-one loses (Pareto).

(2) Can a change be said to be worthwhile if gainers are *able* to compensate losers, whether they do so or not (Kaldor–Hicks).[41]

(3) What happens if, accepting (2), the losers *can* bribe the gainers back to the *status quo* after the change has taken place (Scitovsky's 'problem').[42]

In practice, however, there is a general feeling that it is the distributional effects themselves, rather than any change in relative prices to which they may give rise, which are important, since society is unlikely to be indifferent to changes in income distribution. The practical and theoretical problems involved in some of the proposals made regarding the weighting of costs and benefits between regions and income-groups are however considerable.[43] In their *Manual,* Little and Mirrlees use a crude rule that 'government income counts for one, and that of profit-earners zero, and that of workers unity or less depending on the value the government puts on earnings versus immediate consumption'.[44] Beyond this, though the principle of regional and income-group weightings is recognised, it is broadly assumed that distributional objectives are met by the tax system.[45] But at the very least, for the reasons already given, a distinction has to be made *between nationals and non-nationals,* and this applies both to profit earners and to earners of wages and salaries.[46]

39 Notably the present value – internal rate of return debate.

40 c.f. Pearce (1971) and Mishan (1971).

41 Kaldor (1939) and Hicks (1939), both reprinted in Arrow and Scitovsky (1969).

42 Scitovsky (1941), also reprinted in Arrow and Scitovsky (1969). For situations where this problem can be safely ignored see Scitovsky (1941) Sec, VIII and Pearce (1971) pp. 22–3.

43 Proposals for the weighting of costs and benefits by region and income group have been made by Foster (1966), Maas (1966), Krutilla and Eckstein (1958) and Eckstein (1968). These are discussed in Pearce (1971).

44 Little and Mirrlees (1968). The quotation is from Little and Mirrlees, 'A reply to some Criticisms. . ' *Bull. Ox. Inst. Econs* and *stats,* Feb, 1972, p 166.

45 Little and Mirrlees (1968) pp. 42–3.

46 It is also clear that any position adopted means that any 'consumer's surplus' accruing to foreigners (tourists) should not be counted. In this context, it seems that the Roskill Commission on the Third London Airport (1970) did not make any distinction between benefits to nationals and benefits to foreign travellers. See also Pearce (1971), p. 9 and Chapter 9.

Since projects have different time profiles of costs and benefits, their comparison requires that a discount rate be used. The second area of decision thus relates to the choice of an appropriate discount rate, assuming that, for a number of well-documented reasons, the 'market' rate of interest is not relevant. Three broad approaches to this decision exist. The first relates to the social time preference rate (STPR), according to which the social discount rate (SDR) should reflect society's preference for present benefits over future benefits.[47] The second concerns the social opportunity cost of resources which are used in public sector investment. The opportunity cost rate, as it is usually termed, fails to take account of situations of underinvestment which are due to divergences between the private and social rate of time preference. In this case, public investment will be partly at the expense of consumption foregone, the cost of which would differ from the opportunity cost rate. It is for these reasons that the third approach was suggested, which takes into account both the STPR and the opportunity cost rate expressed in social terms, the resulting discount rate being termed a 'synthetic' rate.

This approach has been adopted by Marglin[48] and by Little and Mirrlees.[49] A project not only 'uses' resources which could have been consumed or invested, but it gives rise to future income which can be consumed or saved. In the Little–Mirrlees method, the STPR is termed the consumption rate of interest (CRI) and this is used in conjunction with the accounting rate of interest (ARI). Basically, the CRI is used to revalue consumption in terms of savings in each time period, and the stream of benefits so derived is discounted back to the present using the ARI. The principle underlying the calculation of the ARI is as follows:

> If all investment were under public control, we would find the rate of interest such that there is a just sufficient number of projects, with positive present social value, to add up to the total amount investment (domestic and foreign) will permit ... In a mixed economy, where only a part of investment is under public control ... planners should try to see that the marginal social yield is about the same in both sectors.[50]

Thus the value which one chooses for the ARI depends on the extent to which available savings are a constraint on the execution of socially profitable projects in the private and public sectors. The ARI and CRI are intimately related through the change over time of the relative value of income freely available for investment in

47 Marglin (1963) pp. 110–3; Pearce (1971) pp. 43–4. Marglin suggests that 'The rates of growth, investment and (social) discount would be selected interatively. The policy-maker might initially propose a high growth rate .... only to be horrified by the rejoinder of his economic advisor that (this) .. would require an enormous sacrifice of current consumption ... and imply an exceedingly low social rate of discount .. The policy maker might then scale down his initial growth rate .. (and) After several iterations .. would presumably converge upon a triple .. which appear to him to represent the optimal balancing of consumption at different times.'

48 Marglin (1963).

49 Little and Mirrlees (1968). This method does not explicitly use a 'synthetic rate', but rather a social opportunity cost rate, the accounting rate of interest. See also below for a further discussion.

50 Little and Mirrlees (1968) p. 95.

the hands of the government as compared with the same income in the hands of consumers (which Little and Mirrlees term s, s_0 being the relative valuation in the base period).[51] The value of s_0 is determined from an inspection of marginal projects and is used to calculate the shadow wage rate (SWR), which is then used to revalue the stream of benefits in each year.[52] It is therefore through the SWR that the CRI achieves its significance. The ARI is determined by trial and error such that the available investable funds are just used up.[53] In principle, then, consistency is required between the values computed for the ARI, the CRI, s_0 and the SWR, since they are all related. In practice, calculations involve a certain amount of trial and error which is not without danger.[54]

The third main area of decision relates to the calculation of surrogate prices. As explained earlier, the term 'surrogate price' is used to cover the prices of 'marketed' goods where the distortions of costs and prices are such as to render actual prices an inaccurate guide to 'real' social costs or benefits, as well as 'non-marketed' inputs and outputs for which no actual price exists to reflect the social valuations which are put on these inputs and outputs. For 'non-marketed' inputs and outputs of tourism specifically, it may be argued that a category of 'diseconomy' exists which is particularly difficult to value in pecuniary terms.[55] In such cases, the nature of these diseconomies needs to be spelt out, and the problem of their pecuniary significance can be faced if and when it is shown that the project is on other grounds socially profitable.

Surrogate prices for marketed inputs and outputs are variously termed 'accounting prices' and 'shadow prices' in the literature. Basically such prices are determined by adjusting market prices to correct for the distortions which are considered to be significant in such a way that they reflect real scarcity and real needs in the economy. In the 'partial' approaches of cost–benefit analysis, some systematic and consistent way of 'correcting' the prices of inputs and outputs is required.

A proposed methodology

The proposed methodology rests heavily on that of Little and Mirrlees,[56] partly because it is thought to be the most thoroughly worked out 'partial' approach to cost–benefit analysis in developing countries, and partly because the Little–Mirrlees 'paradigm' fits the appraisal of tourist projects in 'open' economies quite well. The majority of inputs and outputs are 'fully traded'. Thus, as Joshi states in his

51 Joshi has demonstrated that if the government is acting rationally (assumed by Little–Mirrlees) then $\dot{s}/s = \text{ARI} - \text{CRI}$, i.e. 'the difference between ARI and CRI will equal the rate of fall of s. Joshi (1972).

52 Little and Mirrlees (1968), pp. 166–8.

53 Little and Mirrlees (1968), p. 96, pp. 188–9.

54 Little and Mirrlees (1968) pp. 166–8. The dangers have been discussed by Joshi (1972).

55 See below, p. 90. et seq.

56 Little and Mirrlees (1968).

conclusions 'the main question on which the usefulness of the *Manual* is to be judged is the division of goods into fully traded and less than fully traded goods. The larger the number of goods that fall into the former category the greater the applicability of the distinctive *Manual* methods. This is more likely to be the case in relatively open economies than in relatively closed economies'.[57]   Again, in the same vein, Stewart and Streeten comment that the *Manual* approach is 'best suited to the selection of projects whose sole impact is on international trade, for commodities whose export demand and/or import supply elasticities are infinite'.[58] As has been shown in Chapters 2 and 3, a large part of the impact of tourism is on international trade, while from an individual country's point of view 'export' demand elasticities and import supply elasticities can reasonable be considered as infinitely elastic where the country'has a very small market share. Such would be the case in a relatively large number of tropical countries which have had, or are having, rapid growth in their tourism sectors.

The principle of the method is to value inputs and outputs in terms of 'free' foreign exchange in the hands of the government; in other words foreign exchange 'in the hands of the government' is taken as the numeraire, so that the shadow price of foreign exchange is unity. Traded goods (and services) are valued at their world market prices (c.i.f. for imports, f.o.b. for exports), while non-traded goods are 'decomposed' into their inputs of traded goods and labour input. It is through the shadow wage rate (SWR) that the Little—Mirrlees method allows one to take a scarcity of foreign exchange into account; a low SWR encourages a greater use of domestic resources.[59] Corrections to interest rates are made through the CRI and the ARI, which, as we have seen, are intimately related to the SWR. Basically, then, Little and Mirrlees consider three main sources of 'distortion' to be important — first, those in product markets due partly to factor market imperfections and partly to other features of trade policies etc. in developing countries. Second, labour market imperfections, which tend to mean that the actual cost of labour in 'industry' exceeds the social opportunity cost of that labour. Third, imperfect capital markets, which give rise to a situation of under-saving and under-investing. But other sources of distortion are recognised and can be handled within the Little—Mirrlees method.[60]

What is proposed here is that an input—output table be used to provide estimates of the cost of each 'bundle' of commodities used in producing the pattern of final output implied by the sectoral pattern of tourist receipts. This is done by inverting the open Leontief matrix, multiplying the inverse by the vector of final demand —

57 Joshi (1972) pp. 30—1.

58 Stewart and Streeten (1972), p. 90.

59 Little and Mirrlees (1968), p. 90.

60 E.g. (1) Risk and Uncertainty: 'We do not advocate making any allowances for risk on most projects' but where a project is large and where there is uncertainty which affects society this should be handled by using *expected* values of inputs and outputs rather than use of a higher discount rate or the use of 'pay-back' periods (p. 96). (2) Externalities 'whenever the possibility of an external economy (or any external effect) is suggested, every effort should be made to measure it . . . ' But 'vague and theoretical "external economies" have often been used in support of bad projects' (p. 97).

in this case the vector of investment expenditures and tourist receipts — and applying the primary input coefficients to the resulting gross outputs, discovering the primary input scalar. Thus each commodity in final demand (or 'bundle' of commodities where, as is usual, the transactions matrix is aggregated) has a unique requirement of primary inputs given the assumptions of input—output analysis. It may be necessary in fact to take account of changing coefficients in the matrix — due for example to some or all sectors operating at full capacity — or the evidence of grossly under-utilised capacity in which case the marginal input—output coefficients will differ from the average coefficients. Such amendments are undertaken in the present study.[61]

In the analysis presented in Chapter 10 the primary inputs are defined as:

wages and salaries (labour)

gross domestic profits (domestic capital)

government revenues

imports of goods and services c.i.f. *plus* the remitted profits of foreign enterprise.

Imports of goods and services present no valuation problems in the Little—Mirrlee methodology — c.i.f. prices are used without adjustment. The remitted profits of hotels — which are assumed to be all hotel profits less any interest payments on locally raised loan capital — are valued in foreign exchange, since they represent the cost to society of receiving the original foreign investment.[62] If this approach is adopted, however, the original inflow of foreign capital should be treated as a benefit.

In the particular case of the Caribbean, government revenues do present problems. This is because it has been national accounting practice in the smaller islands of the Caribbean to aggregate the government sectors and thereby to conceal the distinction between revenue and expenditure relating to the provision of goods, utilities and services sold by the government, and general revenue and expenditure.[63] Adjustment must therefore be made for direct and indirect taxes, which are a gain to society, at any rate after the deduction of the social costs of assessing and collecting these taxes. For the involvement of government in utilities, if there were a real surplus at accounting prices, then this would also be counted as a benefit. However, in the case of the Caribbean there is very little — if any — real surplus from such activities and so this problem does not arise.[64] Since government, as part of final demand, is not within the matrix, no direct adjustment of the wage element is possible. However, it is argued that no general case can be made for attaching a shadow wage of less than unity to the government sector as a whole since the employees are, in general, skilled people whose value in alternative occupations is attested for by the list of

61 See below Chapter 9.

62 It is assumed that, for practical purposes, the 'hotel' plant can be assumed to be wholly owned by 'foreigners'. All hotel profits (less interest) are treated as remitted—but even if they are not they can still be regarded as pure cost since they raise the consumption or wealth of foreigners neither of which are part of the 'objective function'. This follows the Little—Mirrlees approach to distributional objectives.

63 See O'Loughlin (1966) and Bryden (1970).

64 See also Chapter 3.

vacancies in most Caribbean governments.[65]

So far as gross domestic profits are concerned, these arise because of the assumption of constant input coefficients. In reality, if these sectors are operating at full capacity, the additional output presumed to occur will only occur if some investment is undertaken. If we had capital coefficients for each sector, this could be accounted for directly. But such coefficients are not available in the Caribbean, nor, it is suspected, in many other small tourist economies. Little—Mirrlees arguments apart, it could be argued that in such circumstances a part of the 'profit' at least should be counted as cost. The Little—Mirrlees argument is that such profits cannot be counted as benefit on distributional grounds, and to the extent that they are consumed they must be treated as pure cost. The treatment of domestic profits as a cost is justified on both of these grounds. The only part of gross profits which counts as a benefit in the proposed approach is profits tax, which accrues to the government.[66]

Wages and salaries do present a valuation problem which is central to the Little—Mirrlees methodology. A wide range of circumstances exist within the Caribbean, and the shadow wage rate is something that can only be adequately worked out after careful on-the-spot analysis. The first point is that the shadow pricing of wages and salaries refers to *national* labour resources. So far as the employment of non-nationals is concerned it is assumed that it is not part of government policy to maximise such employment — indeed the reverse is often the case. To the extent that non-nationals are employed in the construction sectors and in sectors serving tourism, adjustments have to be made to the total wages and salaries bill *before* any shadow pricing takes place. After accounting for any direct taxes paid, the wages and salaries of non-nationals should be treated entirely as a real cost in terms of foreign exchange.[67]

The dichotomy between 'skilled' and 'unskilled' labour which is employed by Little and Mirrlees appears to be rather too simplistic, as reference to Chapter 2 above will confirm. The valuation of skilled labour is largely ignored by Little and Mirrlees, and their recommendation is to 'charge actual salary payments to the project (i.e. to make no reduction on account of direct and indirect taxes paid by salary earners)'. In effect this allows a shadow price of skilled labour of slightly over unity if taxes are paid, thereby allowing for some 'inelasticity' in the education system.[68] But 'since skilled labour inputs are seldom so large a part of costs that

65 *The Tripartite Survey* p. 77 gives some information on this point, though it refers only to professional and technical personnel in ministries of finance, public works and agriculture. However, most unskilled or semi-skilled personnel in government are involved in construction, maintenance work etc., and construction work at least is accounted for separately by assuming that such work is contracted out to the construction sector.

66 Account is however taken of any tax relief measures which operate in different sectors. See below Chapter 10.

67 This seems to follow from the Little—Mirrlees approach. It is intuitively reasonable since that part of the income of non-nationals which is remitted will be largely spent on imports. But it should be clear from the earlier discussion that wages and salaries of non-nationals should, from the national point of view, be counted as a cost whether they are remitted, spent on imports, or spent on domestic goods and services.

68 Little and Mirrlees (1968), pp. 155—6.

variations in their accounting prices would make much difference to project choices' one only needs rough estimates.[69] It is difficult to assess the validity of this statement without a rigid definition of 'skilled' and 'unskilled' and an appraisal of all the opportunities open to the economy. Such a distinction is not easy to make, however as there is generally a spectrum of skills rather than a clear dividing line.[70] One suspects that it may be quite important in some cases to refine the treatment of the SWR to allow for different categories of skills, though clearly this makes the analysis more complex.[71]

In the Little—Mirrlees methodology, all 'unskilled' labour for marginal industrial projects is assumed to come from the (subsistence) agricultural sector, where the consumption of the worker is assumed to be equal to his marginal product, or even somewhat above it owing to the operation of a 'sharing mechanism'.[72] This latter assumption is however highly dubious since it is likely to be the younger, more energetic members of the rural sector who migrate, and their marginal product may well have exceeded the average product of labour in that sector, in which case rural consumption (and possibly also investment) will decline rather than increase when they migrate.[73]

But the SWR should reflect (1) the effect of employment generated on production elsewhere and (2) the effect of employment generated on the commitment to consumption. As with industry, the social significance of the employment of one 'man' in tourism 'depends on where he comes from, how his departure effects the situation he leaves behind, how much he was paid, what he does with the money, and whether the earnings of others are affected by his arrival'.[74]

In the case of tourism in the Caribbean, the evidence of Chapter 2 suggests that much of the unskilled or semi-skilled labour used in tourism came from two main sources, namely agriculture and an increase in the female participation rate. While the valuation of the former is reasonably straightforward, the valuation of the latter poses considerable problems, at least in theory, because national income statisticians in most countries fail to value the services of a housewife to society. There is no clear way of dealing with this problem except to assume that the marginal product of housewives is at least equivalent to that of agricultural workers, though one inference from the lower female participation rates might be that this seriously understates the value of the housewife in rural society.

Assuming that the marginal product in alternative occupations is m, and the wage

69 *Ibid*. p. 114.

70 See also the discussion in Chapter 2.

71 It means detailed knowledge of the availability of each category of skill both now and for the life of the project, and the requirements of each category of skill by all existing and potential activities. A detailed analysis of this kind also raises doubts about the treatment of consumption out of wages in the Little—Mirrlees methodology.

72 Little and Mirrlees (1968), p. 158.

73 Because the average product is *reduced* by their moving rather than increased.

74 Little and Mirrlees (1968), p. 157.

in the new employment is $\bar{w}$, then if taxes paid on wages are t and all (disposable) wages are consumed, the new consumption level of workers will be $c = \bar{w} - t$. The amount of goods and services committed to consumption increases by $(c - m)$ and the new employment reduces the amount available for investment by $(c - m)$.[75]

It now remains to value the new consumption in terms of the investment forgone, and it is here that we must refer back to the discussion of the appropriate rate of discount.

The shadow wage rate (SWR) is given by the formula[76]

$$\text{SWR} = c - \frac{1}{s_o}(c - m)$$

where s_o is the relative value of income freely available for investment in the hands of government as compared with the same income in the hands of consumers. The above formula therefore compares the relative valuation of the consumption and investment effects of new employment, which gives the shadow wage rate.

The value of s_o is given by[77]

$$s_o = \left(\frac{1 + r}{1 + i}\right)^T \left(\frac{(c - m)n}{r - i} + 1\right) - \frac{(c - m)n}{r - i}$$

where $i = $ the CRI (assumed constant)

$r = $ the rate of reinvestment in the 'marginal project'

$n = $ the labour–capital ratio in the 'marginal project'

$T = $ the time period until consumption and investment are equally desirable.[78]

It was stated earlier that s_o, i, the SWR and the accounting rate of interest (R) must all be consistent with each other. An estimate of the ARI can be obtained from the values of the variables in the above equation.[79]

$$R - r + \frac{1}{s_o}(c - m)n \quad \text{('To a reasonable approximation. .')}$$

Since R is determined as the rate which equalises the supply and demand for investible surpluses, the value given by the above equation must approximate to the value of R as determined independently. If the two calculations are inconsistent, then a revision of the SWR is implied, and the inference is that 'the values of r and n have been ill-chosen and do not represent a marginal project in fact'.

In practice, the finer adjustments of the analysis do not greatly affect the present study, for two reasons. First, we are primarily concerned to examine whether the social rate of return is less than the private rate of return, indicating careful examination of tourism projects and the necessity of control. Secondly, we have no other projects to compare with tourism projects on the same analysis, and so one is

75 *Ibid*. p. 158.

76 *Ibid*. p. 167.

77 *Ibid*. p. 167.

78 Thus $s = 1$, and the situation of underinvestment is removed.

79 Little and Mirrlees (1968), p. 168.

left with a *minimal* ARI which represents the rate which can be 'earned by portfolio investment abroad' which Little and Mirrlees suggest may be equal to 5 or 6 per cent per annum in real terms.[80] In these circumstances it seems reasonable to make some fairly crude estimates and to test the sensitivity of the result to the various assumption made. Where sensitivity is marked, the assumptions can then be scrutinised more carefully.

Having computed the shadow prices of primary inputs in the manner outlined earlier, we are now in a position to compute social costs and benefits for the project over the period chosen for the analysis, which in this case is 20 years. The internal rate of return of the net stream of social benefits is computed and compared with the private rates of return in tourism and the minimal ARI. The details are given in Chapter 10 below.

Other pecuniary and non-pecuniary costs and benefits of tourism

So far we have been concerned with arriving at a method of evaluating the complex of investments required by an expansion of the tourist sector, where a number of fairly obvious and quantifiable distortions exist which make the divergences between social benefit (to nationals) and private benefit. At least four areas of costs and benefits require to be discussed further:

(1) Economies of scale.
(2) External economies and diseconomies.
(3) Uncertainty and risk related to the costs of dependence.
(4) The social impact of tourism.

Economies of scale

The present study lays some stress on the heavy burden of infrastructure costs which fall on governments of developing countries when the tourist sector grows. In small islands, a considerable part of this is expenditure on airports, and it might be argued that economies of scale exist in airports which have to be taken into account. In other words, where infrastructure costs are computed over a relatively short period, substantial underutilisation of capacity may exist, particularly in airport facilities. In practice, however, this argument is difficult to accept for small territories which are, by and large, stop-over points rather than terminal points in a route network. The size and speed of aircraft, and consequently the runway length and load capability and other technical characteristics, are determined not mainly by the number of passengers disembarking at any one point, but by the number of passengers on the route as a whole. Thus one finds that many small islands in the Caribbean — for example Antigua and the Cayman Islands — are being continually requested to invest more money in airport facilities by international airlines even though *prima facia* there appears to be a considerable amount of excess capacity if the aircraft *currently used* were to remain in use on the route in question. This is a particular problem of relatively small countries (or regions) which are attempting to develop their tourist sectors. The same argument would apply to some extent to harbour facilities.[81]

---

80 *Ibid.* p. 96.

81 Infrastructure costs are discussed in Chapter 8.

External economies and diseconomies

It is difficult to think of any special case being made for external economies arising from tourist development. It is possible that some exist — for example the existence of an international airport may save some time for local travellers, though these would tend to be the better-off members of the community in any case. Similarly the existence of hotels, casinos etc. may provide some external benefits, again for the better-off. The provision of tourist roads may ease the access of farmers to market centres, though this must be set against the cost of the rapid growth of tourism in terms of competition for resources. Finally, the growth of tourism is likely to benefit large landowners through the effect on land prices of real estate development potential. But again, it seems unlikely that the appraiser would wish to count such gains as benefits to society.

Diseconomies which are not taken into account by the appropriate choice of shadow prices concern the access to amenities (particularly beaches) for nationals, the possibility of pollution, which arises in tourism mainly because of inadequate sewerage disposal, and the much more difficult question of visual pollution via the architectural features of tourist developments. In the case of real estate development, clearance of the natural vegetation may also have some microclimatic effects which could affect water supplies for domestic and agricultural use. Lack of access to beaches (and tourist facilities in general) has been a complaint voiced in the West Indies from time to time. For example, Norris clains that the Jamaican or the casual tourist 'finds it almost impossible to get close to a beach unless he books at a hotel'.[82]

Naipaul, in *The Middle Passage,* commented on the implicit colour bar which operates in the tourist industry in the Caribbean.[83] In the case of access to beaches, this is something which is better handled by legal rights than by attempting to assign a cost and incorporate it into the analysis, Where there is crowding of beaches it is difficult to think of 'a willingness to pay' criterion being applied since this — given the income distribution — would lead to the same result. The apparent colour bar is more often the effect of the high prices of hotels which exclude all but tourists and the wealthier nationals, but it may have an impact on feelings of 'relative deprivation.'[84]

The possibility of pollution being associated with tourism generally relates to the problem of sewerage disposal. Given the heavy burden on government associated with tourist development, it is perhaps not surprising that this has tended to be left to individual hotel proprietors in the Caribbean, and fears have been expressed that this leads to inadequate disposal at sea. the growth of green algae, and the creation of diseconomies through the effect on the beaches and marine life.

As regards architectural features, the fears here relate to the despoiling of the natural landscape by high rise buildings and other architectural features which are not 'in keeping' with indigenous art forms and which tend to be 'borrowed' from

82 Norris (1962).

83 Naipaul (1962).

84 See below p. 91. *et seq.*.

other countries more or less wholesale. It is difficult to handle this complaint other than by suggesting that the scrutiny and approval of plans be as far as is humanly possible in the hands of 'disinterested' indigenes.

Uncertainty and risk related to dependence

In fact the economic disadvantages of tourism in developing countries are generally discussed in terms of the vulnerability of tourism to: (a) fashion; (b) fluctuations in the national incomes in developed countries which constitute the main source of tourists; (c) war, natural disasters or political 'disturbances', and (d) the uncertainty of any industry in which there is a dominance of foreign capital.[85] As Hawkins points out, vulnerability due to fashion is rather outdated by the growth of 'mass tourism', although it was and is a feature of tourism based on catering for the wealthy and eccentric. Vulnerability due to fluctuations in national incomes in developed countries arises because of the high income elasticity of demand for foreign tourism. It is true, however, that such fluctuations have been much less severe in the post-war period, and the effect has been mainly on the rate of growth of tourism rather than by absolute declines in international tourist receipts. Nevertheless the fear is a real one and, together with (c), which is unpredictable, constitutes a good economic reason for viewing too great a degree of dependence on tourism as undesirable, though the limits in this respect are not easy to set.

Similarly, dependence on an industry which seems to be dominated by foreign capital, whatever the economic effects of this, appears unacceptable in many developing countries. This may be for a number of reasons — first, that economic decisions are taken by non-nationals and non-residents and that the objectives of these owners of capital may conflict with national objectives. Second, that the *inflow* of foreign capital will itself be sensitive to national policies and dependence on this inflow will limit the freedom of manoeuvre which government has in its economic policies. Third, that foreign firms may have easier access to local capital through banking institutions which are themselves foreign owned. Finally, it may well be that the economic benefits of foreign capital, viewed within the broader scope of cost—benefit analysis, are frequently insufficient and that this constitutes a major reason for unacceptability. Although there are other reasons why dependence on foreign capital is not liked in developing countries, one may note that these disadvantages apply to any industry developed on the basis of foreign capital and that tourism may be at less of a disadvantage here than other industries in view of the fact that *technological* limitations to local ownership would appear to be less significant.[86]

In the light of the above discussion of dependence on tourism, it is of some interest to note that the Commonwealth Caribbean contains some of the most highly dependent tourism countries in the world, if we take as an indicator of tourism dependence the ratio of tourist receipts to national incomes or visible exports. Table 5.2 gives some comparative data on tourism dependence.

85 Hawkins, H.G.C. (1967), personally communicated.

86 Marketing may, however, be a problem in this respect.

Table 5.2 *Dependence on tourism of tourist countries, 1965*[a]

Country	Tourist receipts as a percentage of national incomes[b]	Tourist receipts as a percentage of visible exports[c]
Morocco	2·8	15·3
Kenya	2·5	14·5
Tunisia	2·3	14·6
Hong Kong	11·9	10·9
Lebanon	9·4	94·9
Jordan	6·3	110·0
Mexico	4·5	68·2
Puerto Rico	4·7	n.a.
Bahamas	about 40·0	316·3
Jamaica	5·9	19·9
Barbados	17·8	40·7
Grenada	15·9[d]	54·4
St Vincent	5·8[d]	23·6
St Lucia	15·0[d]	14·4
Antigua	40·0[d]	275·0
Montserrat	14·6[d]	316·1
British Virgin Islands[e]	49·1[d]	inf.
Cayman Islands[e]	28·5[d]	inf.
Turks and Caicos	3·0[d]	30·4
Malta	5·1	29·2
Greece	2·2	32·8
Spain	6·2	119·8
Portugal	4·8	27·3
Italy	2·8	17·9
Austria	8·0	335·0
Switzerland	4·6	17·8
Ireland	8·5	30·7
Canada	1·9	8·6

Symbols: n.a. = not available
inf. = infinite; visible exports minimal
Notes and sources:
[a] Tourist countries defined as those in which tourist receipts exceed 5% of national income or 10% of visible exports. Some countries omitted because of lack of data.
[b] National income figures from *UN Yearbook of National Income Statistice.*
[c] Export data from *UN Trade Statistics* except for Caribbean.
[d] GDP at factor cost has been used.
[e] 1968 data only available.

The social impact of tourism

Peters stands somewhat alone in contending that tourism creates 'social' benefits arising from a 'widening of people's interest generally in world affairs and to a new understanding of foreigners and foreign tastes'.[87] But it is true, by and large, that the analysis of the social impact of tourism has been ignored by economists in spite of the fact that most of the attack on tourism in developing countries has been levelled at its 'social' effect.[88] This results from the time-honoured, but time-worn,

87 Peters (1969) cited above p. 126.

88 Thus the Report on the 1969 Dag Hammerskjold Seminar on 'The Development and Promotion of Tourism in Africa' commented that 'It was finally felt that even more consideration should have been given to the negative aspects of tourism.' (*Report*, p. 5).

boundaries within the social sciences.[89] It is argued here that tourism in developing countries has social effects, the implications of which cannot be ignored.

The important distinguishing feature of tourism in developing countries is the fact that tourists have to come to the developing country in order to consume the product. This is in contrast with other exporting activities, and indeed most exchange relations, where producers and consumers are separated and rarely confront each other in person. It is the consequences of this confrontation, rather than the consequences of the mode of production *per se* that are the concern of this section.

The impact of large scale tourism on developing countries has not escaped the notice of the World Council of Churches, which commented as follows:

> An excessive number of tourists can generate social strains in small and unsophisticated communities. The human effect, on this scale and on the international scale, of competition for tourist 'consumers' has been given too little attention and deserves serious research.[90]

Some indications that there may be a relationship between tourism density, expressed in the annual numbers of tourists as a proportion of the population or as a proportion of the land area, and the growth of resentment towards tourists, have been expressed elsewhere in relation to the Caribbean.[91] The inference here is that tourism density, which is to some extent related also to dependence, is an indicator of the degree of confrontation between tourists and indigenes and that this confrontation gives rise to resentment of tourists. In addition, it was earlier suggested that tourism *may* have effects on the propensity to import of the indigenous population through social effects on the pattern of consumption.[92]

Evidence regarding the density of tourism in 'tourist countries' is given in Table 5.3 below. It will be noticed that several Caribbean islands exhibit very high tourist densities – especially the Bahamas, Barbados, Antigua, Montserrat, the British Virgin Islands and the Cayman Islands, which have high tourist densities by reference either to population or land area. Four of the ten most dense countries by reference to land area, and five of the ten most dense countries by reference to population, are in the Caribbean region.

A possible theoretical explanation for both the growth of resentment and the effect on consumption patterns is offered by the twin concepts of relative deprivation and reference group analysis.[93] The concepts of 'relative deprivation' and 'reference group' derive from the idea 'that people's attitudes, aspirations and grievances largely depend on the frame of reference within which they are conceived'.[94] Two features of tourism seem to be important in this context; first, the tourist *qua* 'reference group' with which the indigene individually or as a group

89 C.f. Reynolds (1971).

90 *Leisure–Tourism: Threat and Promise*, World Council of Churches Geneva 1970, p. 21.

91 Bryden and Faber (1971).

92 See above, Chapter 3.

93 I lean heavily in this discussion on Runciman (1972).

94 Runciman (1972) p. 10.

Table 5.3 *Density of tourism in tourist countries 1965*[a]

Country	Tourist arrivals per '000 population	Tourist arrivals per sq. mile of land area
Morocco	35	3·0
Kenya	9	0·4
Tunisia	36	2·6
Hong Kong	110	1,019·0
Lebanon	246	200·0
Jordan	264	14·0
Mexico	30	1·6
Puerto Rico	235	177·0
Bahamas	3,691	112·0
Jamaica	109	45·0
Barbados	278	412·0
Grenada	146	104·0
St Vincent	73	43·0
St Lucia	137	54·0
Antigua	805	285·0
Montserrat	450	203·0
British Virgin Islands	1,283	203·0
Cayman Islands	749	66·0
Malta	148	392·0
Greece	99	17·0
Spain	391	63·0
Portugal	166	42·0
Italy	217	9·0
Austria	889	198·0
Switzerland	970	358·0
Ireland	629	66·0
Canada	626	3·0

Note: [a] See previous table for definition of tourist countries.
Source: Tourist arrivals: IUOTO data; population and land area: UN data; and Chapter 2 above for the Caribbean.

compares his own standard of living; second the expectations which are aroused by rather too frequent and optimistic pronouncements regarding the benefits to be derived from tourist development. First of all, then, the pattern of consumption of the tourist[95] may be attractive to the indigene and, while he is economically unable to achieve his desire in this respect, he may nevertheless move along the implied direction, which usually means the importation of commodities from the tourist's own country.[96] In this respect, tourists and/or expatriate employees may be a 'positive' reference group, in which case a relative deprivation follows.[97] The feeling of relative deprivation may be compounded by historical inequalities associated with membership of a racial group.

95 Or, possibly more realistically, expatriate employees in the tourist industry.

96 Thus, for example, is the switch to American cars in the Caribbean unrelated to the growing significance of American tourism?

97 Runciman (1972) p. 13. An exception to this would be the Rastafarians in Jamaica, for whom tourists, expatriate employees and most other Jamaicans broadly represent a negative reference group.

Other possible explanations regarding the growth of animosity toward tourists exist both within and beyond the Caribbean. Demas has raised the problem of the relationship between tourist development in the Caribbean and inflation of land prices 'where it is often impossible for a local resident to acquire land to build a house or for any other purpose in his own country', and in addition the associated problem of large scale alienation of land.[98] This, of course, is one aspect of the competition for resources, but it does indicate that certain income groups at least may suffer rather than gain from tourist development, and resentment in such cases would be understandable. It is a major criticism of the analysis that it does not identify the gainers and losers in greater detail.[99] A similar problem has been raised in relation to Switzerland by Raymond, who points out the effects of high land prices tempting small farmers to sell for a large profit.

> At first he would feel he had done well. But the money would only have its full value if it were reinvested properly – and he would have no skill or knowledge of this kind. What is likely to happen in consequence? When the tourist facilities are built, he is left landless, and trained only in agricultural skills which are no longer relevant. Accordingly, the only work he can get is low-status work. He feels robbed of his dignity and has a chip on his shoulder against tourists.[100]

Another type of explanation of animosity and the 'social' costs of tourism rests on the 'corrosive' effects of tourism on the culture and value system of the indigenous population. Thus, according to Bishop Ban It Chiu:

> People in South East Asia who were at the receiving end of the tourist-boom often felt that they were made into something like a human zoo. Tourists came along to see 'the natives' and to study the odd habits of the natives. Local people were thus encouraged to be 'interesting natives' and go through traditional movements for the benefit of goggling strangers. It robbed a people of their dignity to be treated as zoo-objects.[101]

Similar points have been made by Naipaul and others in respect of the Caribbean.[102] Taken in isolation, it is difficult to know how to handle these points, though they are clearly important to some people in the sense that they represent a largely unavoidable 'cost' related to tourist development.

Another explanation of changing relationships between tourists and indigenes may be found simply in the effects of commercialisation. In the early stages of tourist development the tourist may find himself treated to traditional hospitality

·

98 Demas, W. G. Feature Address for the Fifth West Indian Agricultural Economics Conferenc *Proceedings* (1970) p. 4.

99 This aspect would seem to be highly deserving of further research.

100 Raymond, quoted in *Leisure–Tourism: Threat and Promise*, World Council of Churches (1970) pp. 30–1.

101 Ban It Chiu, quoted in World Council of Churches (1970) p. 31.

102 Naipaul (1962), p. 76. Also a recent study paper on 'The Role of Tourism in Caribean Development', Caribean Ecumenical Consultation for Development, CADEC, Barbados 1971, p. 27 *et seq*. Demas (1970) also raises the problem of 'loss of dignity'.

ree from market calculation. The tourist is subsumed under the traditional category
of 'guest', while the behaviour of the indigene most appropriate to their relationship
s that of host. Such factors as increasing density of tourism, the growth of commercial outlets in general, the exposure of indigenes to the predominantly western value
system which the tourist industry reflects, and so on, will cause a change in this
relationship as it becomes less and less practical to treat increasing numbers of
ourists as guests, and for most of the indigenes the appropriate behaviour towards
ourists moves to that of the seller—customer type, in which calculations of the
market place assume an increasing role. Tourists who have experienced the same or
a similar community at an earlier stage are likely to feel that the indigenes are now
ess 'friendly'. Similarly, if promotion and advertising campaigns are based on por-
raying an image of the host country which is false, the tourist may feel that he has
been cheated. This could lead to dissatisfaction and resentment which, if reflected
n the behaviour of tourists, may be heartily reciprocated. This type of explanation
would seem to have implications for promotional policies.

But there are many possible explanations for animosity, the important point
here being that a perusal of the literature seems to indicate a general feeling that
ourism has 'costs' associated with it which are not easily enumerated, and that these
costs' form part of an explanation for animosity towards tourists in some developing countries. Some of these 'costs' are part of the problem of competition for
esources engendered by the rapid growth of tourism, some of them may be associated with the *distribution* of benefits and costs from tourist development, while
others may not be amenable to inclusion within an empirical study of the impact of
ourism, in which case other approaches would seem to be necessary.[103]

As regards the effect on consumption patterns, it seems important to discuss
whether this effect is associated with particular forms of development; whether, as
Adams has suggested for Jamaica, it is due to an 'adverse secular trend in tastes'[104]
which is related generally to increases in incomes; or whether it is simply due to
hanging income distributions and differences in consumption patterns between
ncome groups. Analytical frameworks tend to ignore the effects of different
trategies on patterns of consumption, concentrating on the effect on production
atterns instead.

Confronted with this problem in other parts of the developing world, economists
ave tended to call up that all-embracing concept, the 'demonstration effect'. Some-
imes this demonstration is a 'good thing' because it encourages people to work for
hings they have not already got.[105] Sometimes it is a 'bad thing' because it leads to
higher marginal propensity to import.[106] This latter interpretation is becoming
nore familiar in the writings of Latin American economists, who are concerned with
he effects of foreign domination of industry and the apparent tendency for import
atterns of foreign capitalists or upper income groups to set the style for others in

03 I return to these issues again in Part V.

04 Adams (1968).

05 E.g. Nurkse (1953), pp. 58, 63–7 etc.

06 E.g. Griffin (1969) pp. 99–100 and pp. 271 *et seq.*

the community.

The demonstration effect is, however, a vague and unsatisfactory concept. It does not, by itself, explain who is demonstrating what to whom and why, or to what extent and at what pace such 'demonstration' is occurring. For example, why is it that it is the tastes of foreigners which are assumed to be adopted by indigenes, and not *vice versa*? But if the 'demonstration effect' is observable in the pattern of relationships between outsiders and indigenes in many parts of the developing world, then it seems highly likely that whatever it is that the concept is trying to express will be extremely important in the case of tourism, which involves a relatively greater exposure to foreigners and foreign tastes. It is the feeling of the present author that theories of relative deprivation suggest a fruitful starting point for an analysis of these problems.

Summary

The starting point of this chapter was Peters' statement of the potential benefits of tourism. The paucity of the popular 'multiplier' approach to the benefits of tourism was demonstrated. Alternative approaches to the problem of the social costs and benefits of tourism were discussed, and the approach adopted in this study explained in some detail. Finally, the more serious omissions from the proposed methodology were discussed. Viewed as a whole, the discussion of the methodology has revealed several important areas of 'cost' which have to be compared with the 'potential' benefits. By and large, these costs tend to be ignored by most studies of tourism.

The growth and structure of Caribbean tourism in the 1960 s and the role of government s

Introduction to Part III

The purpose of this section is to examine the basic data relating to the growth and structure of the Caribbean tourist industry in general and the hotel industry in particular, together with the role of governments, especially in the smaller islands, in promoting and controlling the tourist industry. Such an examination is regarded as essential firstly because much of the subsequent analysis in Part IV is based on the data presented in this section, secondly because it is necessary to highlight the areas in which basic data are likely to be weak and therefore requiring cautious interpretation, thirdly because a comparative analysis of the basic data relating to tourism in the Caribbean has not been previously carried out. In fact, since the 1958 study by the Institute of Economic Research of the University of the West Indies into the distribution of tourist expenditure in Jamaica*, very little 'in depth' work has been carried out in this field of study in the region as a whole.

* Reported in Cumper (1959).

6   Growth in Caribbean tourism 1961–8

It was in the 1900s that a steady stream of travel journals, tourist guides and handbooks for the Caribbean began to emerge.[1] Aspinall's *Pocket Guide*, published in 1907, was able to comment that 'Every year our beautiful and historic possessions in the West Indies attract an increasing number of visitors from England, who find in them a pleasant refuge from the rigour and fogs of winter. To our American cousins these colonies have long been a profitable hunting ground for health and enjoyment.'[2] But while it would be an error to suggest that tourism in the West Indies was of very recent origin, it is certainly in the post-war period that it has reached any significant size as an industry in most of the islands of the Commonwealth Caribbean. During the 1960s the growth of tourism in the Caribbean, if measured by tourist numbers, was very rapid indeed, comparing closely with the growth of international tourism in the world as a whole.[3]

This chapter examines, first, the growth, structure and other characteristics of tourist arrivals in the Commonwealth Caribbean, and second, the growth and pattern of tourist receipts, particularly in relation to the 1960s.

Tourist arrivals: growth, structure and other characteristics

Table 6.1 shows the growth and geographical structure of tourist arrivals in the Commonwealth Caribbean during the 1960s.

Owing to the absence of regional institutions and the very varied quality of the statistical units in the islands, data for the early years of the decade in particular can only be taken as indicative of orders of magnitude. Even for later years different sources give different figures. So far as has been possible, the figures for 1967 and 1968 have been double-checked for accuracy, and most of these have been derived from figures produced by individual tourist boards, who obtain their information from the respective immigration authorities.[4]

Problems of definition have arisen in the collation of such data. A 'tourist' is normally defined as any non-resident visiting a country for more than 24 hours, having an intention to return to his place of permanent residence and not being remunerated

---

1   Aspinall, (1907) (1930) together with Rutter (1933) are among the best known.

2   Aspinall (1907) Preface.

3   See also Chapter 4.

4   Unfortunately this is still no guarantee of accuracy.

Table 6.1 *Growth and geographical structure of tourist arrivals in the Commonwealth Caribbean*

Territory and geo-graphical grouping	Tourist arrivals				Growth rates	
	1961	1962	1967	1968	1961-7 %	1962-8 %
Windward Islands	20,460	20,853	51,963	67,901	16·7	21·5
St Vincent	3,100e	3,500e	7,242	12,107	15·2	23·0
Grenada	7,970	8,181	20,549	23,164	17·1	18·9
Dominica	3,535	3,417	7,465	9,977	13·3	19·6
St Lucia	5,855	5,755	16,437	22,653	18·8	25·7
Leeward Islands	23,554	33,908	73,535	72,560	20·8	13·4
Montserrat	2,000e	2,200e	5,373	6,925	17·9	21·1
St Kitts–Nevis	5,554	6,708	8,988	9,797	8·4	6·5
Antigua	16,000	25,000	59,174	55,838	24·4	14·3
Barbados	37,060	44,258	91,565	115,697	16·2	17·3
Northern Group	8,000e	10,000e	28,641	38,188	23·7	25·0
Turks and Caicos	n.a.	248	769	1,514	n.a.	35·2
Cayman Islands	n.a.	n.a.	10,328	14,496	n.a.	n.a.
Virgin Islands	n.a.	n.a.	17,544	22,178	n.a.	n.a.
Jamaica	224,492	206,838	235,025	258,460	0·8	3·8
Trinidad and Tobago	70,000e	70,000e	77,790	91,660	1·7	4·6
Bahamas	336,211	444,870	915,273	1,072,213	18·1	15·8
Total Commonwealth Caribbean	719,777e	830,727e	1,473,522	1,716,679	12·7e	12·8

e: estimate

Source: Individual tourist boards, government departments, or survey data for all islands except Jamaica and Trinidad and Tobago, for which IUOTO statistics were used.

from within the country visited.[5] This definition will include visitors on holiday, business visitors, diplomats and other persons on foreign government missions, visiting relatives of nationals or immigrants and some other less common categories. It will exclude cruise ship visitors or in transit passengers who normally stay for less than 24 hours in any island. Most of the territories have now adopted this definition of tourists, although confusions still arise, for example when an in transit visitor has to spend a night in an island before catching his onward flight.[6] Another factor of importance in some islands is temporary migrants seeking work who do not always declare their intentions on entering.[7]

One exception appears to be the Bahamas. The figures in this case include cruise ship passengers who are included in the general category of visitors arriving by sea. The reason for this seems to be that cruise ships visiting the Bahamas stay for more

5 This is the definition of 'tourist' approved by the 1963 UN Conference on International Travel and Tourism. See International Travel Statistics, IUOTO (1965).

6 For example, in Antigua.

7 For example, in the British Virgin Islands.

than 24 hours even though the passengers do not use accommodation capacity on the land.[8]

From Table 6.1 above it can be seen that the region as a whole experienced a growth of nearly 13 per cent per annum in tourist arrivals during the 1960s. If Jamaica and Trinidad were omitted, this growth would be substantially higher.[9] The growth of arrivals in the Leeward Islands, which is primarily determined at present by Antigua, has been slower in recent years due to the failure of Antigua to maintain its initial momentum in the late 1950s and early 1960s which gave it a major share of the small island market. The Windward Islands, on the other hand, were enjoying a banana boom in the late 1950s and early 1960s and it was only in the second half of the decade that tourism began to grow rapidly. Grenada and St Lucia in particular, perhaps because of their greater natural endowment of beaches than the other Windwards, have established themselves firmly in the tourist market. Barbados is the major tourist island in the East Caribbean, and has shown consistently high growth during the decade.

Of increasing importance in relation to their size is the Northern Group of islands comprising the Turks and Caicos Islands, the Cayman Islands and the British Virgin Islands, all of which have shown very high growth rates during the second half of the decade. In the Cayman Islands recent growth in tourist arrivals has been of the order of 30 per cent per annum (1968–70), while the experience of the British Virgin Islands has been very similar.[10]

In terms of market shares, Table 6.2 shows the picture in 1962 and 1968.

Table 6.2 *Commonwealth Caribbean: geographical distribution of tourist arrivals expressed as percentages of total arrivals, 1962 and 1968*

	1962	1968
	%	%
Windward Islands	2·5	4·0
Leeward Islands	4·1	4·2
Barbados	5·3	6·7
Northern Group	1·2	2·2
Jamaica	24·9	15·1
Trinidad and Tobago	8·4	5·3
Bahamas	53·6	62·5
Total	100·0	100·0

Source: As for Table 6.1.

It shows that the share of Trinidad and Jamaica fell between 1962 and 1968, while the rest of the region collectively and individually succeeded in increasing their share of the market. The Eastern Caribbean and the Northern Group of islands

8 See 1969 *Annual Report on Tourism in the Commonwealth of the Bahamas Islands,* pp. 11 and 12.

9 I have not been able to double check the data for the larger Islands, i.e. Jamaica, Trinidad and the Bahamas. *Prima facie* the apparently slow growth in Trinidad and Jamaica looks rather strange.

10 *Economic Surveys and Projections.* The British Virgin Islands and the Cayman Islands.

together increased their share of the market from 13·1 per cent in 1962 to 17·1 per cent in 1968.

Sources of visitors to the Commonwealth Caribbean

It is difficult to obtain comparative data for each island for any single year. However, assuming that the proportion of visitors from any one source will not vary greatly from year to year, it has been possible to compile aggregates giving a general picture for most areas in the middle of the decade. The following table gives the results of this analysis.

Table 6.3 *Sources of visitors by declared residence to the Commonwealth Caribbean[a]circa 1965*

| Arrivals in | Proportion of total arrivals from | | | | | |
	USA	Canada	UK	W Indies[b]	Other	Years
Windward Islands	25·1	8·0	13·9	39·8	13·2	1964, 1965 1966
Leeward Islands	46·1	13·0	5·4	25·3	10·2	1965, 1966
Barbados	29·0	20·7	9·7	32·0	8·6	1965
Northern Group	n.a.	n.a.	n.a.	n.a.	n.a.	n.a.
Jamaica	78·2	9·8	3·2	2·5	6·3	1965
Trinidad and Tobago	31·8	7·8	8·8	16·6	35·0	1965
Bahamas	87·8	5·1	1·4	0·8	5·2	1969

Source: As for Table 6.1.
Notes:
[a] Residence as declared on immigration cards.
[b] There may be some confusion here − some islands include only British West Indies.

Figures for the Northern Group of islands are not available, but the impression is that the picture in these islands would reflect that of the Bahamas rather than that of the East Caribbean islands. An interesting feature of these figures is the relatively high proportion of visitors from the West Indies in the Windward Islands, Barbados, and to a lesser extent the Leeward Islands and Trinidad.

Part of this is no doubt due to family connections, travelling for business reasons and travelling for higher education. Nevertheless, there is a significant amount of inter-island movement for holidays, particularly in the summer months when accommodation rates are cheaper, and special tours have been arranged by British West Indian Airways (BWIA) in conjunction with various hotels. This has been important in taking up the excess capacity which arises in the summer months, and has helped to alleviate the problem of seasonality.[11]

The most important non-regional source of visitors is the USA, which is only to be expected on account of the vast travel market which it represents and its geographical proximity. In general, Canada is the next most important source, the exceptions being Trinidad and the Windward Islands where UK visitors are seemingly more important. The main sources of visitors under the residual category 'other' are Central and South American and North European countries, in particular Germany and Scandinavia.

11 See also Chapter 7.

Seasonality in Caribbean tourism[12]

Tourism in the Commonwealth Caribbean in general shows quite marked seasonality, with peak arrivals occurring in February/March and July/August. The slackest months appear to be May/June and September/October. Table 6.4 gives some evidence on this point for 1965.

Table 6.4 *Seasonal distribution of tourist arrivals: Commonwealth Caribbean, 1965*

Proportion of total arrivals in	St Vincent and Grenada	Antigua (1966)	Barbados	Jamaica	Trinidad
January	7·3	10·1	8·8	9·1	7·5
Feburary	9·7	12·1	9·3	9·3	12·8
March	10·4	11·4	9·4	10·5	8·6
April	8·9	9·3	9·3	7·9	7·9
May	6·7	5·8	6·8	8·1	7·1
June	5·5	5·6	5·8	6·2	6·9
July	10·0	10·5	10·1	9·4	9·5
August	12·5	8·2	11·0	10·9	10·2
September	7·4	4·6	6·5	6·3	7·4
October	5·9	5·3	6·2	6·4	6·7
November	7·4	7·3	7·1	8·4	6·5
December	8·2	9·7	9·6	7·6	8·9

Source: As for Table 6.1.

Only partial data are available showing monthly arrivals classified by country of residence. However, the evidence provided by these data, which cover Barbados, St Vincent, St Lucia and Grenada, shows that seasonal patterns differ significantly between different countries of residence. Table 6.5 summarises the data.

Table 6.5 *Peak months of visitors from different countries, circa 1965*

| | Visitors from | | | | |
	USA	Canada	UK	West Indies	Other
St Vincent (1966)	Feb. Mar.	Feb. Mar.	Mar. Nov.	April Sept.	n.a.
St Lucia (1969)		Feb. Mar.		April Aug.	Apr. Aug.
Grenada (1965)	Feb. Mar.	Feb. Mar.	Feb. Aug.	August	August
Barbados (1964)	Feb. July December	Feb. Mar.	Jan. Feb.	August	August

Source: As for Table 6.1.

Although North American visitors tend to be concentrated in the winter months for climatic reasons, minor peaks emerge in July and August. Visitors from all sources tend to show a slack period in May/June and September/October, which are the worst months for the tourist industry in the Caribbean. As might be expected from the above analysis, seasonality tends to be a more serious problem in islands with a low proportion of visitors from the West Indies, for example Antigua.

12 The problem of seasonality is a common one in the tourist trade. Its significance in the Caribbean has been stressed in numerous reports, for example the *Tripartite Survey*.

The fastest growing sources of visitors tend to be the USA and Canada, although visitors from the UK have grown more rapidly in Antigua. This has not affected seasonal patterns greatly because promotion tends to be concentrated on the summer months, and, although time series data here are inadequate, the inference is that these promotional campaigns have been successful in attracting visitors from North America in the summer months.[13]

Length of stay characteristics

The main method used in the Caribbean for estimating average length of stay involves the use of 'intended stay' as recorded on immigration cards taken from incoming passengers. Occasionally actual length of stay is computed by matching entry and exit cards, but this is rare because the process involved using traditional types of immigration card would place a considerable strain on the government departments involved.[14]

This method is inadequate insofar as intended length of stay differs from actual length of stay, as it often does in practice. Consequently, and with the exception of the data for Barbados, the Cayman Islands and Antigua, where detailed surveys were made, too much reliance should not be placed on the length-of-stay estimates.

Table 6.6 *Average length of stay of visitors to the Commonwealth Caribbean, 1967*

Island	Length of stay, days	
St Vincent	7·8	
Grenada	8·1	
Dominica	4·8	
Montserrat	n.a.	
St Lucia	10·0	
St Kitts—Nevis	5·7	
Antigua	4·7	Hotels and guest houses only
Barbados	7·0	(1965) Excluding apartments and cottages
Cayman Islands	7·4	(1968)
Virgin Islands	n.a.	

Source: Economic Surveys and Projections of individual islands.

The evidence available also suggests that visitors to hotels have a shorter length of stay than visitors staying in other forms of accommodation. In St Lucia, for example, a 50 per cent sample of hotels indicated an average length of stay of 4—5 days in 1966.[15] In the Cayman Islands, length of stay for visitors in hotels was 6·5 days, while that of visitors staying in guest houses and cottages was 13 days and that of visitors staying with friends and others 9·6 days.[16] There is also evidence that the length of stay varies with seasonality. Again in the Cayman Islands, visitors to hotels

13 This needs further study: the direction of causality is always difficult to determine.

14 See, for example, *Report on Statistical Collection in the Leewards and Windwards,* Regional Development Agency (Antigua) 1968.

15 British Development Division. Personal correspondence.

16 Cayman Islands, *Economic Surveys and Projections* 1969—75.

during the high season stayed an average of 7·4 days while out of season (1 May—31 October) they stayed only 4·9 days. The difference in length of stay for visitors in other forms of accommodation was not so great.[17] In Antigua, visitors to hotels and guest houses in the second quarter of 1966 stayed 5·9 days, but only 3·2 days on average in the third quarter.[18] The *Tripartite Economic Survey* of the Eastern Caribbean also gave further evidence of this tendency, which indicates in addition that different *categories* of hotel and guest house accommodation show different length of stay characteristics.[19]

Table 6.7 *Barbados: Average length of stay, by class of hotel, 1965*

	Jan—April	May—Sept.
Luxury	12·9	8·3
'A' class	6·8	4·6
'B' class	7·5	7·1
Guest houses	11·2	8·8

Source: Tripartite Survey p. 153.

These factors, which tend to reduce the length of stay in the off-season, serve to exacerbate the problems of seasonality which arise from fluctuations in visitor arrivals.

The Caribbean offers some range in the type of accommodation available to visitors, although this range is generally limited. Nevertheless, it is useful to gain some idea of the types of accommodation used by visitors. Here again, data are only available for a few islands, but they are indicative of the general pattern. In Barbados, a survey by the Statistical Service revealed the following stratification.

Table 6.8 *Barbados: visitors classified by country of residence and proposed address, 1964*

	Total	Luxury clubs	'A' class hotels	'B' class hotels	Guest houses	Private homes, apartments and cottages and n.s.
USA	15,138	5,127	4,578	781	446	4,206
Canada	10,923	1,366	6,101	522	696	2,238
UK	6,174	1,635	1,968	381	299	1,891
W Indies	20,096	233	2,971	584	2,129	14,187
Other	5,286	817	1,898	226	390	1,955
Total	57,617	9,178	17,516	2,494	3,960	24,477

Source: Barbados Statistical Service, *Digest of Tourism Statistics* 1964, Special Studies No. 9, Table VIII.

17 Cayman Islands, *Economic Surveys and Projections*.

18 Antigua, *Economic Surveys and Projections*, July 1969.

19 *Tripartite Survey*.

Table 6.9 *Percentage breakdown of visitors from different countries classified by proposed address: Barbados 1964*

	Total	Luxury clubs	'A' class hotels	'B' class hotels	Guest houses	Private homes, apartments and cottages and n.s.
USA	100	33·9	30·2	5·2	2·9	27·8
Canada	100	12·5	55·9	4·8	6·4	20·5
UK	100	26·5	31·9	6·2	4·8	30·6
W Indies	100	1·2	14·8	2·9	10·6	70·6
Other	100	15·5	35·9	4·3	7·4	37·0
Total	100	15·9	30·4	4·3	6·9	42·5

Source: Derived from Table 6.8.

Table 6.10 *Source of visitors to various categories of accommodation: Barbados 1964*

Visitors from:	All	Percentage staying in each category of accommodation				
		Luxury clubs	'A' class hotels	'B' class hotels	Guest houses	Private homes, apartments and cottages and n.s.
USA	26·3	55·9	26·1	31·3	11·3	17·2
Canada	19·0	14·9	34·8	20·9	17·6	9·1
UK	10·7	17·8	11·2	15·3	7·6	7·7
W Indies	34·9	2·5	17·0	23·4	53·8	58·0
Other	9·2	8·9	10·8	9·1	9·8	8·0
Total	100	100	100	100	100	100

Source: Derived from Table 6.8.

Thus, about 58 per cent of visitors to Barbados in 1964 stayed in hotels and guest houses. This compares with about 73 per cent in Antigua (1967 data) and 79 per cent in the Cayman Islands (1968 data).

One of the reasons for these differences may be the lower population of West Indian visitors in Antigua and the Cayman Islands. The above table indicates that 71 per cent of West Indian visitors to Barbados stayed in private homes, apartments or cottages. Recent data from St Lucia indicate that between 30 and 34 per cent of West Indian visitors stayed in hotels and guest houses, which tends to confirm the belief that many West Indian visitors stay with friends and relatives.[20]

Nevertheless, the fact that some 30 per cent West Indian visitors stayed in hotels and guest houses, coupled with their large numbers in the 'off-season', makes the West Indies market an important one in itself.[21]

Table 6.10 also shows that Americans tend to patronise luxury clubs, 'A' class hotels and apartments and cottages, while Canadian visitors tend to stay in 'A' class hotels and apartments etc. In both cases, only a small percentage patronise 'B' class hotels and guest houses. Different markets appear to require different kinds of

20 British Development Division—sample survey. Personal communication.

21 The *Zinder Report* on the Future of Tourism in the Eastern Caribbean, for example, did not mention the West Indian market.

accommodation, as one might expect from the different income levels of tourists from different countries. For those who see the future of tourism in more and more luxury-type hotels, perhaps the point should be made the other way round: namely that there are markets which manifestly opt for hotels of a less sophisticated standard.

Cruise ship and other visitors

Two other significant categories of visitor to the Caribbean remain for discussion, namely cruise ship visitors who stay for less than 24 hours in any one island, or yachting visitors who charter yachts from the islands, with or without a crew. The latter are important in Antigua, Grenada and St Lucia where centres exist for chartering yachts, but little is known about this aspect of tourism.

From the data which are available,[22] it seems that some 60,000 cruise ship arrivals were recorded in the Windward and Leeward Islands in 1966. In some islands, arrivals on the Federal boats, *Federal Maple* and *Federal Palm* of the West Indies Shipping Service, which ply between the islands from Trinidad to Jamaica, are included in 'cruise ship' visitors, while in others they are not. If passengers on the Federal boats are excluded, the above total would probably drop to about 50,000. As with aggregate figures for tourist arrivals, but more so, these figures do *not* represent total arrivals to the region since cruise ships visit several territories. Between 1964 and 1966, the only period for which data are available, cruise ship arrivals grew by some 26 per cent per annum, or somewhat faster than other tourist arrivals. However, as cruise ship passengers stay under 24 hours and use no shore accommodation facilities, they are obviously of far less economic importance than other visitors.

Little information is so far available on yachting visitors. There were about 23 yachts based on Antigua in 1968 for charter, with a total passenger capacity of about 122 persons. Most charters are for a week or fortnight. Grenada had about the same number of yachts for charter in 1966. Little chartering is so far done in the 'off-season', partly due to hurricane danger and partly to general seasonality in demand. Both Grenada and Antigua now have full facilities for slipping, repairing and servicing yachts. St Vincent and St Lucia are also yachting centres, and in 1967 it was estimated that 8,921 yacht days were spent on St Lucia – over half the number of cruise ship visitors in the same year.[23]

Tourist receipts: growth, structure and composition

Because of price rises and, latterly, sterling devaluation in 1967, tourist receipts (expressed in current prices) in the region have grown more rapidly than tourist arrivals.[24]

---

22 Mainly from the various *Economic Surveys and Projections* which, in turn, got data from individual government departments and tourist boards.

23 St Lucia. *Economic Survey and Projections*, 1968.

24 The EC $ was devalued in line with sterling in 1967. Hotel rates were usually quoted in US $ since this was the currency used by the majority of tourists. Other prices were marked up to a greater or lesser extent depending on the sources of imports, and, no doubt, some sections of the commercial and trading community took advantage of the confusion. For the tourist, most prices rose in terms of the EC $ by close to the full extent of devaluation.

Figures for tourist receipts are notoriously prone to error in any country, and those for the Caribbean are no exception. Sample surveys of tourist expenditure are few and far between, and those that have been carried out have not been too reliable – apparently many tourists just do not like to reveal how much they spend.[25] The methods which have been used in collating most of the figures for the smaller islands are discussed below. These methods are seldom satisfactory and suggest that a good deal of caution should be used in interpreting the data.

The starting point in these investigations has normally been the receipts of hotels. Three broad methods of approach have been adopted here.

(1) Analysis of income tax or hotel tax data. The latter are most useful if hotel tax is in effect a sales tax applied as a percentage of hotel bills. Even in this case, certain items are excluded, particularly cash sales in the bar, and allowance has to be made for this. In cases where a flat rate tax is applied per bed night, receipts can be analysed by hotel and used for weighting purposes in conjunction with method (2).

(2) A weighted average of hotel rates in winter and summer is applied with allowances for other purchases not included in the tariff. This is inferior to the first method, but has to be used where income tax data are of poor quality or lacking entirely (many hotels are under concessionary tax arrangements and do not file income tax returns) or, where there is no sales tax, in conjunction with method (1). There is a complex tariff structure in many hotels since apart from the choice of American Plan (AP) which is full board and lodging, Modified American Plan (MAP) which excludes lunch, and European Plan (EP) which excludes lunch and dinner, special rates often apply to groups and business visitors, and single rates are more than the 'half-double' rate. Solo visitors are often penalised by excessively high single rates, especially during the 'season'. In practice, experience seems to show that the average charge per bed in any hotel lies much closer to the 'half-double' rate than the simple average of 'single and half-double' which assumes implicitly that fifty per cent of visitors are 'single' and fifty per cent are 'double'.[26] This method is often supplemented by method (3).

(3) The third method involves a direct survey of hotels and guest houses, although this has seldom covered more than fifty per cent of available beds, and usually the number of hotels willing to reveal data to the investigator is strictly limited.[27]

---

25 The most detailed survey of tourist expenditures was that in Jamaica already cited. Although this survey was in 1958, where data are presented in a comparable form, use will be made of them in an attempt to gauge major areas of disagreement, and to suggest reasons for this. Cumper (1959).

26 I am indebted to W. R. Nanton of the Statistical Unit, British Development Division in the Caribbean, for this point.

27 For the distribution of hotel expenses, such an approach is often necessary in view of the lack of income tax data. Even the 1958 Jamaica Survey used the accounts of only four hotels in reaching their estimates of the input structure of the industry.

Other items of tourist expenditure, either by tourists staying in hotels or by tourists staying in other forms of accommodation, are less reliable. Basically, these expenditures fall into the following categories:

(a) Purchase outside hotels of gifts, souvenirs etc.
(b) Transportation — taxis, buses, and internal flying.
(c) Finance — financial services, mainly commissions on travellers cheques.
(d) Services such as hairdressing, beauty salons, plus non-hotel entertainment (night clubs etc).
(e) Rent — by visitors staying in rented accommodation or imputed rent of visitors who maintain residences.
(f) Payments to government — mainly airport or departure taxes, hunting licences and direct stamp sales.
(g) Direct payments to households, mainly domestic staff for persons living in rented accommodation or non-residents who maintain a vacation home.

Of the above, items (a), (c), (d) and (g) are the most intractable in the absence of reliable surveys of tourists, and they are the most likely items in which to expect large errors. Item (b), expenditure on transportation, is estimated by direct approach to taxi drivers, or the taxi drivers' associations, together with an estimation of the minimum cost of taxi fares required to take tourists to and from their various hotels, normally weighted by differential occupancy rates where available. Item (e) is obtained from rental rates and the number of visitors staying in this type of accommodation adjusted by length of stay. Item (f) is mainly departure tax which is partly paid by residents travelling abroad and partly by visitors. The weighting is found from data on departing passengers, while receipts from departure tax are easily obtained from the government accounts.

With these factors in mind we may now examine the growth and structure of tourist receipts in the Commonwealth Caribbean. Reference to Table 6.1 shows that these growth rates are generally in excess of those for tourist arrivals for the reasons given above. This tendency would have been even more marked but for two factors, namely:

(1) A tendency for average length of stay to decline.
(2) A tendency for a higher proportion of visitors to come in the 'off-season' when prices are lower.

Tourist receipts per tourist arrival may now be computed, and this is done in Table 6.12. On the whole, and with the possible exception of Barbados and Antigua, little reliance can be placed on the 1962 data. The variations are less than credible, as are the high figures for St Vincent and the very low figure for Dominica. *Some* variation is of course to be expected for the following reasons:

(a) Differences in the proportion of visitors staying in hotels and other more expensive forms of accommodation.
(b) Differences in expenditures outside hotels of different nationalities.
(c) Differences in length of stay.
(d) The fact that cruise ship visitors are included in tourist receipts but not in arrivals data.
(e) Different amenities offered to tourists.
(f) Variations in costs between territories.
(g) Different methods used in compiling data.

(h) Expenditure of passengers in transit, which may be significant in Barbados, for example.

Table 6.11 *Growth and geographical structure of tourist receipts in the Commonwealth Caribbean, 1961/2 to 1967/8*

| | Tourist receipts $m EC[a] | | | | Growth rates % p.a. | |
	1961	1962	1967[b]	1968	1961−7	1962−8
Windward Islands	3·8	6·1	12·1	15·6	21·3	16·9
St Vincent	0·8	1·4	1·9	2·9	15·5	12·9
Grenada	1·8	2·6	5·4	6·4	20·1	16·2
Dominica	0·2	0·2	1·0	1·3	30·8	36·6
St Lucia	1·0e	1·8	3·7	5·1	24·4	19·0
Leeward Islands	7·9	9·7	22·5	26·7	19·1	18·4
Montserrat	0·2	0·2	2·4	2·6	51·3	53·3
St Kitts−Nevis	0·5	0·6	2·1	2·9	27·0	30·0
Antigua	7·2	8·9	18·1	21·2	16·6	15·6
Barbados	15·9	18·9	34·8	53·9	14·0	19·1
Northern Group	n.a.	n.a.	7·8	11·2	n.a.	n.a.
Turks and Caicos	n.a.	n.a.	0·1	0·2	n.a.	n.a.
Cayman Islands	n.a.	n.a.	2·8	4·3	n.a.	n.a.
Virgin Islands	n.a.	n.a.	5·0	6·6	n.a.	n.a.
Jamaica	64·8	59·9	134·2	175·6	12·9	19·6
Trinidad and Tobago	n.a.	n.a.	24·7	33·8	n.a.	n.a.
Bahamas	n.a.	n.a.	269·0	380·0	n.a.	n.a.
Commonwealth Caribbean	n.a.	n.a.	505·1	696·8	n.a.	n.a.

e: estimated on the basis of arrivals.
Sources: Windward and Leeward Islands and Northern Group: *Economic Surveys: and Projections.* Barbados: *Economic Surveys.* Jamaica, Trinidad and Tobago and Bahamas, IUOTO data converted at prevailing exchange rates. For some E. Caribbean Islands, data for 1961/2 are from UWI (ISER) *Abstract of Statistics* (1964).
Notes:
[a] Totals may not add up due to rounding.
[b] Sterling devaluation in November 1967 affected the value of tourist receipts expressed in $EC since most receipts are in $US and most hotel rates are quoted in $US. See also footnote (24) above.

These estimates may be compared with those in Table 4.6 which calculate average *expenditures* per tourist. For example, US travellers to regions other than Canada, Mexico and Europe spent on average $300 US in 1965 ($515 EC). Other travellers tended to spend less than this. Given that US travellers will be'diluted' by less pecunious travellers from other regions, and also that some US travellers visit several islands, the average figure of $400 EC given in Table 6.12 for the Caribbean as a whole may be a fair guide.

Composition of tourist expenditures

Estimates of the composition of tourist expenditures in the Commonwealth Caribbean also differ quite markedly, for the same reasons given for variations in average receipts per tourist. As can be seen from Table 6.13, receipts of hotels usually

Table 6.12 *Tourist receipts per arrival 1962 and 1968: Commonwealth Caribbean*

	Tourist receipts per arrival $EC	
	1962	1968
Windward Islands	292	230
St Vincent	400	240
Grenada	318	276
Dominica	59	130
St Lucia	311	225
Leeward Islands	286	368
Montserrat	91	377
St Kitts–Nevis	89	296
Antigua	356	380
Barbados	426	465
Northern Group	n.a.	294
Turks and Caicos	n.a.	133
Cayman Islands	n.a.	297
British Virgin Islands	n.a.	297
Jamaica	289	678
Trinidad and Tobago	n.a.	368
Bahamas	n.a.	354
Commonwealth Caribbean	n.a.	406

Sources: Computed from Tables 6.1 and 6.11.

Table 6.13 *Composition of tourist receipts*

Category of tourist receipt	British Virgin Is.[a] 1968 %	Cayman Is.[b] 1968 %	Antigua[c] 1963 %	Antigua[d] 1967 %
1 Gifts and commodities	12·8	9·7	27·5	17·9
2 Taxis, boats, internal flights	12·8	3·0	8·1	3·7
3 Financial services	1·0	negligible	2·1	2·6
4 Other services	3·0	0·7	1·6	7·8
5 Hotels and guest houses	68·9	79·0	49·0	61·2
6 Rent-of-dwellings	1·2	3·4	2·2	1·9
7 Government taxes, etc.	0·4	0·8	0·2	0·4
8 Households (direct receipts)	negligible	3·4	9·2	4·4

Notes on sources:
[a] Derived from *Economic Survey and Projections, 1969.*
[b] Derived from *Economic Survey and Projections, 1969.*
[c] Derived from O'Loughlin (1965).
[d] Derived from *Economic Survey and Projections, 1969.*

comprise some fifty per cent or more of aggregate tourist receipts; commodities and gifts purchased outside hotels some ten to twenty per cent; hire of taxis, boats and internal flying between three and thirteen per cent; payments for other services from 0·7 per cent to 8 per cent; direct payments to government between 0·2 per cent and 0·8 per cent; and other payments between 2·2 per cent and 4·5 per cent.

Since different categories of tourists will have different spending patterns, the structure of tourist arrivals will clearly influence the overall composition of tourist receipts. Expenditure by cruise ship visitors will be mainly on items 1 and 2 in Table 6.13, while that of visitors not staying in hotels will be mainly on items 1, 2, 4, 6 and 8 of the same table.

The above estimates may be compared with the 1958 estimates for Jamaica which are summarised in Table 6.14.

Table 6.14 *Composition of tourist receipts: Jamaica 1958*

	Percentage composition of all tourist receipts[a]
1 Shopping	27·7
2 Food, drink, tobacco	5·9
3 Transport	5·3
4 Services	1·4
5 Entertainment	3·4
6 Tips	3·9
7 Charity	0·3
8 Hotel bills	52·0
Total	99·9

Source: Cumper (1959).
Note:
[a] Items 1–7 were based on sample surveys of 'long stay' and 'other' visitors in winter and summer, but summer season visitors were asked only to distinguish between shopping and other expenditure, the distribution of the latter being assumed to be the same as that of winter visitors. Hotel bills were not included in these surveys and were estimated separately from hotel rates and occupancy patterns. Item 8 will understate hotel sector receipts because it *excludes* cash expenditures in hotels on items 1, 2, 4, 5 and 6.

The chief differences between these estimates and those contained in Table 6.13 concern the proportions of tourist expenditure represented by 'shopping' and 'hotel and guest house receipts', the former tending to be a higher, and the latter a lower, proportion of total receipts in the case of Jamaica. While this is partly due to the exclusion of cash purchases in hotels in the Jamaican data, commented on in Table 6.14, another important feature is the heavy weight of 'other visitors' expenditure in Jamaica, of which cruise ship visitors are the most important. A very high proportion of expenditure of this group (about 90 per cent) is represented by 'shopping', which raises the relative importance of this item. In fact about half of all expenditure in this category is derived from cruise ship and other short stay visitors.

Some analysis of the expenditure patterns of different categories of visitor has been carried out in Antigua and in the Cayman Islands. Tables 6.15 and 6.16 below show the results of this analysis.

Table 6.15 *Expenditure patterns of hotel visitors: Antigua 1963*

Category of expenditure	Percentage distribution of expenditure	
Expenditure outside hotel		
Purchases	26	
Taxis	12	
Finance, insurance	2	
Entertainment, professional services	2	
Total outside hotel		42
Expenditure in hotel		
Bills, including gratuities	51	
Bar and extra meals	7	
Total in hotel		58
Total expenditure		100

Source: O'Loughlin (1965) Table 14.

Table 6.16 *Expenditure patterns by category of visitor: Cayman Islands 1967–9 (average)*

	Average percentage 1967–9
A Visitors in hotels	
Accommodation and meals	67·1
Bar and extra meals	13·9
Taxis, cars and boats	2·7
Gratuities	5·4
Tourist tax (hotels)	2·4
Airport tax	0·6
Purchases in shops	7·9
Total	100
B Visitors in cottages	
Accommodation	50·0
Meals and food (purchased in shops, hotels and restaurants)	22·1
Drinks and bar (purchased in shops, hotels and restaurants)	7·6
Taxis, cars and boats	6·1
Tourist tax (computed liability)	0·7
Airport tax	0·6
Gratuities	1·5
Purchases in shops	11·3
Total	100
C Visitors with friends and relations	
Notional rent and meals	83·0
Drinks and bars	5·0
Taxis, cars and boats	3·4
Purchases in shops	5·6
Airport tax	3·0
Total	100

Source: Economic Survey and Projections, Cayman Islands. Based on a special survey carried out by R.E. Crum.

In the Cayman Islands the results of a sample survey indicated varying absolute levels of expenditure as between different categories of visitor in 1968.

Table 6.17 *Expenditure levels of visitors staying in different types of accommodation: Cayman Islands 1968 ($ Jamaican)*

| | Hotels | Visitors staying in/with | |
		Cottages and apartments	Friends and relatives
Expenditure per day	$ 21·52	$ 12·02	$ 3·22
Average length of stay	6·6	12·9	9·7
Expenditure per visitor	$142·00	$155·00	$31·00

Source: Derived from *Economic Survey and Projections,* Cayman Islands.

Thus, although expenditure per day of visitors in cottages and apartments is lower than that of visitors in hotels, their total average expenditure is higher because the latter stay for a shorter period. Expenditure of visitors staying with friends and relatives is naturally much lower.

Cruise ship visitors

Expenditure of cruise ship visitors has been variously estimated at between $5 and $10 US each per visitor or approximately $10 to $20 EC. On this basis, tourist receipts from this category of visitor in 1967 in the Windward Islands would be approximately $720,000 EC or about 5·9 per cent of total tourist receipts. Receipts from cruise ship visitors in the Leeward Islands would be about $360,000 EC or some 1·6 per cent of total tourist receipts.[28]

Yacht visitors

In the Eastern Caribbean most yachts are at present chartered with a crew, bare-boat chartering being at present mainly confined to the more sheltered waters of the US and British Virgin Islands. Average charter rates vary with the size of the yacht and facilities included in the charter rate. The average weekly rate for the 23 charter yachts based in Antigua was about $1600 US in the season and $1200 US out of season in 1968. Running costs were normally additional to this sum, ranging from about $25 US for two people to $48 US for six people per day. It was estimated that the average yacht would be chartered for between 14 and 15 weeks in the year, of which 11 to 12 weeks would be during the season and 3 would be in the off-season summer months.

From these data, it was estimated that the total revenue from yacht chartering activities in Antigua plus revenue from the visiting yachts was some $1·1 millions EC in 1968, or just over 5 per cent of total tourist receipts.

Although yachts call in at most islands, it is the yacht centres of Antigua, St Lucia and Grenada which benefit most since it is here that crews are employed, stores replenished and yacht repairs and maintenance carried out.

Unfortunately, few data are available for yachting revenues in islands other than Antigua. From experience, capital costs of the type of yachts used in the Caribbean

---

28 But a very high proportion of this expenditure is on imported goods.

would originally be some $4,800 EC per ton, and the size of yacht used would be anything between 14 and 60 tons.[29] Annual maintenance and docking charges would be upwards of $2,400 per yacht, and doubtless the costs of food and drink would be similar to those experienced in hotels. There may, therefore, be a good deal of expenditure generated by this type of activity in the local economy, while it has the added advantage of utilising a natural asset with which the Caribbean abounds, namely good sailing waters. In addition the maintenance of yachts enables men who looked after the now disappearing inter-island ships and schooners to find new opportunities for their skills. On the other hand, it appears that there may be little direct employment of West Indians as crew on charter yachts, and little local expenditure content apart from maintenance and docking.[30]

29 But these are all imported.

30 Alan Whicker's recent programme on ITV (UK) suggested that most skippers in Antigua prefer to employ young expatriates—known as the 'beard and bikini' brigade. I have no quantitative evidence to offer on the matter, however.

7 The hotel industry in the Caribbean

Since visitors staying in hotels and guest houses comprise usually between 60 and 80 per cent of all tourists,[1] and the actual receipts of hotels from tourists usually comprise somewhere between 50 and 80 per cent of all tourist receipts,[2] a good case can be made for concentrating on the hotel industry as opposed to real estate and holiday home development or the cruise ship and yacht charter business.[3] It is also the case that a high proportion of total private investment in tourism has been in hotels and, further, that a major part of this is private foreign investment.[4]

The purpose of this chapter is therefore to examine the growth and structure of hotel tourism in the Caribbean and to analyse the structure of inputs and outputs in the hotel industry and the principal factors affecting the input coefficients, both to support earlier assertions in the Introduction and Part I and to serve as a prelude for the multiplier and cost–benefit analysis in Part IV below.

Growth and geographical structure of the hotel industry

The growth and geographical structure of hotel capacity in the region is as shown in Table 7.1.

The total number of hotel beds in the region in 1967 was about 27,900, excluding Jamaica. A reasonable estimate for Jamaica, bearing in mind the number and structure of visitor arrivals, might be 4,000, bringing the overall total for the region to roughly 31,900.

The growth in hotel beds has kept pace with the growth in arrivals, but since the proportion of total arrivals staying in hotels has probably increased over the decade it seems likely that utilisation of hotel capacity has improved slightly in the region as a whole.

The regional structure of the hotel industry in the Commonwealth Caribbean is as shown in Table 7.2.

---

1 See Tables 6.8, 6.9 and 6.10 and comments in the text on these tables.

2 See Tables 6.13 and 6.14 and Chapter 6 *passim*.

3 This is not, of course, to say that studies of the impact of real estate type development, cruise-ship tourism and yacht chartering are not urgently needed, so that the standard of policy-making in relation to these developments can be improved for the benefit of the nationals. The hotel industry has been chosen for more intensive study in this case both for the reason given above, and because of more severe data constraints in respect of these other types of tourist development.

4 See also Chapter 3, section on Construction and Investment, and below pp. 121–2.

Table 7.1 *Growth and structure of hotel capacity in the Commonwealth Caribbean*

	Number of hotel and guest house beds in use				Growth rate % per annum	
	1961	1962	1967	1968	1961–7	1962–8
Windward Islands	694	910	1626	2180	24·5	15·7
St Vincent	170e	246e	386	432	14·7	9·8
Grenada	260	400	630	750	15·9	11·0
Dominica	50e	50e	130	174	17·2	23·1
St Lucia	214	214	480	824	14·4	25·2
Leeward Islands	672	1,120	2,260	2,383	22·4	13·4
Montserrat	12e	88e	213	213	61·5	15·9
St Kitts–Nevis	100e	114e	358	370	23·7	21·7
Antigua	560	918	1,689	1,800	20·1	11·9
Barbados	1,995	2,061	4,795	5,420	15·7	17·5
Northern Group	n.a.	n.a.	950	1,093	n.a.	n.a.
Turks and Caicos	n.a.	3	30	50	n.a.	59·8
Cayman Islands	n.a.	n.a.	656	622	n.a.	n.a.
British Virgin Is.	n.a.	n.a.	364	421	n.a.	n.a.
Jamaica	n.a.	n.a.	n.a.	n.a.	n.a.	n.a.
Trinidad and Tobago	n.a.	n.a.	1,987	n.a.	n.a.	n.a.
Bahamas	5,700	6,700	16,300	16,500	n.a.	n.a.

e = estimated.
Sources: As for Table 6.1. For the Bahamas, *Visitor Statistics,* 1969, published by the Ministry of Tourism.

Table 7.2 *Regional structure of the hotel industry, 1967*

	Percentage of total beds
Windward Islands	5·1
Leeward Islands	7·1
Northern Group	3·0
Barbados	15·0
Jamaica[a]	12·5
Trinidad and Tobago	6·2
Bahamas	51·1
Total	100

Note:
[a] Assuming 4,000 beds for 1967 in Jamaica and a total for the region of 31,900.

The smaller islands of the region, that is the Windward Islands, the Leeward Islands, the Northern Group and Barbados, together had 30·2 per cent of hotel capacity in the region. This compares with some 16·7 per cent of total arrivals and suggests that occupancy rates were generally much lower in these islands, although part of the difference is explained by the inclusion of cruise ship visitors in the figures for arrivals given by the Bahamas. As was pointed out in Chapter 6, these cruise ship visitors appear to stay for more than 24 hours but do *not* use hotel capacity.[5]
5 See Chapter 6, pp. 100–1.

Figures obtained directly on utilisation of hotel capacity[6] are rather sketchy, but those that are available are summarised in Table 7.3.

Table 7.3 *Utilisation of hotel capacity in the Commonwealth Caribbean, 1967*

	Bed nights available[a] ('000)	Bed nights utilised[b] ('000)	Occupancy rate[c] %
Windward Islands	593·5	297·2	50·1
St Vincent	140·9	53·6	38·0
Grenada	229·9	151·5	66·0
Dominica	47·5	30·8	65·0
St Lucia	175·2	61·3	35·0
Leeward Islands	824·9	281·2	34·1
Montserrat	77·7	27·2	35·0
St Kitts–Nevis	130·7	52·5	40·0
Antigua	616·5	201·5	32·7
Barbados	1,750·2	655·0	37·5
Northern Group	346·7	141·8	40·9
Turks and Caicos	10·9	2·7	24·6
Cayman Islands	239·4	53·6	22·4
British Virgin Islands	132·9	85·5	64·5
Jamaica	1,460·0	n.a.	n.a.
Trinidad and Tobago	725·3	n.a.	n.a.
Bahamas	5,950·0	3,360·0	56·5

Sources: Table 7.1 for beds available. Bed nights utilised are sometimes directly available, or can be derived from visitor statistics and length of stay, or can be obtained from occupancy rate data derived from surveys.
Notes:
[a] Beds × 365 (no account is taken here of hotels which close for parts of the year).
[b] Visitors to hotels and guest houses × average length of stay.
[c] Bed nights utilised as a percentage of bed nights available.

The evidence shown in Table 7.3 suggests quite marked variations in occupancy rates. As might be expected from the evidence on seasonality in Chapter 6, occupancy rates tend to be worst where seasonal variations are largest.[7] The seasonality problem is exacerbated by the tendency of off-season visitors to stay for shorter periods of time, and the higher proportion of West Indian visitors in the summer months, a larger number of whom do not apparently utilise hotel capacity.[8] Some indication of this problem may be obtained from Table 7.4.

6 Utilisation of hotel capacity is expressed in terms of 'occupancy rates' which measure the proportion of bed nights available which are actually filled by guests. For simplicity, a room is normally assumed to have two beds available for the entire year. In other words, the annual capacity of one room is 365 × 2 = 730 bed nights.

7 See Tables 6.4 and 6.5.

8 See Chapter 6, p. 106.

Table 7.4 *Seasonal occupancy rates in hotels and guest houses in the Commonwealth Caribbean*

	Summer (off) season %	Winter (in) season %	Year	Source
St Lucia	28	43	1969	Survey data [c]
Cayman Islands	14	44	1968	Survey data [c]
Antigua	18 [a]	58 [b]	1967	Survey data [c]
Barbados:				*Tripartite Econ-*
'A' class hotels	30	60–5	1965	*omic Survey*
'B' class hotels	25	40–5	1965	*Tripartite Econ-omic Survey*

Notes:
[a] Third quarter data.
[b] First quarter data.
[c] As prepared for *Economic Surveys and Projections*.

The fluctuation in occupancy rates causes even greater fluctuations in the earnings of the hotel industry since hotel charges are lower in the off-season in an attempt to attract business.

Investment in the hotel industry

Data on actual gross fixed investment either *in toto* or by categories are rather unsatisfactory for most of the islands over the time period required.[9] The best that can be done in this regard is to make global estimates based on evidence regarding unit investment costs.

Investment costs of between $12,000 EC and $40,000 EC per room have been reported as obtaining in the Caribbean in 1966.[10] The *Tripartite Economic Survey* of the Eastern Caribbean in 1966 used a range of $25,000–30,000 EC per room. There is evidence of a considerable range in building costs per square foot in the Caribbean, although this range tends to be much less in the case of larger, more sophisticated hotels, which are often built by international contracting firms.[11]

Using a figure of $25,000 per room as an estimate for the period under analysis, the following table shows the estimated investment in hotel and guest house facilities between 1961 and 1968.

Expressed in annual terms, this level of investment may be compared with estimates of total gross domestic fixed capital formation for a single year.[12]

Table 7.6 indicates the importance of hotel investment in terms of total private investment during the decade, which has been reflected in the impact on the construction sectors in the various islands.[13]

9 See also Chapter 3 and Bryden (1970).

10 Feasibility Study by C. Laird and Associates, kindly made available to the author.

11 The author himself collected data for building costs in many of the smaller Islands of the Leewards, Windwards and the Northern Group. This tended to confirm the range used by the *Tripartite Survey*.

12 C.f. Chapter 3 where it was estimated that about 18 per cent of all private investment in the Windwards and Leewards during the period 1964–7 was investment in hotels.

13 See Chapter 3 for a further discussion of this point.

Table 7.5 *Commonwealth Caribbean: estimated investment in hotels 1961–8*[a]

	Increase in rooms 1961–8	Estimated investment in $EC millions
Windward Islands	743	18·6[b]
St Vincent	131	3·3
Grenada	245	6·1
Dominica	62	1·6
St Lucia	305	7·6
Leeward Islands	855	21·4[b]
Montserrat	100	2·5
St Kitts–Nevis	135	3·4
Antigua	620	15·5
Barbados	1,712	42·8
Total, E. Caribbean	3,310	82·8

Notes:
[a] Data not available for Northern Group, Jamaica, Trinidad and Tobago. The increase for the period in the Bahamas was 5,427, but I have no reliable cost estimates for the Bahamas.
[b] See also Table 3.6 for the period 1964–7.

Table 7.6 *Average annual investment in hotels 1961–8 and total GDFCF for 1965 in $000 EC*

	1 Average annual hotel investment 1961–8[a]	2 Total private fixed capital formation 1965[b]	3 Col. 1 as a % of col. 2
Windward Islands	2,654	16,023	16·5
St Vincent	468	2,759	17·0
Grenada	875	6,193	14·1
Dominica	221	2,350	9·4
St Lucia	1,089	4,721	23·1
Leeward Islands	3,054	12,579	24·3
Montserrat	357	2,107	16·9
St Kitts–Nevis	482	4,058	11·9
Antigua[c]	2,214	6,414	34·5
Barbados	6,114	n.a.	n.a.

Notes:
[a] Total estimated investment in Table 7.5 above divided by 7 years.
[b] Taken from *Economic Surveys and Projections* of the various islands excluding government investments.
[c] Antigua data are for 1964 and are derived from O'Loughlin (1965).

Establishment size in the hotel industry

Individual hotels in the Eastern Caribbean tend to be small in size. Most have less than 40 rooms, and under 10 per cent have more than 60 rooms. In Antigua, for example, 29 hotels and guest houses had 1,689 beds – an average of about 58 beds or 29 rooms per establishment. Only five hotels have over 100 beds, and one has 200 beds or more. Again, in the 13 hotels and guest houses in the British Virgin

Islands there were 364 beds available in 1968; an average of 28 beds and 14 rooms per establishment. Only one hotel had over 50 beds. The average number of beds per establishment in the Cayman Islands was 34·5 in 1968. Finally, the *Tripartite Economic Survey* noted that most hotels in Barbados in 1966 had between 10 and 40 rooms and only three had more than 60 rooms.[14]

Over the decade a significant proportion of investment in hotel capacity was in additions to existing establishments, and since the number of establishments has not grown as rapidly as the number of beds, one may infer that the average size of establishments is increasing. New hotels being built in the region are also tending towards larger sizes.

Hotel ownership

The observation is made at various points in this study that a very high proportion of hotels in the smaller Caribbean islands are foreign-owned. Generally speaking, involvement of indigenous entrepreneurs is confined largely to small guest houses which generally account for a smaller proportion of beds and a smaller proportion of gross tourist receipts. At a rough count, fewer than 90 hotel and guest house beds were owned by indigenes in the British Virgin Islands out of a total of 421 beds in 1968, and about 54 of these were guest house beds. In Antigua something under 200 hotel and guest house beds out of a total of about 1,780 in 1968 were locally owned, and of these about 135 were guest house beds. Similarly, most of the other small islands of the region exhibit the same type of ownership patterns. Moreover, since it is the capacity of hotels rather than guest houses which has been growing rapidly in the decade under investigation, and since many of the guest houses are of older origin, an examination of the pattern of ownership in the latter half of the decade would tend to understate the extent of private capital inflows for the purposes of hotel construction during the decade.[15]

The reasons for the reluctance of indigenous owners of capital to enter the new hotel industry may be summarised as follows:[16]

(a) A lack of past experience and expertise in the hotel industry, or perhaps more important, in any bureaucratically organised business. This applies particularly to the larger hotels beyond the capacity of 'family' management.

(b) The highly skewed distribution of wealth in the Caribbean.

(c) A relative shortage of domestic savings associated with highly restricted capital markets, discussed in Chapter 3.

14 By comparison the distribution of hotels by size in Scotland and Wales in 1968 was as follows:

	Less than 25 rooms	25–74 rooms	75+ rooms
Scotland	51%	34%	15%
Wales	35%	45%	20%

Source: Manpower Studies No. 10. Hotels. Department of Employment, HMSO, 1971. This survey, however, excludes small hotels and guest houses employing less than six staff.

15 In other words, the marginal proportion of foreign investment in the hotel industry tends to exceed the average.

16 These reasons are not of course exclusive, but as the point is not crucial for the findings of Section IV, they are put forward as reasonably plausible in the circumstances of the Caribbean. Further research is necessary to establish the point.

(d) Associated with (c), the relatively easier availability of financing of foreign entrepreneurs.

The second explanation, relating to the distribution of wealth, seems likely to be important. In most Caribbean territories, wealth has traditionally been concentrated in the hands of the large landowners and the trading community. For the latter, the evidence of Chapter 3 suggests that tourism enhanced rather than detracted from their economic strength, which has sometimes also been protected by other means.[17] Landowners, on the other hand, tended to view tourism with mixed feelings. On the one hand, the value of their land was possibly increased; on the other hand, they feared that labour would be withdrawn from agriculture, thus tending to lead to rising wages. In addition, they might fear that their dominating position in society was being threatened.[18] Yet another reason which may have been important in some cases was the anxiety of the wealthy to avoid steep rates of local income taxation and estate duties through loopholes in the law and the difficulties facing small tax administrations in tracing assets held overseas.

Nevertheless, in certain cases foreign owned hotels were able to obtain local loan finance, principally through the banking sector, it being in the interest of foreign investors to obtain such finance so long as their expected rate of return exceeds the rate of interest on local loans. This source of finance was, however, limited by the traditionally negative attitude of the banks to loans of more than 3 to 4 years' duration, although subsidiary organisations, such as Barclays Overseas Development Corporation, provided longer term funds of this nature.[19]

Hotel revenues and output structure

For most islands in the region, expenditure by visitors in hotels is the major single item in tourist receipts. Although complete time series data regarding the gross receipts of the hotel industry are not generally available, some information is available for the region, and this is summarised in Table 7.7.

The data given in Table 7.7 have been compiled in various ways. One method has been to use a weighted average of hotel rates and apply the number of visitors staying in hotels multiplied by average length of stay. Sometimes this has been supplemented by sample surveys of the hotel industry.[20] It should also be noted that the above figures include local expenditure in hotels for entertainment etc., although this is a minor item. In Antigua expenditure in hotels by residents amounted to only 4·6 per cent of total hotel receipts.

From these estimates we can calculate average revenues per hotel bed, per tourist night and per tourist.

Average revenues per hotel bed vary from about $3,500 EC to $10,000 EC with an average of something over $6,000. The figures for St Lucia are currently being

17 For example the operation and control of business licences is effectively controlled by the trading community in the Cayman Islands.

18 In St Kitts, where a white plantocracy has survived, the planters viewed tourism with considerable suspicion. See also Lewis, G. K. (1968) p. 135

19 See also the discussion in Chapter 3, p. 39.

20 See also the discussion of methods of compiling tourist receipts in Chapter 6.

Table 7.7 *Hotel revenues in the Commonwealth Caribbean 1964–7 $000 EC*

	1964	1965	1966	1967	1968
Windward Islands	5,924·5	7,753·8	10,103·0	11,145·5	n.a.
St Vincent	898·0	1,126·0	1,340·0	1,403·0	n.a.
Grenada	2,010·0	2,625·0	3,582·0	3,980·0	n.a.
Dominica	337·0	431·0	554·0	656·0	n.a.
St Lucia	2,679·5	3,571·8	4,626·0	5,106·5	n.a.
Leeward Islands	n.a.	n.a.	12,332·7	13,819·7	n.a.
Montserrat	n.a.	638·0	849·0	902·0	n.a.
St Kitts	n.a.	760·0	1,140·0	1,510·0	n.a.
Antigua	5,739·5	n.a.	10,343·7	11,407·7	n.a.
Barbados	n.a.	n.a.	n.a.	n.a.	n.a.
Northern Group	n.a.	n.a.	n.a.	5,586·5	n.a.
Turks and Caicos[a]	38·9	65·2	102·2	106·5	n.a.
Cayman Islands[b]	n.a.	n.a.	n.a.	2,310·0	3,540·0
Virgin Islands[c]	n.a.	n.a.	2,260·0	3,170·0	4,810·0
Jamaica	n.a.	n.a.	n.a.	n.a.	n.a.
Trinidad and Tobago	n.a.	n.a.	n.a.	n.a.	n.a.
Bahamas[d]	n.a.	n.a.	n.a.	n.a.	n.a.

Source: *Economic Surveys and Projections* of the various islands.
Notes:
[a] Local currency is £ sterling. $4·80 EC = £1.00
[b] Local currency is $Jamaican. $2·40 EC = $1·0 J
[c] Local currency is $US exchanging at $1·72 EC = $1·00 US before sterling devaluation in 1967, at $2·00 EC = $1·00 US after.
[d] Local currency = $ Bahamas

Table 7.8 *Estimates of hotel revenues per hotel bed, per tourist night and per tourist staying in hotels ($ EC) 1967*

	Average revenues per hotel bed	Average revenues per tourist night	Average revenues per tourist
Windward Islands	$6,860	$33·2	$252
St Vincent	3,640	26·2	203
Grenada	6,310	26·3	212
Dominica	5,050	21·3	102
St Lucia	10,600	52·3	418
Leeward Islands	6,120	49·0	246
Montserrat	4,240	33·1	198
St Kitts	4,220	28·8	164
Antigua	6,760	56·7	266
Barbados	n.a.	n.a.	n.a.
Northern Group	5,880	39·4	242
Turks and Caicos	3,560	39·6	143
Cayman Islands	3,520	43·0	283
Virgin Islands	8,700	37·1	223

Source: Tables 7.1, 7.3 and 7.7 above.

revised and preliminary indications are that this figure given is an over-estimate.[21] Revenues per hotel bed will of course be affected by hotel charges and occupancy rates, as well as the structure of the industry in terms of the type of accommodation offered.

Average hotel revenues per tourist night vary from $21.3 in Dominica to $56.7 in Antigua, with a mean of $35—40. Much of this variation will result from differences in hotel charges and occupancy rates in the winter and summer seasons.

Revenues per tourist, which vary with average length of stay, range from $102 in Dominica (average stay 4·8 days) to $418 in St Lucia (average stay 8 days). In spite of the differences in length of stay, the figures for St Lucia again seem on the high side.

To all intents and purposes the receipts of hotels from tourists can be taken as their gross output. Some idea of the *structure* of this output in terms of the goods and services supplied by or through hotels can be obtained from Tables 6.15 and 6.16.

The input structure of hotels in the Commonwealth Caribbean

A few sample surveys of the hotel industry have been carried out in the Caribbean with the object of elucidating the input structure of hotels.[22] These surveys were used in the preparation of national accounts statistics which can be used to show the structure of operating costs in hotels.

The two most important groups of payments by the hotels sector are those for commodities, with variable proportions being imported directly and purchased locally, and payments to households. Gratuities and tips are a fairly important part of payments to households, but these do not normally enter into the *financial* accounts of hotels as they are either paid directly to staff or through a separate accounting procedure. This finding is very similar to that of the 1958 Jamaica survey which is shown in Table 7.9 for comparative purposes. Payments for commodities ranged from about 30 per cent of sales in the Cayman Islands to some 37 per cent of sales in Antigua. Of these, direct purchases from the agricultural sectors were but a small proportion. Payments to households varied from some 26—7 per cent of sales in Jamaica and the Cayman Islands to 40 per cent of sales in Antigua. Some of these differences are explained by the different occupancy rates obtaining in the three territories. In Antigua, the occupancy rate for hotels and guest houses was only 29·3 per cent in 1963. In the British Virgin Islands the occupancy rate for 1967 was estimated at 64·5 per cent. In the Cayman Islands occupancy rates were estimated at 33·2 per cent for 1968, while in Jamaica an occupancy rate of around 60 per cent in 1958 seems probable. Other factors which could explain the differences are:

(a) Different levels of expenditure by *residents* in hotels due to different income levels in the islands.

(b) Different cost and wage structures, and levels of labour organisation. For

---

21 The figures given in Table 7.8 certainly suggest that those for St Lucia are over-estimated as there are no *a priori* reasons which might explain the very high average revenues per tourist night.

22 The author is aware of three such surveys in the smaller Islands, namely those of Antigua, the Cayman Islands and the British Virgin Islands.

Table 7.9 *Operating costs as a proportion of total sales: hotels and guest houses in three territories*[a] *compared with Jamaica (1958)*

Category of payment	Percentage distribution of operating costs in			
	Cayman Is. 1968	B. Virgin Is. 1967	Antigua 1963	Jamaica 1958
1 Direct purchases from agriculture	0·849	1·125	2·749	d
2 Private and public utilities electricity	3·499	1·277	0·779	2·16
other	0·251			
3 Maintenance	14·572	0·641	8·248	3·67
4 Financial and other services incl. transport	7·303	4·635	6·085	16·45
5 Local retail and wholesale purchases	13·370	21·662	30·894	31·81
6 Direct imports of commodities	15·632	11·267	3·668	d
7 Other overseas payments incl. promotion	8·336	16·639	10·085	3·76
8 Payments to households wages and salaries	19·355	28·265	27·283	} 25·89[e]
free meals	1·651	3·358	4·685	
gratuities	5·938	6·772	8·626	
9 Payments to governments hotel tax	1·603	nil	1·919	} 1·25
import duty	2·480	1·642	0·550	
other	0·272	1·389	3·110[b]	
10 Gross profit (loss) before tax and depreciation	4·925	1·327	(8·692)[c]	15·00
Total sales	100	100	100	100

Sources: National Accounts of Antigua 1954–64. Working papers for National Accounts of the Cayman Islands and the British Virgin Islands, 1969. Jamaican data are derived from Cumper (1959). All relied on relatively small sample sizes.
Notes:
[a] Adjusted for comparison from national accounts data.
[b] Includes casino licence (1·833%)
[c] Hotels sector apparently made a gross loss in 1963 – c.f. O'Loughlin (1965).
[d] Included in item 5.
[e] May not include gratuities as these do not normally pass through hotel accounts.

example employees in Antigua have a union organisation, while those in the British Virgin Islands and the Cayman Islands do not. It is certainly possible that this could have some effect on wage rates.

(c) Different employee : room ratios.

(d) Different sample sizes and hence degrees of error in the estimates.

The effect of occupancy levels on revenues and costs in hotels is clearly important in any discussion of the tourist industry. An indication of the structure of revenues and costs at different occupancy levels may be obtained from Table 7.10 below which summarises data presented in a feasibility study prepared by a firm of chartered accountants for a 100-room hotel in Antigua.[23]

23 This study, which was prepared by a well-known international firm of accountants, was kindly lent to the author by the manager of the hotel in question.

Table 7.10 *Structure of revenues and costs at different occupancy levels — a 100-room hotel project in Antigua*

	Revenue and costs in $000 US at:		
	45% occupancy	65% occupancy	percentage change
Revenue			
Rooms	447·6	600·7	34
Food	234·6	333·0	43
Beverages	119·3	172·8	45
Laundry	4·2	6·0	43
Other	8·8	11·6	32
Total revenue	814·5	1,124·1	38
Expenses			
Cost of sales	130·9	176·7	35
Administration payroll	36·3 ⎫	42·0	16
Other payroll	101·0 ⎬137·3	121·1	20
Administration and other costs	43·9	50·8	16
Advertising	44·8	60·0	34
Heat, light, power	36·4	43·6	20
Repairs and maintenance	23·6	28·8	22
Other inputs	162·0	190·0	17
Total expenses	578·9	713·0	23
Net income before fixed charges	235·6	411·1	75

From this table it can be seen that cost items increase less than proportionately with revenue as occupancy rates increase, and in some cases considerably less. In this example revenue increases by 38 per cent, cost of sales by 35 per cent, non-administrative payroll by 20 per cent, and total expenses by 23 per cent. Net income before fixed charges increases by 75 per cent, and since fixed charges are by definition fixed, net profits before tax would increase by a substantially higher percentage. On the basis of this example, it seems likely that the assumptions regarding utilisation of capacity are likely to be important in determining the input—output coefficients in the hotel industry.

Employment in hotels and guest houses
Firm estimates of employment in the hotels sector are rather scarce in the Commonwealth Caribbean. Table 7.11 shows the information that is available from published sources.

Thus the number of employees per room varied from 0·89 in the Antigua 'off-season' of 1963—4 to 1·38 in the British Virgin Islands in 1968, where occupancy rates were much higher. These estimates compare with O'Loughlin's estimate that about 531 man-years of employment had been created by the Antigua hotel industry up to 1963—4, or just over one man-year per room available.[24] The employee

24 O'Loughlin (1968) p. 147.

Table 7.11 *Employment in hotels and guest houses*

Territory	Year	Estimated employment:		Number of hotel rooms
		in season	out of season	
Antigua[a]	1963–4	715	475	535
Antigua[b]	1967–8	1,235	806	860
Cayman Islands[c]	1969 (Nov)	n.a.	350	324
Cayman Islands[d]	1970	329	254	268
British Virgin Islands[e]	1968	290	n.a.	210

Sources:
[a] *Tripartite Economic Survey* p. 95.
[b] *Economic Survey and Projections,* Antigua, 1969.
[c] *Economic Survey and Projections,* Cayman Islands, 1969.
[d] *'Manpower Survey'* 1970, Table 17-3(A), Grand Cayman only.
[e] *Economic Survey and Projections,* British Virgin Islands, 1969.

Table 7.12 *Employee/room ratios in three territories*

Territory	Year	Number of employees per room	
		In season	Out of season
Antigua	1963–4	1·33	0·89
Antigua	1967–8	1·43	0·94
Cayman Islands	1969	n.a.	1·08
Cayman Islands	1970	1·23	0·95
British Virgin Islands	1968	1·38	n.a.

Source: Derived from Table 7.11

room ratios are shown in Table 7.12 above and show a reasonable degree of consistency between the different islands.

The sex of hotel employees appears to be quite variable in the region, presumably depending on the relative cost and availability of male and female workers. In the Cayman Islands, 67 per cent of all hotel and guest house employees were women, although this dropped to 50 per cent in the off-season, reflecting a tendency for the burden of seasonality in employment to fall on women.[25] By contrast, in the British Virgin Islands only about 45 per cent of employees in hotels and guest houses were women in April 1970.[26] Female participation rates in general are much lower in the British Virgin Islands, however, and it is true to say in both cases that the male–female ratio is much lower in the hotel and guest house sector than for the economy as a whole. In a sample survey covering about 29 per cent of available hotel and guest house beds in Antigua in 1968, women comprised 62 per cent of employees in the season, and 57 per cent out of season.[27]

However, the opportunities for women in the hotel and guest house sector are principally in unskilled categories – waitresses, kitchen and room maids and

25 *Manpower Survey*, 1970, Table 17.3(A).

26 Elkan and Morley (1971) Tables 2.5 and 1.6. About 26 per cent of the total labour force in the British Virgin Islands were women according to this survey.

27 Bryden and Pollard, unpublished survey, 1968.

domestics accounting for a high proportion.[28]

A high proportion of employees in skilled and professional categories are of foreign nationality and, as would be expected from the previous comments on the nature of female employment, the proportion of 'expatriates' tends to be higher among males. For example, in the Cayman Islands 46 per cent of males employed in hotels and guest houses were non-Caymanian as compared with 22 per cent of females.[29]

Table 7.13 below identifies the structure of hotel employment in the Cayman Islands in terms of occupational category and identifies the proportion of females and 'expatriates' in each of these occupational categories. This table is in the same form as Table 2.7 in Chapter 2, which relates to the whole economy, thereby allowing a comparison with other sectors to be made.

Table 7.13 *Structure of hotel employment by occupational category, sex and nationality: Grand Cayman 1971*

Occupational category	All hotel employees	Percentage of females in each category	Percentage of expatriates in each category
	%	%	%
I Higher and lower professional	12·0	37	87·0
II Clerical and allied	6·0	94	50·0
III Skilled	17·5	33	41·0
IV Semi-skilled	34·0	75	15·0
V Unskilled	30·0	84	13·5

Source: Taken from the Establishment Survey which formed the basis of Hart and Hart (1971).

The most important features of hotel employment may be summarised as follows:
(1) The relatively high proportion of employees in semi-skilled and unskilled categories (64 per cent for hotels; 42·7 per cent for all sectors).
(2) The relatively high proportion of females in semi-skilled and unskilled categories.
(3) The high proportion of expatriates in higher and lower professional grades (87 per cent for hotels as compared with 64 per cent for all sectors), and also in clerical and allied and skilled categories.

Similar data for the British Virgin Islands are summarised below in Table 7.14.

Again one may note the very high proportion of expatriates in the occupational categories which are likely to be best paid.

Some evidence on wage and salary differentials is available from the Cayman Islands survey and is shown in Table 7.15 below.

28 About 66 per cent of female employees in the British Virgin Islands were in those categories, and while figures for the Cayman Islands are not strictly comparable, 73 per cent of female employees in the hotel and guest house sector returned an answer of 'N.A.' or 'None' to the query regarding training in relation to present job. *Manpower Surveys* – personal communication.

29 Manpower Survey, taken from coded cards which were made available to the author.

Table 7.14 *Structure of hotel and guest house employment in the British Virgin Islands,*
1970 (April)

Category of employment	All hotel employees %	Proportion of females in category and hotel employees %	Proportion of expatriates in category and all employees %
1 Professional, entrepreneurs, administrative, executive and managerial staff	12	32	60
2 Clerks and typists	8	77	48
3 Bar, waitresses and waiters	26	18	34
4 Cooks/chefs	4	100	32
5 Seamstresses and domestics	25	100	47
6 Electricians, plumbers, painters, carpenters, masons	5	0	46
7 Gardeners, foremen, supervisors	5	0	43
8 Labourers, drivers and other	15	4	45
Total	100	44·5	48·5

Source: Elkan and Morley (1971). Derived from Tables 2.5, 2.6, 2.14 and 2.15.

Table 7.15 *Cayman Islands – hotels, level of weekly earnings × occupational category, 1971*

Occupational category	Proportion of individuals in each occupational category earning						Median earnings
	$0–20	$21–40	$41–60	$61 +	N.A./refusal	Total	
	%	%	%	%	%	%	$
I	–	–	3	30	67	100	81·1
II	12	50	31	6	–	99	36
III	2	32	32	34	–	100	50
IV	40	37	14	2	7	100	24
V	39	56	4	2	–	101	23

Source: Hart and Hart (1971) working papers.

The very high proportion of refusals in relation to occupational category I reflects the modesty of high income earners which is well known in surveys of this nature. Nevertheless, ignoring refusals, median earnings for each occupational category may be calculated and these indicate the crude differentials between occupational categories, thereby enabling estimates to be made of the distribution of the wage and salary bill between occupational categories and also between nationals and non-nationals.[30]

It can therefore be seen that, while non-Caymanians account for just over 30 per cent of the total labour force in hotels, the proportion of earnings which accrues to

30 But because of the high proportion of refusals in the highest income group, these estimates will be biased in such a way as to understate the proportion of wages and salaries going to the occupational category I and, hence, to expatriates who form a high proportion of this group.

Table 7.16 *Estimate of the proportion of earnings accruing to non-nationals employed in the hotel and guest house sector: Grand Cayman 1971*

Occupational category	Median earnings[a]	Distribution of earnings[b]	Proportion of earnings accruing to non-Caymanians[c]
	$J	%	%
I	81	27·2	23·6
II	36	6·1	3·0
III	50	24·5	10·1
IV	24	22·8	3·4
V	23	19·4	2·6
		Total 100	Total 42·7

Notes:

[a] Approximate. It is assumed that the median is sufficiently close to the mean that the outcome of the analysis is not materially affected.

[b] Derived by multiplying the median earnings of each category by the proportion of employees in each occupational category and reducing to percentage terms.

[c] Derived by multiplying the distribution of earnings by occupational category by the proportion of non-Caymanians in each category. It is assumed that there is no significant difference in earnings *within* categories of different nationalities.

this group is likely to be at least 42·7 per cent.

Similar data which would allow such estimates to be made for other islands in the region are not available at the time of writing, but although the Cayman Islands and the British Virgin Islands are to some extent special cases in so far as it is generally believed that there is no significant unemployment, observations of a more casual nature would suggest that the general situation of a high proportion of wages and salaries accruing to non-nationals in the labour force of hotels and guest houses, who are mainly in the higher paid occupational categories, is one which is fairly common in the region as a whole.[31]

In the Cayman Islands, at least, the median earnings in the unskilled and semi-skilled categories of hotel employees which generate the bulk of employment for nationals lie fairly close to the median earnings for the economy as a whole, but particularly in the case of unskilled categories.[32] In the case of semi-skilled categories, median earnings for the hotel employees are *less* than those of the rest of the economy — $24 as compared with $34, but this is almost certainly due to the high proportion of females in this category in the hotel industry. Median earnings for females in the economy as a whole were $28·1 J as compared with $54·7 J for males, although this covered all occupational groups.[33] This reflects the relative lack of opportunities outside the home for unskilled and semi-skilled female labour.

In the British Virgin Island, female domestics 'typically' earned between $41 and $60 US per month which, according to the *Manpower Survey* 'is low compared with

31 See also Chapter 2 for evidence on this point relating to the labour force as a whole.

32 The median for the economy as a whole is $ 22·7 J. *Manpower Survey* Table 26.3.

33 *Manpower Survey*, Table 3.7.

other female occupations'.[34] But it is not possible in this case to carry out a detailed analysis of earnings in comparable occupations.

Similarly, data for earnings in comparable occupations which can be thought of as alternatives to employment in hotels are not available for other islands in the region. Two things can, however, be said on the basis of the evidence presented above. First, most of the employment of *nationals* in hotels appears to be female employment in unskilled and semi-skilled categories. Second, the wages paid to this category of employee appear to be, if anything, lower than for similar categories in the rest of the economy. These features are considered further in Chapter 9 when the problem of calculating a 'shadow wage' for hotel employees is discussed.

It is of some interest in this context that of a sample of 100 employees in the hotels sector in the Cayman Islands, 24 had no previous job, and of these 21 were female. Bearing in mind that 46 came from a previous job in the same sector (32 female) this illustrates the lack of alternative opportunities. When asked about their job prospects in 1975, 66 per cent had no idea or saw themselves in the same job; no respondents saw themselves with a better job in the same establishment. This illustrates that the perception of hotel employees regarding opportunity for advancement or career prospects in the industry tends to be very low. When asked why they took their present job, 15 per cent of women indicated that they needed any kind of job and a further 46 per cent indicated that financial reasons were paramount.

As questions regarding employment and earnings in the hotel industry are of prime importance for this study, the main conclusions of the foregoing section are summarised below.

(1) Employment in the hotel industry tends to be highly seasonal, with employee room ratios varying from a high of around 1·4 'in season' to a low of around 0·9 'out of season'. Some evidence exists to suggest that the burden of seasonal employment may fall more heavily on female employees.

(2) The male/female employment ratio tends to be lower in hotels than for the economy as a whole. Indeed, during the season females account for over 60 per cent of all hotel employees in both Antigua and the Cayman Islands, and around 45 per cent in the British Virgin Islands.

(3) A relatively high proportion of hotel employees are in unskilled or semi-skilled occupational categories, and within these categories the proportion of female employees tends to be even higher than for all categories.

(4) A relatively high proportion of the hotel employees in better-paid professional grades were non-nationals in the Cayman Islands and the British Virgin Islands. The same tends to be true for clerical and skilled grades in the Cayman Islands.

(5) In view of the wage and salary differentials and the low proportion of nationals in higher paid jobs, the proportion of the wages bill going to non-nationals is higher than the proportion of employment represented by this group would suggest — an estimate for the Cayman Islands in 1971 suggests that a minimum of 42·7 per cent of the wage and salary bill of hotels accrues

34 The *median* lies at around $60 US, which is equivalent to about $50 J per month $12 J per week —a very much lower rate, apparently, than that in the Cayman Islands, in spite of reasonably comparable costs of living. Elkan and Morley (1971), p. 29.

to non-nationals, who only account for 30 per cent of the labour force in hotels.

(6) For the unskilled and semi-skilled employees, there is little evidence to suggest that earnings in hotels are higher than those elsewhere in the economy, and some evidence to suggest the reverse may be true. This is largely due to the lack of employment opportunities elsewhere in the economy for the women who form the bulk of these categories of hotel labour.

Coefficients of resource use and output levels in hotels

Capital gross output ratios in the hotel sector may be computed for different occupancy levels from the investment and income data given earlier in this chapter. Table 7.17 summarises the results of one such analysis which assumes a unit investment cost of $25,000 per room, and a range of revenue per bed-night.

Table 7.17 *Capital gross output ratios for different occupancy levels and revenues per bed-night assuming investment costs of $25,000 per room*

| Revenue per bed-night in $ EC | Occupancy rates | | |
	30%	40%	50%
25	4·57 : 1	3·42 : 1	2·74 : 1
35	3·26 : 1	2·45 : 1	1·96 : 1
40	2·85 : 1	2·14 : 1	1·71 : 1
55	2·88 : 1	1·56 : 1	1·24 : 1

Reference to Tables 7.8 and 7.3 above shows that revenues per tourist night are commonly in the range of $25–40, while occupancy rates are usually between 30 and 40 per cent. A capital/gross output ratio of 3 : 1 would thus be a reasonable rule-of-thumb to apply under Caribbean conditions, although some hotels will be doing better than this, and others worse. Since value added (net output) lies between roughly 32 per cent and 41 per cent of gross output for the four islands cited in Table 7.9, capital/net output ratios of up to 9 : 1 would seem to apply to the hotels sector of the Caribbean.

Capital/employment ratios in the hotel sector

With the number of man-years of employment created per room approximately equal to one, it follows from the discussion of hotel investment costs that investment costs per man-year of work created will be in the range of $20,000 to $30,000 in the Commonwealth Caribbean.

Summary and conclusions

In this chapter an attempt has been made to support the earlier contentions that the hotel industry is dominated by foreign ownership, contains a substantial proportion of expatriates in the better paid jobs which it creates, pay a substantial proportion of wages and salaries to foreigners, requires few locally produced inputs, and generally has underutilised capacity, especially in the summer (off-season) months. Although detailed surveys are necessary in every island, those that are available suggest that these contentions retain their validity.

8 The role of government in the growth of Caribbean tourism

It has been argued that the governments of the smaller islands of the Commonwealth Caribbean have made a substantial contribution to the growth of tourism in the region and, further, that this contribution tends to be ignored in most studies of the economic impact of tourism.[1] The purpose of this chapter is to examine the role of governments in promoting tourist development in the Caribbean and, wherever possible, to attempt to measure the cost of these measures in monetary terms for the purposes of subsequent analysis. It goes without saying that the conclusions of this chapter will not be generally applicable to all developing countries which are promoting tourism. Small islands, acting alone, are at a substantial disadvantage in many aspects of economic life, and the promotion of tourism is one of them.[2] But although the factor of small size is important, it remains true that even in larger countries tourism *can* involve very substantial costs for the government, and many of the points raised below will apply in a number of developing countries beyond the Caribbean.[3] Their empirical significance, however, remains to be determined.

The role of Commonwealth Caribbean governments in the growth of tourism during the 1960s may be conveniently examined under four different heads, namely:

(1) *Fiscal policies.* Including incentives offered to hoteliers, real estate developers, and other activities related to tourism.

(2) *Infrastructure and utilities.* Including the cost of provision of tourist-related infrastructure and public utilities, e.g. airports of international standard, roads, water supplies and deep water harbour facilities for cruise ship visitors.

(3) *Staff training and promotional activities.* Including the provision of hotel schools and tourist boards or other educational and promotional activities related to tourism.

(4) *Physical planning and controls.* Legislative provisions for the control of direction of tourist development, in particular the location of hotels and other tourist facilities.

1 See especially above Chapter 1, Chapter 3 and Chapter 5.

2 See also Chapters 2 and 3 above and Demas (1965).

3 Many developing countries have introduced fiscal advantages for tourism, and are responsible for the provision of infrastructure. A bibliography of tourism legislation has been compiled by the IUOTO, with continued accretions. A number of countries (e.g. Yugoslavia, Ceylon) operate a system of especially favourable exchange rates for tourists, but this system has not been introduced in the Caribbean. Still others offer especially low rates of interest on loans to hotel developers. See also Peters (1969), pp. 249–52.

Fiscal policies

The biggest single contribution to revenues in the islands of the region is made by import duties, the yield from which is commonly 10 to 15 per cent of GDP.[4] This is a logical consequence of the open nature of the economies and the relative ease with which this form of impost may be collected on small islands. Generally speaking, income tax is second in importance, although this source is non-existent in the Bahamas and the Cayman Islands, while in the British Virgin Islands and Montserrat greatly reduced rates of income tax apply. For the other islands, rates of income tax are progressive and marginal tax rates at income levels of £2,000–3,000 are usually in the region of 60 per cent. Company tax is normally 40 per cent, but reduced rates apply in Montserrat and the British Virgin Islands, and there is no company tax in the Bahamas or the Cayman Islands.

Other important sources of revenue are sales of postage stamps (a high proportion of which comes from stamp collectors), export duties (mainly in the Windward Islands), currency profits (from sterling assets held by the Eastern Caribbean Currency Authority), excise duty (mainly on rum), licences, fees and fines, revenue from operation of government utilities, and airport tax and tourist tax. The latter is of increasing importance in Antigua (where it is a flat rate levied per bed-night and collected from hotels), Grenada, the Cayman Islands (where it is a percentage of hotel bills, with certain exclusions), the British Virgin Islands and the Bahamas.

Tourism can affect the general revenue system in a number of ways. The most obvious of these is through the fiscal incentives offered for hotels and for related activities, which are discussed below. Perhaps less obviously, where taxes on 'luxuries' have been kept low to encourage tourists to buy these commodities, the degree of progression or regression in the tax system as a whole is affected. This is important in smaller islands for whom the establishment and administration of duty-free facilities at ports of exit would be *prima facia* very costly.[5] In such cases there may be considerable conflict between the distributional objectives of the fiscal system and the desire to increase tourist expenditure. This conflict may, however, be more apparent than real since the income generated by this type of luxury expenditure is of necessity minimal.[6] Finally, the point was made in Chapter 3 that dependence on flows of foreign capital in general introduces a constraint on the freedom of manoevre which government has in relation to fiscal structure.[7]

Incentives

Given the similarity in fiscal structure in the region, it is not surprising that incentives offered to hotel investors are very similar in form, generally dating back to the early

---

4 See also Chapter 3 for the details of revenue structure in the Commonwealth Caribbean.

5 For example, the Cayman Islands, the British Virgin Islands, and most of the Leewards and Windwards tend not to have duty-free facilities at airports and harbours.

6 The outcome of this conflict is of some economic and political significance for the Cayman Islands and the British Virgin Islands where the tax system is regressive in any case. My own view is that the manipulation of rates of duty in order to encourage this kind of expenditure by tourists is almost always self-defeating and inconsistent with declared national objectives.

7 Chapter 3, p. 31.

1950s, and concentrating on reducing liability for import duties and income taxes.[8]

The basic provisions of the incentives legislation for hotels (commonly termed hotels aid ordinances or acts) cover duty-free importation of raw materials and equipment for the original investment in hotels licenced under the legislation and the granting of a 'tax holiday' for a period of years, usually ten. To obtain a licence, hotels must be over a minimum size, normally ten rooms (although in the British Virgin Islands it is six rooms) with a differential tax holiday period for hotels of 6–9 rooms and hotels with ten or more rooms.

Provision for duty-free importation of raw materials and equipment is sometimes also made for hotel extensions and replacement equipment for a specified period (e.g. the British Virgin Islands). In one case, duty relief is graded according to the siting of the hotel (the Cayman Islands).[9]

In the case of income tax relief, which is granted in all islands except St Lucia (where accelerated depreciation provisions apply) and in the islands which have no income tax, relief is normally granted for hotel profits and distributed income in the hands of the shareholders. The reason for this is that income from unincorporated businesses is income of the proprietors and partners and, consequently, when the former is exempted so is the latter. It is logical that the income from incorporated businesses should be treated in the same way. Provision may also be made for the extension of the tax holiday period by decision of Executive Council or Cabinet.[10] Employment provisions are normally included in the relevant laws to ensure that a certain proportion of employees engaged in the construction and running of the hotels granted these concessions are nationals (normally 60–75 per cent of all employees are to be indigenes).[11]

Effect of incentive provisions

It is inevitably difficult to assess the effect of those incentives on investment in the hotel industry. Hotel investment has remained at a high level in the region during the decade and a very high proportion of investors have taken advantage of the incentives offered. Nevertheless, other factors have also favoured hotel investment in the region. Demand has been growing rapidly, particularly in North America which is the principal market for the region as a whole. Wages, prices, building and land costs are also generally lower in most of the region than in competitive resort areas like Florida, Miami and Puerto Rico. Finally, the decade was one of general political stability in the region. On the other hand, investors often use the fact of the existence of incentives in other tourist areas as a bargaining point in their negotiations with governments, and it is probably true that once incentives had been introduced in one island, others found themselves forced to follow suit. The timing of the legislative measures would seem to support this argument.[12]

8 Examples of such legislation are given in Appendix 8.A.

9 This is an attempt to influence location.

10 Thereby avoiding debate in the legislative assembly or parliament.

11 But there are no provisions regarding the *structure* of this employment, so that, effectively, there is nothing to prevent a hotel from employing 'expatriates' in all senior and skilled positions.

12 See Appendix 8.A.

There is, however, little doubt in most people's minds that a substantial proportion of investment in hotels would have taken place even in the absence of incentives, or at any rate with substantially reduced incentives. If this is true, or rather to the extent that it is true, then the incentives represent a cost to the governments concerned. To the extent that the investors are foreign, it will also be a cost to the nation, while in the case of local investors it will represent a redistribution of income within the nation.[13]

The maximum extent of this cost is measurable for a given pattern of incentives if the following information is given:

(a) The import-content of hotel investment.
(b) The normal rate of duty on these imports.
(c) Or, simply, imports and duty refunds and drawbacks under the hotels aid legislation for a relevant series of years if these are distinguished in the trade returns and statistics of import duties collected.
(d) Profits (losses) in hotels for the relevant years.
(e) Normal rate of profits tax
(f) Length of tax holiday period.

Thus, if T = taxes and duties sacrificed
I = initial investment in year 0
m = proportion of initial investment imported
d = normal rate of duty on these imports
$p_1 - p_n$ = profits in years 1 to n
t = normal rate of profits tax
n = length of tax holiday period
r = normal rate of interest or discounting rate to be used in such calculations (the social rate of discount).

Then

$$T = (I \times m \times d) + t(p_1(1+r)^{-1} + \ldots + p_n(1+r)^{-n})$$
$$= I.m.d. + t(p_1(1+r)^{-1} \ldots p_n(1+r)^{-n})$$

in present value terms.[14]

A slight complication arises if hotels make losses in any years. Normally losses may be offset against the following year's profits for income tax purposes. The same may be done in this case. If there are no profits over the tax holiday period, then there is no incentive offered by the relief of income tax and no loss to government in offering that relief.

Additional refinements would be necessary to take account of the extent to which additional capital expenditures incurred during the tax holiday period could be carried forward and, should losses be made throughout the tax holiday period, the extent to which they could be carried forward to offset against future profits.

---

13 Which, depending on the distributional objectives of the nation, may well represent a real cost to the nation also. See also Chapter 5 and footnote 14 below.

14 In fact, the problem is more complex than this, as reference to Chapter 5 will suggest. T is income in the hands of government, while p is income in the hands of 'capitalists'. The above formula will tend to *understate* the social cost of incentives.

Nor are there any savings in administrative costs to be offset against the revenue lost by incentives of this kind since, although no taxes or duties are paid, the administrative procedures are still carried out. Indeed it would be argued that the average administrative costs would be higher because of the non-routine nature of the work involved and the additional policing required, for example, to ensure that goods imported free of duty are not re-sold. In any examination of a 'with' and 'without' case, administrative costs should be added, and a first approximation of these could be derived from the above formula through a consideration of costs of collection of import duties and income taxes.

Thus, if c = average proportionate costs of collecting import duties, and s = average proportionate costs of collecting company taxes, then the amount which should be added on for administrative costs is

$$A = I.m.d.c. + s.i. \, (p_1(1 + r)^{-1} \ldots p_n(1 + r)^{-n})$$

in its discounted form.

Taking reasonably 'typical' values for the variables in the above equation gives us values of T and A which indicate a maximum 'money' cost in present value terms of around 25 per cent of the initial private investment.[15] This assumes, however, that the investment would have taken place in the absence of incentives provisions, which is probably not realistic. Nevertheless, it does indicate the potential cost of such measures, and suggests that their quantitative significance is likely to be important in any study of tourism in the Caribbean.

Of less concern to us in the context of tourism is the pioneer industries legislation, which is again common and fairly uniform throughout the region. Some tourist-orientated industries such as yacht-slips or souvenir manufacture will, however, be included under the provisions of this legislation. The inducements offered are very similar to those offered under the hotel aid legislation, that is, duty free imports for construction purposes and tax free profits for a period of years, normally seven to ten.[16] Occasionally, raw materials for production processes are also admitted free of duty although this is a very 'expensive' concession to give for obvious reasons. The same comments and criticisms apply to this legislation as to that covering hotels.

One criticism that has been made of both hotels aid and pioneer industries legislation as it stands today in the Caribbean is that it tends to benefit temporary investors who sell out at the end of a tax holiday period, reaping large capital gains, no part of which goes to the government.[17] It seems possible that a large proportion of 'investment' in the Caribbean has been made with a view to tax-free capital gains rather than potentially taxable income. It is also true that a high proportion of hotels seem to change hands at the end of the tax holiday period. Where losses made in Caribbean enterprises owned by individuals resident and operating other businesses in the USA can be offset against liability for corporation tax in the USA, the operation of enterprises with a strong capital gain potential is a

15 See Appendix 8.B.

16 For a survey of incentives in the Caribbean and elsewhere, see Andic (1968).

17 The tax concessions may then be re-applied to the new owner. See also comments below on the question whether such concessions apply to individuals (or companies) or to the hotel.

method of converting a tax liability into a non-taxable capital gain. To the extent that this capital gain is due to the accretion of 'external economies' resulting from government capital expenditures, these gains of foreign entrepreneurs are a loss to the nation.[18]

One legal complication here is the question of liability of hotel owners selling their hotels at the end of the tax holiday to repay the import duty concessions granted to them. Usually the *licence* under hotels aid legislation is given to *individuals* who are actually investing, and one interpretation of the sections dealing with the sale of materials and equipment imported by licensed individuals would seem to include sale of the completed hotel, although this interpretation has not in fact been applied. If it were applied, there would still be an incentive to hotel investors since the duty concession would represent an interest-free loan to the hotel operator during the period in which he owned the hotel. It would also encourage longer term involvement by hotel owners and reduce the speculative element in hotel investment in the region. This is important since, so long as current profitability is only a minor concern of hotel owners, the task of promotion and advertising tends to be left to the governments.[19]

Special concessions

In addition to incentives offered to investors under the hotels aid and pioneer industries legislation, it has been customary in the islands to offer additional incentives to especially large investors or land developers offering the prospect of large real estate developments in the future. These inducements may take the following form:

(a) Provision of a large block of financing at favourable rates and over a long term, as for example in the case of the Barbados Hilton.[20]

(b) Provision of Crown lands either as a grant or on favourable leasehold terms for up to 100 years, of which the Rockefeller and Bates agreements in the British Virgin Islands, the Ranfurly agreement in the Bahamas, and the various agreements concerning the St Vincent Grenadine Islands are the most outstanding examples.[21]

(c) Free port or tax haven concessions as in the case of the Ranfurly (Nassau) agreement in the Bahamas and the Bates agreement concerning Anegada in the British Virgin Islands.

(d) Special tax treatment of key employees as in the case of Antigua oil refinery and the proposed intercontinental hotel in Antigua.

(e) Special rates and guaranteed supplies of electricity, water and other utilities.

18 Thus a hotel and its land become more valuable as access and facilities improve.

19 But the fact that promotion etc. tends to be left to government is not, of course, evidence that current profitability is not a major concern of hoteliers. Indeed, hotel associations and tourist boards are most vociferous in their demands for higher levels of government expenditure in this area.

20 The Barbados government owns the Hilton hotel, Hiltons undertaking the management for a fee. This type of arrangement is, I understand, quite common with Hilton hotels.

21 Some examples are given in Appendix 8.C.

(f) Provision and maintenance of access roads.

(g) Exclusive casino licences such as the Mamora Beach hotel and casino in Antigua.

These concessions are normally *in addition* to concessions granted under the Hotels aid and pioneer industries legislation. They have normally been granted only in periods of particular economic stress for the islands concerned, when such action seemed necessary to 'get development moving' or prevent large scale unemployment, for example in Antigua after the collapse of sugar in the middle of the decade, and the consideration of the longer term effects of these concessions, particularly through the wide differences in tax treatment which emerge and the erosion of benefits to the nation, has seemed to be at most of secondary importance.

Government bargaining strength in negotiations for special concessions

The cost of these additional concessions is difficult to assess. At the time when they were granted there was no 'free market' situation, and with governments faced with economic problems and very limited recourse to deficit financing (which, in any case, would only be of limited usefulness in such open economies), the large investors were in a seller's market, so to speak. Negotiations were often initiated and concluded at Cabinet level, with little coordination or consultation within the administrations. Serious investors came equipped with a team of highly qualified and experienced negotiators and a well thought out negotiating position, while on the government side there was generally an absence of a firm and agreed negotiating position and a lack of experienced and qualified negotiators. It would be very surprising indeed if, in these circumstances, governments were able to get anything like a fair share of the potential benefits. Finally, renegotiation of such agreements has proved difficult since it is felt that any such move would endanger the confidence and goodwill of future investors.[22]

Infrastructure and utilities

Governments of the Commonwealth Caribbean are responsible for the financing of a very substantial proportion of tourist-oriented utilities and infrastructure, particularly roads, airports, electricity, telephones, water supplies and harbours. In some cases electricity or telephones may be run by the private sector or corporations such as the Commonwealth Development Corporation (CDC) and Cable and Wireless Limited, but the other utilities are the responsibility of government.[23]

It is unfortunately not possible at this stage to give firm figures for past investment in infrastructure and public utilities which has been exclusively related to tourism since, although in some cases the division between tourism and other uses may be fairly clear (e.g. airports), in most cases it would be very difficult to do this without a series of intensive surveys. Moreover, analysis of data for a few years would

---

22 This fear was raised when attempts—which failed—were made to renegotiate the Bates agreement relating to Anegada following public concern regarding this agreement. Eventually, compensation was agreed between the British Virgin Islands and Mr. Bates following nationalisation by the government. See *Financial Times* 18 November 1970, Buying out the Developer and subsequent correspondence.

23 See also Chapter 3.

not be particularly useful since many of the investments are extremely 'lumpy' in nature, especially major road, harbour and airport constructions or reconstructions. Nevertheless, with tourism being one of the few 'dynamic' sectors during the decade, particularly in the smaller islands, it is useful to start by examining the capital expenditures incurred by governments on infrastructure and utilities in relation to the increase in hotel beds over a period. We may then compare this with the capital needs of the islands as identified by the *Tripartite Economic Survey*, a careful reading of which yields some estimates of requirements for 'tourist-orientated' investments in infrastructure and public utilities. These estimates can then be compared with Zinder's estimate, that related infrastructure requirements 'typically' are 20 per cent of hotel capital costs excluding major rebuilding or relocation of roads and airports.[24]

Table 8.1 *E. Caribbean: government capital expenditures 1964–7 showing the number of hotel beds in addition built over the same period and capital expenditures per new hotel bed.*

	Capital expenditures 1964–7 $ m EC	Number of new hotel beds 1964–7	Capital expenditures per new bed $ 000 EC
Windward Islands	25·6	895	28·6
Grenada	6·0	250	24·0
St Vincent	4·9	112	43·8
St Lucia	8·0	434	18·4
Dominica	6·7	99	67·7
Leeward Islands	30·8	989	31·1
Antigua	18·7	730	25·6
St Kitts	8·0	170	47·1
Montserrat	4·1	89	46·1
Total	56·4	1,884	29·9

Sources: Figures for public capital formation from Table 3.5 above. Records of hotel capacity from *Economic Surveys and Projections* and other sources. See also Chapter 7.

As might be expected, the level of capital expenditures per new hotel room varied quite widely between the various islands. The reasons for this may be as follows:

(a) Greater capital availability or 'absorptive capacity' over the years concerned.[25]

(b) Different degrees of importance of tourism, and different growth of the hotel sector between islands. Amounts per bed tend to be high where other activities are important and tourism (expressed in the number of new hotel beds) has grown relatively slowly, for example, in Dominica, Montserrat and St Kitts, and low where tourism is already an important sector and the number of hotel beds has increased rapidly, for example, in Antigua and

24 *Zinder Report* p. 112.

25 The term 'absorptive capacity' is used here in the restricted sense of the capacity of *government* to undertake and supervise investment projects.

St Lucia. We may postulate that these differences are due to the varying proportion of total government capital expenditure which is tourism-related investment in infrastructure and utilities, which in turn will depend on the degree of dependence on tourism and the growth of tourism *vis-à-vis* other sectors.

A further point of interest which emerged from the above analysis is that capital expenditures on public utilities represented some 22 per cent of total government capital expenditures in the region.

These figures may be compared with the estimates of total capital needs and tourist-related capital needs derived from the *Tripartite Economic Survey* which, in turn, obtained most of the projects included from the five year plans prepared by the individual islands covering the period 1965–6 to 1970–1.[26]

Table 8.2 *E. Caribbean: capital needs 1965–6 – 1970–1 as compared with the projected increase in hotel capacity*

	Additional hotel beds projected[c]	Total capital expend- itures[a] $ 000 EC	Tourist infra- structures[b] $ 000 EC	Tourist inf. as a % of total inf.	Tourist inf. per hotel bed $ 000 EC	Total capital needs per bed $ 000 EC
Windwards	3,500	128,197	22,015	17·2	6·3	36·7
Grenada	1,200	39,268	8,726	22·2	7·3	32·7
St Vincent	800	31,653	2,480	7·8	3·1	39·6
St Lucia	1,000	27,570	6,729	24·4	6·7	27·6
Dominica	500	29,706	4,080	13·8	8·2	59·4
Leewards	1,785	92,404	36,061	39·1	20·2	51·7
Antigua	705	53,314	25,599	48·0	36·4	75·5
St Kitts	740	26,244	87,451	33·3	11·8	34·2
Montserrat	340	12,846	1,717	13·4	5·1	37·8
Totals	5,285	220,601	58,076	26·4	11·0	41·8

Notes on sources:
[a] Source: *Tripartite Economic Survey,* Islands chapters, Tables A, B and X of capital needs.
[b] Source: As a; derived as estimates from a reading of the Islands chapters, which give indications of infrastructure needs of tourism.
[c] Source: As a; page 30.

A great deal of caution must be exercised in using these figures. For one thing, even the aggregate totals for capital needs are of uncertain reliability in view of the lack of detailed costing of projects. Secondly, it is not always easy to work out from the *Tripartite Economic Survey* exactly what projects *are* priorities for tourism, what the costs of these projects are, and to what extent other users will benefit.[27]

26 See also comments by the leader of the Tripartite Economic Survey Mission, Professor J. R. Sargent, in the preface to the *Report*.

27 There *will* be other users for most of the facilities, but, if the argument of Chapter 5 is accepted, it is necessary to go further and identify these users and the extent to which they benefit. If it is argued that they are mainly upper income groups, then it is reasonable to neglect the benefits.

It is of some interest that, in both the Windwards and the Leewards, estimated requirements for investment in tourist-related utilities represented 61·1 per cent of the total requirements for tourist-related infrastructure investment. In view of the fact that the figure were not 'arranged' in this way, that is, by using this ratio in the calculations, this coincidence is remarkable.[28]

It is also of some interest to use the ratios of tourist infrastructure to total infrastructure requirements given in Table 8.2 to calculate tourist infrastructure investment over the period 1964—7 assuming these ratios to have some constancy for the individual islands over a time period.

Table 8.3 *Estimated investment in tourist infrastructure and tourist infrastructure investment per new bed, 1964—7 inclusive.*

	Estimated investment in tourist infrastructure 1964—7 $ 000 EC	Estimated tourist infrastructure investment per new bed $ 000 EC	
Windward Islands	5,417	6·0	(6·3)[a]
Grenada	2,021	8·1	(7·3)
St Vincent	420	3·8	(3·1)
St Lucia	2,035	4·7	(6·7)
Dominica	941	9·5	(8·2)
Leeward Islands	13,430	13·6	(20·2)
Antigua	9,420	12·9	(36·5)
St Kitts	2,910	17·1	(11·8)
Montserrat	1,100	12·4	(5·1)
Totals	18,847	10·0	(11·0)

Notes:
[a] Figures in brackets are for 'requirements' as calculated in Table 8.2 above from *Tripartite Survey* data and are inserted for ease of reference.

The above table reveals some interesting features. First, there is a remarkable similarity between the estimated tourist infrastructure investment per bed for the period 1964—7 and the figures derived for the required tourist infrastructure investment per bed from the *Tripartite Economic Survey*. Where significant differences do emerge between the two figures (for example, in Antigua and Montserrat) this could be explained by underinvestment or overinvestment in tourist infrastructure in the period 1964—7 requiring to be corrected in the later period with which the *Tripartite Survey* was concerned. This is certainly a plausible argument in the case of Antigua where relatively large investments in roads, water and electricity were required by the middle of the decade, and one of the key justifications for the expensive deep water harbour built in the second half of the decade was expected income from cruise ship visitors. Furthermore, much of the government's capital budget in 1964—5 was absorbed in attempts to prop up the dying sugar industry in order to prevent widespread unemployment.[29]

28 The author, as one of the survey's research assistants, can vouch for this coincidence.

29 See also Chapter 3.

142

The second interesting feature to emerge from Table 8.3 is the significant differences between both the estimated and the required infrastructure investment per hotel bed in the Leeward and the Windward Islands. One explanation for this is that facilities such as roads and harbours are more overtly tourist orientated in the Leewards than they are in the Windwards, where there are considerable agricultural exports also requiring roads and harbours.

In any event, the conclusion would seem to be that the Zinder hypothesis that infrastructure requirements represent 20 per cent of hotel capital costs is likely to be a serious underestimate in the Eastern Caribbean. If the figures in Table 8.2 above can be accepted as roughly correct, and if our estimate of hotel capital costs of $25,000 EC per double room is reasonable, then the ratio is more likely to be in the region of 80 per cent with intra-regional variations, the ratio being higher where there are fewer alternative uses for the infrastructure facilities required for tourism and *vice versa*.

The distinction between directly related government investment in infrastructure for tourism and 'general infrastructure' related to general growth in the economy becomes redundant if we accept a model in which tourism is the only 'engine' of growth and evaluate the 'benefits' in terms of both direct, indirect and induced accretions to GNP after the operation of the 'multiplier'.[30] In this case we have to evaluate the benefits not only in terms of investment in hotels, and directly related infrastructure investment, but *also* in terms of other private and public investment required to realise the output levels in other sectors of the economy implied by the use of multiplier analysis. This point is discussed at greater length in Chapters 9 and 10.

Public utilities

The importance of the distinction between investment in general infrastructure and investment in public utilities related to tourism lies in the fact that the latter earn revenue directly, whereas the former do so only indirectly and very inadequately. For example, revenue from 'tourist' roads comes from the relevant proportion of taxi and hire-car licences and, it could be argued, from import duties on these taxis and hire-cars plus duties on current inputs of the relevant portion of the transport sector, which are nowhere near covering the recurrent costs of maintaining roads, let alone capital charges.

Public utilities earn revenue, but even in this case there are many instances of these utilities making recurrent losses even before capital charges, and these losses have to be subsidised from general revenue.[31] Furthermore, it must be remembered that a large proportion of the capital costs of general infrastructure and public utilities has been met by capital grants from aid donors, particularly from the UK, and debt charges which do exist consequently understate the true economic capital costs of these facilities. Of all the costs which fall upon the government, it therefore seems likely that those relating to the provision of infrastructure and utilities which

30 Or even if we take direct and indirect benefits only—since indirect 'benefits' will require at least some infrastructure component.

31 See also Table 3.13 and comments in Chapter 3.

are directly and indirectly related to tourism will be the most empirically significant. While the evidence presented above regarding the relationship between investment in hotels and investment by government is unsatisfactory and in need of more detailed enquiry, it is sufficient to cast considerable doubt on the estimates contained in the *Zinder Report,* and to suggest the importance of including this element of cost in any analysis of the economic impact of tourism.[32]

Staff training and promotional activities

In the smaller islands of the Commonwealth Caribbean, the contribution of governments towards training of hotel staff has been minimal. Hotel schools or related training facilities do exist in Antigua, Barbados, the Bahamas, Jamaica and Trinidad, but that in Antigua is largely financed and run by the UNDP and is mainly concerned with catering. There is, so far as is known, no institution where hotel managers and higher grade chefs can be trained in the region. One of the reasons for this lack of training facilities is simply small scale on the one hand, and an absence of regional co-operation on the other. One of the consequences is that higher income skilled jobs in the hotel industry tend to go to expatriates.[33]

With regard to the promotion of tourism, nearly all of the islands have tourist boards and these are mainly statutory bodies. These tourist boards are primarily concerned with advertising and promotional activities, and usually have no more than one or two full-time employees.[34] The boards usually contain a mixture of various interests from hoteliers through commercial interests to government representatives. The functioning of these bodies is rarely satisfactory, and their structure and the many proposals for their reform are fields of study in themselves.[35]

Expenditures by governments on tourist boards and promotional activities are shown in Table 8.4.

Promotional expenditures per visitor arrival vary enormously in the region as a whole — from below $1 per tourist in the British Virgin Islands to above $10 per tourist in the Bahamas, Trinidad and the Cayman Islands, with an approximate average of $10 including the Bahamas and Trinidad and $4 excluding the latter. Assuming that the average hotel bed is occupied for 180 days, and that the average

32 An interesting comparison may be made with the Languedoc–Roussillon tourist development initiated by the French government. According to a report in the *Economist* (5 June 1971), the state has spent $ 80 millions to date and an additional $ 80 millons or so is scheduled to be spent up to the end of 1975. This all on drainage, road works, water supplies and major road works. A local consortium of state, local government and private interests has spent an additional $ 35 millions on local services like drains, new roads, electricity and telephone cables, and are committed to at least another $ 15 millions by the end of 1975. Although the plan was for private investment in housing, hotels etc. to run at eight or nine times the level of state investment, in fact, to date only $ 260 million has come forward from the private sector. It would be interesting to see the social cost–benefit analysis of this project if one exists.

33 Most hotel employees in unskilled or semi-skilled categories receive only 'on the job' training. In the Cayman Islands, 80 per cent of hotel employees had no training or practical experience, or 'on the job' training only. See also Chapter 7.

34 It seems that the focal interest of the boards concerns getting tourists to come to the Islands, rather than trying to increase the benefits to nationals of tourist expenditure.

35 See also Bryden and Faber (1971).

Table 8.4 *Expenditures by Commonwealth Caribbean governments on tourist boards, advertising and promotional activities $000 EC*

	Expenditure on tourist boards etc. $ 000 EC	Visitor arrivals 000	Promotional expenditure per arrival $ EC	Year
Grenada	57 Z	23·2	2·46	1968
St Vincent	24	6·5	3·70	1965
St Lucia	60	12·9	4·65	1966
Dominica	6	6·0	1·00	1966
Antigua	75 Z	55·8	1·34	1968
St Kitts	18 Z	9·8	1·84	1968
Montserrat	20 Z	6·9	2·90	1968
Turks and Caicos	n.a.	n.a.	n.a.	n.a.
Cayman Islands	175	14·5	12·07	1968
Virgin Islands	6	22·2	0·27	1968
Barbados	846 Z	115·7	7·31	1968
Bahamas	12,074	1,072·2	11·22	1968
Trinidad	924Z	91·7	10·08	1968
Jamaica	n.a.	n.a.	n.a.	n.a.

Notes on sources:
Z = *Zinder Report* data, Table no. 3. Obtained during their field studies. Other data from tourist boards or government departments and estimates.

visitor stays 6 days, then the average cost per bed on promotional expenditures by government is $120 exclusive of the Bahamas and Trinidad and $300 inclusive of the Bahamas and Trinidad, per annum.[36] It is difficult to judge the efficiency of such expenditures, in terms of attraction of new visitors. Most reports[37] have urged increases in promotional expenditures by island governments, but without any cost—benefit analysis or even any attempt to evaluate, *ex post*, the extent to which tourists are attracted by such methods.

Physical planning and controls of land use
From the point of view of tourist development, at least two aspects of land and its distribution are important in the Caribbean context.

(a) Land values rise at least partly as a result of the actions of the community as a whole. Obvious examples of this occur when a new road or an airport is built and financed partly or wholly from local revenues. The provision of these facilities raises land values, the benefit of which accrues to land-owners. Furthermore, land values are maintained only by the collective, if unconscious, efforts of the community as a whole. Thus, to the extent that the distribution of land is unequal, these benefits accrue unequally and if the fiscal system lacks the appropriate redistributive mechanism the effect

36 Moreover, these expenditures are almost entirely a cost in foreign exchange. See also Chapter 10 and Bryden and Faber (1971).

37 For example, the *Tripartite Economic Survey* and the *Zinder Report*.

is to make the landowner richer at the expense of the taxpayer. This, in turn, encourages speculative land holding activities which reduces the supply of land to the market, raising prices still further. Under these conditions a syndrome of rising land prices and increasing inequality of wealth is set up.[38]

(b) The second problem concerns the effects of unplanned and uncontrolled physical development which affect the long term growth potential as well as the costs of government utilities, services and infrastructure which are to some extent borne by the community as a whole. In the absence of adequate controls, long term growth potential can be affected by the type of physical developments initiated, whether adequate provision has been made for sewage disposal,[39] water supplies, road maintenance, as well as such things as building and architectural standards and the more complex questions of aesthetics. Damage to long term growth is *ex definitio* a long term cost and thus more likely to be borne by the community as a whole than the private developer or speculator who tends to operate in the short term.

These problems, by and large, remain untackled by governments in the Eastern Caribbean, primarily because to tackle them adequately presents formidable political economic and administrative problems. In most of the islands, complex problems of land ownership arising from, in the first place, divergences between customary practices regarding the transfer of rights and what constitutes legal transfer under the law and, in the second place, inadequate registration procedures, remain to be overcome. Again, where large landowners are politically powerful they resent restrictions on their freedom to do what they like with their land. Finally, the ordinary West Indian often forced to build their own houses over a period of years for economic reasons, resent the complex restrictions inherent in modern practices developed in the very different conditions of Europe or North America.

Conclusions

The role of the governments of the Commonwealth Caribbean in promoting tourism during the 1960s has been examined under four principal headings: fiscal policies and incentives; the provision of infrastructure and utilities; staff training and promotional activities, and physical planning and controls. For the period under study, the first two areas have probably been the most important from the point of view of their empirical significance for any analysis of the costs and benefits of tourism. In particular, previous estimates of the cost of infrastructure and utilities may have been seriously underestimated in the context of the Caribbean. In fact, taking incentives and infrastructure together, it would not be unduly misleading, on the evidence of this chapter, to suggest that governments have had to match the contribution of the private investors almost 'dollar for dollar' in monetary terms.

---

38 See also Chapter 5.

39 Sewage disposal in the smaller Caribbean Islands tends to be left to individual hotels, who dispose by means of septic tanks, soakaways or by pipes out to sea. The longer run implications of this situation require urgent study. However, if governments were required to provide public systems, the cost, given the geographical dispersion of hotels, would be enormous.

Although some of this public investment earns revenue over and above tourist receipts, it is suggested that, even taking this factor into account, it would be highly misleading to ignore the cost which is borne by the government in any calculation of the costs and benefits of tourist development. Finally, in the light of the discussion on training and physical controls, and the comments in Chapter 5, there is reason to believe that the *actual* cost as derived for a period of years understates the *real* cost if only because the failure to introduce adequate physical controls and complaints of 'inadequate' infrastructure – for example, sewage disposal – imply that associated 'diseconomies' of tourist development have been incurred. But there are other reasons why the real cost to the 'nation' has been understated, as the arguments in Chapter 5 suggest. An attempt to identify the real cost to the 'nation' is embodied in Chapter 10.

APPENDIX 8-A EXAMPLES OF INCENTIVES LEGISLATION RELATING TO HOTELS IN THE COMMONWEALTH CARIBBEAN

Some examples of the main provisions of the incentives legislation in respect of hotels in the smaller islands of the region are given below. As these are cited as examples only, no attempt has been made to ensure that the position as outlined is that actually in force in 1972. Doubtless some minor amendments have been made, but to the author's knowledge, no major changes have taken place that would seriously affect the general picture which is presented by these examples. References are to the principal ordinances and amendments unless otherwise stated.

Grenada **Ordinance No. 12 of 1953** granted relief of customs duties on building materials and equipment to licensed persons constructing a hotel (Sec. 3). A 'hotel' in this context was defined as any building with twenty or more rooms for the accommodation for reward of guests. The definition of 'constructing' includes repairs, alterations, reconstruction or extension (Sec. 2). In the case of items imported from UK colonies and other countries for which 'imperial preferential' rates apply, total relief of customs duty was granted, while for 'foreign' imports the rate of duty was 'equivalent to the difference between the General Tariff and the Imperial Preferential Rates' (Sec. 5). Provision for drawback of duties is made in respect of imported commodities which are purchased locally (Sec. 6). Goods imported with duty relief are marked and inventories kept in order to minimise fraud by re-sale on the local market (Secs. 9 and 10). Two other important provisions of the principal ordinance were as follows:

(i) 75 per cent of employees in the construction, maintenance and operation of a hotel which was given a licence under the provisions of the ordinance should be 'British subjects' (Sec. 12).

(ii) If any hotelier (or employee) refused accommodation or service to a member of the public without lawful excuse they would be liable to a fine and/or imprisonment and revocation or suspension of any licence granted under the Ordinance.

Ordinance No. 19 of 1956 made a number of important changes to the principal ordinance. Minor amendments concerned an extension of the original definition of 'equipment' and reduced the number of rooms in the definition of 'hotel' to ten or more, thereby admitting smaller hotels and guest houses to the ambit of the incentive provisions. In addition, replacement items of equipment were specifically excluded from duty relief. However, imports from *any source* were now granted full relief of duty. Of more significance, however, was the introduction of a new section exempting licensed hotels from income tax for a period of eight years. Moreover, proprietors of licensed hotels were entitled during the tax holiday period and within two years thereafter to distribute a sum equal to the income arising during the tax holiday period from such hotel, to the members of the company, and every such sum should be exempt of income tax in the hands of such members. Subsequent ordinances extended the tax holiday period from 8 to 10 years (Ordinance No. 14 of 1958) and simplified the provisions regarding the relief of import duty (Ordinance No. 16 of 1965).

St Vincent
According to the principal ordinance (Hotels Aid Ordinance, 1954) and later amendments of 1958 and 1963, the provisions relating to import duty and income tax relief almost exactly parallel those of the Grenada legislation discussed above. However, the legislation was intended to apply only to *new* hotels with ten or more bedrooms. The period of income tax relief, originally eight years, was subsequently extended to ten as it was in Grenada.

Dominica
The provisions of the Dominica hotels aid ordinances are essentially the same as those for Grenada, viz. 'freedom from income tax for a period of ten years, and duty free importation of raw materials and hotel equipment' for hotels of ten bedrooms or more (See *Financial Times* 21 August 1970).

Montserrat and *Antigua* have very similar provisions to those already discussed.

St Lucia
According to *Ordinance No. 22 of 1961,* which amended *No. 25 of 1959* and repealed No. 20 of 1961, the approach in St Lucia was somewhat different to that of the other islands. Although in this case the provisions relating to relief of customs duty on materials used in the construction or extension of hotels were very similar to those already discussed (Sections 12–18, 22/1961), in place of total relief of income tax there were provisions for accelerated depreciation in respect of hotel investments and additions. Basically, such expenditures were allowable deductions in respect of the annual profits of the hotel, and could be carried forward for a further seven years if as is almost inevitable they exceeded the profits in the first year (Sections 5–10, 22/1961). The effect of these provisions would, in all probability, be very similar to a tax holiday period of eight years.

British Virgin Islands
Under the provisions of the principal ordinance (No. 1 of 1953) as amended in 1961 and 1967, duty free imports are allowed for both the construction and equipping of new hotels and extensions to existing hotels. In addition, there is provision for the duty free importation of replacement equipment for up to three years after construction has been completed. In this case, however, hotels or extensions were to be of only *six* or more rooms. There are also provisions relating to the employment of British Virgin Islanders, who should represent 60 per cent of those employed on the construction, maintenance and operation of hotels.[1] In spite of the low rates of income tax in the British Virgin Islands, a 'tax holiday' period is given, the length of which varies with the size of hotel. For hotels of nine bedrooms or less it is seven years; for those with ten or more bedrooms it is ten years. But these periods can be extended by the Administrator-in-Council for ten and twenty years respectively. Dividends paid for the period of the tax holiday are tax-free in the hands of the shareholders. Additional capital expenditures on improvements or extensions which are incurred during the tax holiday period may also be partly allowable as a deduction in the year following the end of the tax holiday period.

Cayman Islands
The principal ordinance (*Law 1 of 1955*) and its amendments (5/1960, 46/1966, 29/1967) relate solely to the granting of relief of import duty, there being no income tax in the Cayman Islands. Again, there is a lower size limit of ten bedrooms. A subsequent amendment (1967) removed overall duty relief and introduced a special rate of 7½ per cent in the popular West Bay Beach area and 2½ per cent elsewhere in the Cayman Islands, this being a crude and probably ineffective attempt to encourage dispersion of hotel development.

1 It seems probable that this provision has not always been strictly adhered to. In 1971, 55 per cent of all employees in the construction industry and 38 per cent of employees in hotels and related activities were non-Virgin Islanders according to Elkan and Morley (1971).

APPENDIX 8.B THE COST OF INCENTIVES PROVISIONS FOR HOTELS IN THE COMMONWEALTH CARIBBEAN

The following assumptions are made:

I = \$25,000 per room (see also Chapter 7)

m = 0·60 (See also Chapters 9 and 10)

d = 0·15 (see Tables 3.1 and 3.11. This is about the average rate of duty on imports)

t = 0·40 (see p. 133)

n = 10 (see p. 134)

i = 0·08 (i.e. the SDR is taken, for the purpose of this exercise, to be 8 per cent p.a. See also Chapter 5)

p, profits rise slowly over the period to 10 per cent on invested capital in year 10.

p		$(1 + i)^{-1 \ldots n}$	$p_{1 \ldots n}(1 + i)^{-1 \ldots n}$
p_1 =	0	0·925926	0·0
p_2 =	500	0·857339	428·7
p_3 =	1,000	0·793832	793·8
p_4 =	1,500	0·735030	1,102·5
p_5 =	1,500	0·680583	1,020·9
p_6 =	2,000	0·630170	1,260·3
p_7 =	2,000	0·583490	1,167·0
p_8 =	2,000	0·540269	1,080·5
p_9 =	2,300	0·500249	1,150·0
p_{10} =	2,500	0·463193	1,158·0
			9,161·7

T = (25,000 × 0·6 × 0·15) + 0·40 (9,161·7)

= 2,250 + 3,660

= \$5,910 per room

Now, if c = 0·08

and s = 0·15

A = (2,250 × 0·08) + 0·15 (3,660)

= 180 + 549

= \$729 per room

Thus $T + A$ = \$6,639 per room or 26·5 % of original investment on the above assumptions. This, of course, assumes that the investment would have proceeded in the absence of the incentives provisions.

APPENDIX 8-C EXAMPLES OF SPECIAL AGREEMENTS WITH FOREIGN INVESTORS[1]

The following notes attempt to summarise a few of the specially negotiated concessions related to tourist development in two of the smaller islands of the region, notably St Vincent and the St Vincent Grenadines, and the British Virgin Islands. The form of these agreements differs considerably, and they are often very complex indeed. Further research is necessary to examine *ex post* the distribution of costs and benefits from such concessions, but, implicitly, they represent concessions *in addition to* those offered by hotels aid legislation.

Special agreements relating to St Vincent and the St Vincent Grenadines

1 Canouan Island (Grenadines)

This agreement relates to a lease of the major part of Canouan Island for a period of

[1] For special concessions in St Vincent and the St Vincent Grenadine Islands, I lean very heavily on a paper prepared by Ivor Martin, Government Economist, which was prepared for the St Vincent fiscal survey team with which both he and I were associated. For those in the British Virgin Islands, I have referred to the original agreements. Agreements of this kind are normally available from the Registrar of Companies etc. in the various Islands.

ninety-nine years. The lessor was the government and the lessee a Mr. Rupert Findlay. *Property:* All land owned by the government and not subject to any lease. When land at present leased reverts to government, it was to be passed over to the new lessee immediately. Government can use its powers to acquire more land.

Considerations: Construction of an 'A' Class hotel of not less than 100 rooms with a casino. Option to construct other hotels, casinos, etc. Provision of electricity, fresh water, shopping centre and facilities for servicing boats and yachts. Airport, road, deep-water harbour, police station, health centre, hospitals, schools and customs houses to be constructed by lessee but *to be managed and maintained by the government.*

Income to government: 8% of the gross takings *of the casino* in the first two years. 10 per cent in the next five years. 20 per cent in the remainder. These provisions can be reviewed at the end of the first two years and every succeeding five years. Rental of island $1·00 per year.

The lessee was to have power to sub-let lands under the Alien Land Holding Ordinances. The government was to receive, for any lands so rented:

25 per cent of rent in the first two years
30 per cent of rent in the next five years
50 per cent of rent in the following years.

Concession: Freeport to be constructed, but not all imported items were to be duty free. In fact the freeport was to be governed by legislation enacted by the government of St Vincent. In addition, the developer was allowed all concessions granted under the Pioneer Industries and Hotels Aid Ordinance. Finally, provision was made for exemption from land tax and inheritance tax.

2 *Mustique Island* (*Grenadines*)

This agreement related to special concessions granted to Mr Tennant, owner of the island of Mustique.

Concessions: Materials, supplies and things of every kind and description to be used for construction and erection of hotels, marines, office buildings, housing and roads (and for administrative, medical and educational purposes) were free of custom duties for thirty-five years.

No real property taxes or rates and no real property levies to be collected for thirty-five years.

No personal property taxes or rents and no capital levies. No death duties. No taxes on capital appreciation. No taxes charged on the company's earnings. No stamp duty to be collected by government for thirty-five years.

No taxes imposed on the salaries of the persons employed by the company for thirty-five years. No export duty on anything harvested, processed, assembled, refined or repaired or services by the company.

Consideration: The developer was committed to invest between $5,000 and $10,000 per annum for the next five years; including building and equipping a hospital either in Mustique or the island of Bequia within the next five years to serve both islands and in general to develop tourism and maintain government offices.

Income to government: 5 per cent of net income from all sources for a period of 10 years. 7½ per cent of the next period of 10 years. 40 per cent for the remainder of the agreement. 'Net income' meant the gross income less all expenses, directors' fees, proper depreciation and costs incurred by the company in respect of government offices and all other costs incurred by the company except those which in the opinion of the auditors ought properly to be charged to capital.

Palm Island (*Grenadines*)

This is a lease agreement between the government and Palm Island Resorts Limited for a period of ninety-nine years.

Property: Palm Island, one of the smaller Grenadines.

Consideration: Rent to government of $100. In addition the government to hold 12½ per cent of the share capital.

Concessions: Everything granted under the Pioneer Industries Ordinances and Hotels Aid Ordinance. Profits can be repatriated.

Petit St Vincent (*Grenadines*)

Property: Island sold to Petit St Vincent Company.

Concessions: A large number of duty free concessions and income tax holiday for ten years.

Special agreements relating to the British Virgin Islands
The most important agreements were those signed with Mr Bates and with Mr Rockefeller. In view of his threat to publish a book on his experiences[1] I have chosen to summarise those made with Mr Bates. That signed with Mr Rockefeller related to a large tract of land on the island of Virgin Gorda.

Agreements with Mr Bates
There are three such agreements, two of which relate to the development of Wickham's Cay and adjoining areas on the island of Tortola, the third relating to the development of Anegada Island.

1 *Agreement No. 1 (Tortola)* In return for allowing the Tortola Development and Trust Company Ltd. to reclaim some 60 acres of land, the government were to receive not more than 5% for roads, car parking and amenity space (3 acres) – a Crown grant being given to the company for the remainder of the land. In addition the government undertook to: (a) waive customs duties payable on plant, equipment and materials for the purposes of the reclamation works; (b) great privileges and concessions identical with those granted by the Pioneer Services and Enterprises Ordinance, 1966 (re. customs duty and income tax relief) to the company, any subsidiary company, any associated company, all shareholders to the extent of at least 5% of issued share capital of the company or any subsidiary or associated company, and, further, all companies formed by such shareholding persons or companies with the intention of carrying out commercial activities on the reclaimed land *including* the construction of buildings, but such concessions shall not extend so as to include occupation of private residences or the conduct of retail shops.

2 *Agreement No. 2 (Tortola)* Relates to the reclamation and development of Wickham's Cay and Wickham's Cay Reef, giving the *right without obligation* for a period of 15 years to reclaim a further area of land adjoining that covered by Agreement No. 1. Upon reclamation the government shall: (a) give a Crown grant to the company for the land reclaimed, the mangrove island, *and* a certain area of foreshore by the agricultural station. (b) give the company the right *in perpetuity* to 'control, restrict and govern the use of the Marine Area' created by the reclamations, 'and to levy tolls' save in respect of local bona fide fishermen. In return for this the company should cede 1½ acres of land to government on the reclaimed area. However, the government is also committed to provide sewage to each plot – the cost of which is to be met:
(1) $50,000 over 5 years after completion of the scheme;
(2) Liabilities in excess of $50,000 to be met out of rents receivable under the Anegada Agreement;
(3) Interest on these liabilities at ½% *above* the company's borrowing rate;
(4) In the event of government being unable to raise $50,000 in the first five years, government is to *cede back* the 1·5 acres of land (i.e. at the equivalent 76·5 cts. per sq. ft.). However, this will not be accepted as payment for the interest on the $50,000.

Further, government agreed to provide water and electricity supplies to consumers on the reclaimed land. The same concessions are given in respect of concessions under Agreement No. 1 (see para. 1(a) and (b)).

3 *Agreement No. 3 (relating to Anegada)* For the sum of $1·00 the government granted the option to lease the greater part of Anegada Island (about 8,000 acres) to the Development Corporation of Anegada, which has now been taken up. The agreement specified the terms of this lease, which is for a period of 199 years. In return for this, the following rents are payable:
(a) Year 1 – a peppercorn
(b) Year 2 – $5,000
(c) Year 3 – $10,000
(d) Year 4 – $20,000
(e) Year 5–199 – $30,000 per annum
In addition, 'the Lessee shall pay to the Lessor and the Government sums equivalent

1   Letter from Mr K. Bates to the *Financial Times*, published 2 June 1971.

to five per centum of all rents and premiums ... *actually received by the Lessee* arising under all sub-leases hereafter granted by the Lessee in respect of all or any part or parts of the Lessee's land'.

There are virtually no restrictions on the type or density of development permitted on the land. The lessee is responsible for the provision of electricity, drainage, sewage. The lessee is entitled to draw upon underground water supplies and charge for this service. Roads will be constructed by the company, but maintained by government. Furthermore, the company undertook to meet the *initial* cost in the *first instance* of:

the public service portion for an air terminal

the fire safety equipment for an air terminal

a police station

customs offices

a small hospital

a post office

The government shall be 'liable to repay all such costs to the Lessee with interest' at ½% above the company's borrowing rate, such liabilities being met out of the rents payable to government under this agreement.

The company undertook to put up a jetty capable of taking medium-sized cargo boats 'for a deep water harbour', which facilities 'will be operated on a commercial basis for the benefit of the Lessee or its successors or assigns'.

In addition the government covenanted to procure that throughout the term of the lease 'all persons, firms, companies or corporations whatsoever *resident or conducting activities* of whatever description' within the area of and on the lessee's land shall be exempt from all taxation on profits, income, capital or death duties arising by reason of such residence or the conduct of such activities. However, this present covenant does not grant exemption from customs or import duties.

However, the company will be exempt from customs duties in respect of plant, equipment and materials imported for the carrying out 'by or at the instance of' the lessee of all public services or utilities on Anegada, and *also* for all construction works in relation to the lessee's land for a period of ten years.

Other clauses of the agreement relate to the granting of licences under the Aliens Land Holding Act and steps to be taken should the lessee fail to pay rents due or fail to undertake the commitments made.

Analysis: tourist multipliers and social costs and benefits in the Caribbean

Introduction to Part IV

The theoretical basis of the 'tourist multiplier', which purports to relate foreign exchange receipts of tourism to value added in 'real' terms, and the limitations of the multiplier approach were discussed in Chapter 5. It is nevertheless useful and instructive, in view of the important place granted to tourist multipliers in past studies of the significance of tourism for developing countries, to attempt to derive estimates of the value of the multiplier and to analyse the effects on this value of relaxing various key assumptions. Chapter 9 attempts to carry out such an analysis for the smaller territories of the Commonwealth Caribbean, based primarily on interindustry transactions tables for Antigua.

Chapter 10 moves on to derive estimates of social costs and benefits of hotel development in the Caribbean using a single hotel project as an example and using the methodology proposed in Chapter 5. The sensitivity of the results to alternative values of various key variables is also analysed.

Finally, in Chapter 11 an attempt has been made to reduce the key proposals and forecasts contained in two recent reports concerned wholly or mainly with the future of tourism in the Eastern Caribbean to cost—benefit terms.

9 The tourist multiplier in the Caribbean

A number of previous estimates of the tourist multiplier have been made in relation to the smaller islands of the region. These estimates are summarised in Table 9.1 below.

Table 9.1 *Previous estimates of the tourist multiplier in the Commonwealth Caribbean*

Date	Author(s)	Estimated value of the tourist multiplier
1966	*Tripartite Survey*[a]	0·873
1969	*Zinder Report*[b]	2·3
1970	Levitt and Gulati[c]	1·27
1971	Bryden and Faber[d]	0·88

Notes:
[a] *Tripartite Economic Survey.* Derived from the estimates on page 13 which suggest that, neglecting associated construction activity, an increase of $10 million in tourist expenditure would generate an increase in GDP at market prices of $8·73 millions.
[b] *Zinder Report* pp. 37–46. See also Bryden and Faber (1971).
[c] Levitt and Gulati (1970), p. 337. This is a recalculation of the Zinder multiplier, using Zinder's data but correcting the (faulty) Zinder methodology. Levitt and Gulati also amend the assumptions made by Zinder as regards the values of key variables, and suggest a more 'realistic' multiplier of 1·073 (Table 8).
[d] Bryden and Faber (1971), p. 69.

The principal objections to Zinder's multiplier, which is by far the highest of these estimates, concern the procedure of summing the gross totals of the nominal value of a number of sequential transactions instead of adding only the *value added* by these transactions.[1]

The computation of the tourist multiplier in this chapter is based very largely on the inter-industry transactions table for Antigua relating to 1963.[2] Some basic adjustments were, however, made to the original transactions table, and these are detailed below.

Adjustments made to the basic transactions matrix
(1) The savings-investment sector was removed for the determination of the short period multiplier on the grounds that the factors determining

---

[1] See also Levitt and Gulati (1970) and Bryden and Faber (1971) for detailed criticisms of the Zinder multiplier.

[2] Based on O'Loughlin (1966). The table is reproduced in Appendix Table 9.A1.

investment are much more complex than could be described by a simple mechanistic relationship with domestic savings. It will be noted that in 1963 net capital inflows represented over half of gross 'savings' in Antigua.[3] Also, the banks are foreign owned and they can decide whether to invest local savings at home or abroad. However, it is recognised that this adjustment will reduce the value of the multiplier slightly, since related replacement investment must be carried out. But in practice, this is likely to be small when the capital stock in hotels is young and long-lived. Some related replacement investment in the transport sector will, however, be necessary.

(2) The rest of the world sector was treated as the exogenously determined final demand (column) vector on the one hand and the endogenously determined primary input (row) vector on the other.

(3) Households, government and profit appropriation were treated as endogenous producing sectors subject to the same input—output assumptions as other producing sectors. In other words, the system is 'closed' in respect of all final demand elements except those relating to transactions with the rest of the world.

The matrix of technical coefficients for the resulting 13 X 13 matrix is shown in Appendix Table 9A.2. This table also gives the coefficients for the primary input vector and the values for the vector of final demand, which for our purposes consists not of total exports, but only of tourist receipts of each sector.

The vector of final demand — sectoral tourist receipts — is shown in greater detail in Table 9.2 below.[4]

Table 9.2 *Sectoral tourist receipts, Antigua, 1963*

Sector	Direct tourist receipts ($000 EC)	explanation
1 Export agriculture	0·0	No direct receipts
2 Other agriculture	0·0	
3 Construction and engineering	0·0	
4 Manufacturing	0·0	
5 Distribution	2,900·2	Retail and wholesale purchases by tourists
6 Transport	860·0	Taxis, charter planes, boats, etc.
7 Finance and insurance	220·0	Financial services and insurance
8 Hotel industry	5,176·1	Hotel board, accommodation and gratuities (inclusive of tax) extra meals and bars
9 Other services	170·0	Entertainment and services outside hotel
10 Rent-of-dwellings	230·0	Rent of housing by tourists
11 Households	975·0	Direct wages paid by tourists
12 Profit appropriation	0·0	Nil
13 Government	22·0	Licenses and fees to government

Source: O'Loughlin (1966), Table 12.

3 See also Chapter 3.

4 See also Chapter 6, especially Table 6.13, for comparative data.

The assumptions on which the subsequent calculations are based are no more than the standard assumptions of input—output analysis, namely:[5]

(1) Each commodity or service (or group of commodities and services) is supplied by a single sector of production.

(2) Inputs purchased by each sector are a linear function of the gross output of that sector, and, in a closed system, consumption of each sector's output is a linear function of total consumption by households and government, and profits distributed to households are a linear function of total profits.

(3) Absence of external economies and diseconomies, so that the sum of individual activities is equal to the total effect of these activities.

In practice the high degree of aggregation involved in compiling a 13×13 transactions matrix and, in particular, the treatment of the distribution sector in most national accounts statistics of the smaller Caribbean islands, makes the validity of these assumptions highly doubtful.[6]

However, accepting these assumptions for the present it is possible to proceed mechanically by inversion of the Leontief $(I - A)$ matrix which is derived by subtracting the matrix of technical coefficients (A) from the identity matrix (I).[7] The multiplication of the Leontief inverse $(I - A)^{-1}$ by the vectors of final demands shown in Appendix Table 9.A1 yields estimates of direct, indirect and induced requirements of primary inputs — in this case imports — and value added to support these levels of final demand.[8]

The results of this computation are given below:

Table 9.3 *The tourist multiplier in Antigua, 1963*

	$ million
Total tourist expenditures	10·6
Imports from tourism	9·1
Wages, salaries and interest from tourism	6·7
Gross profits before tax from tourism	2·6
GDP at factor cost from tourism	9·3
Tourism multiplier $= \dfrac{9·3}{10·6} =$	0·88

5   Chenery and Clark (1967) pp. 33–4.

6   Most imports are channelled through the distribution sector along with a heterogeneous bundle of locally produced goods and even some services. It is very difficult in practice to identify which of the purchases of each sector from distribution are imports and which are not. C.f. O'Loughlin (1966) and Bryden (1970).

7   The A matrix is given in Appendix Table 9A.2. The I matrix is simply a matrix of corresponding size which has unity in its leading diagonal and zeros elsewhere.

8   The computations were carried out on a computer using the MM–1A program kindly suggested and compiled by Mr Ian Gillespie. This program is loosely based on one prepared by Lucy Joan Slater described in detail in *Fortran Programs for Economists,* University of Cambridge Department of Applied Economics Occasional Papers No. 13, Cambridge University Press, 1967.

In other words, on average, and making the usual input—output assumptions, the tourist dollar yielded only 88 cents of GDP at factor cost. Direct, indirect and induced imports were a very high proportion of tourist expenditures, showing the very high import content of elements of tourist expenditure and expenditures in general in Antigua.

It is implicit in the above analysis that by utilising fixed coefficients in production, it is assumed that the output of each supplying sector will grow as total final demand grows. But the analysis in Chapter 3 identified at least one important sector in which this is not likely to be the case, namely domestic agriculture. Although the purchases of the tourist sectors directly from domestic agriculture are in most cases very small, the treatment of the distribution sector may partly conceal this fact.[9] One rather crude way of dealing with these problems is to exclude the agricultural sectors from the matrix.[10] The inputs which would have been purchased from the domestic agriculture sector — mainly food — are then transferred to imports, which is what has tended to happen in practice in most of the islands during the decade.[11] Excluding the agricultural sectors yields an 11 X 11 matrix with adjusted coefficients for the sales of the distribution sector (through which the bulk of the inputs are shown as being purchased) and for the direct input coefficients. The adjusted A matrix is given in Appendix Table 9A.3.

The exercise is then repeated, and the revised multiplier is shown in Table 9.4 below. The increased imports and reduced value for the multiplier are not unexpected in the light of the adjustments carried out. The fact that the changes are not more significant only reflects the already small role of domestic agriculture in Antigua's economy in 1963, and the very small purchases from this sector directly or indirectly as a result of tourist expenditures.

Table 9.4 *The tourist multiplier with static domestic agriculture*

	$ million
Imports	9·2
Wages, salaries and interest	6·2
Profits and rent	2·3
Total GDP	8·6
Tourist multiplier	0·81

A second adjustment is required to take cognisance of the very considerable underutilisation of capacity in the hotels industry during the period in question. Clearly if one is attempting to approach some concept of a 'marginal tourist multiplier', this will be important as hotel profits are highly dependent on adequate utilisation of capacity, and input coefficients in the hotel sector can be expected to change significantly as occupancy rates change.[12] Hotel capacity is generally defined

9 See footnote 6 above.

10 The export agriculture sector is redundant in any case, since its sales are almost exclusively to the rest of the world, by definition.

11 See Chapter 3.

12 This was demonstrated in Chapter 7.

in terms of bed occupancy rates over the year. That is, if all beds were full for every night in the year 100 per cent occupancy would be achieved. This is clearly almost impossible to achieve for three main reasons:

(a) Hotels often close for a period at least for maintenance work and sometimes for several months during the quiet period.
(b) Seasonal fluctuations in tourism in general.
(c) A substantial proportion of visitors are single, but rooms are overwhelmingly double.

The prevailing occupancy rates in the Caribbean were discussed in Chapter 7. In Antigua, occupancy rates were 29·3 in 1963, improving slightly to 32·7 per cent by 1967.[13]

At occupancy rates of 29·3 per cent, profitability cannot help but be low in spite of relatively high charges. The data presented in Chapter 7 suggest that if the incremental tourists are increasing the occupancy and revenue of existing hotels to any significant degree (rather than merely moving to new hotels operating at the same occupancy levels), then the input structure will change. This changing input structure will affect the size of the multiplier. In order to illustrate this, the data in Chapter 7 were used to compute possible changes in the input coefficients as occupancy rates increased. The revised coefficients for the hotel sector are shown in Table 9.5 below.

Table 9.5 *Revised input structure and input coefficients assuming that marginal tourist receipts accrue to existing hotels, effectively increasing capacity utilisation*

Recipient sector	Base year input[a] $000 EC	Percentage[b] increase %	Revised input $000 EC	Revised coefficients
1	450·0	+ 11	499·5	0·06948
2	0·0		0·0	0·00000
3	1,685·5	+ 13[c]	1,904·6	0·26494
4	80·0	+ 9	87·2	0·01213
5	82·6	+ 12	92·5	0·01287
6	0·0	–	0·0	0·00000
7	170·0	+ 8	183·6	0·02554
8	0·0	–	0·0	0·00000
9	2,214·7	+ 9	2,414·0	0·33580
10	85·7	+ 38.4	118·6	0·01650
11	346·9	+ 9	378·1	0·05260
12 (imports)	900·3	(residual)	1,510·7	0·21015
	6,015·7	+ 19·5[d]	7,188·8	1·00001

Notes:
[a] Already adjusted to take account of the static agricultural sector – see above.
[b] Based on Table 7.10.
[c] This is lower than might be expected, referring as it does to purchases from the distribution sector – a large part of the 'cost of sales' element. However, the evidence suggests that a large part of marginal purchases may be imported directly by the hotel and this is taken into account in the above.
[d] Represents a resonable annual increase in tourist receipts (c.f. Chapter 6, Table 6.11).

13 *Economic Survey and Projections,* Antigua. British Development Division in the Caribbean, 1969.

These revised coefficients replace the original coefficients in the A matrix and the computation is repeated using the same final demand vector and holding the other coefficients constant. The results are given in Table 9.6

Table 9.6 *The tourist multiplier with rising utilisation of hotel capacity*

Tourist receipts	$10·6 m. (EC)
Imports	9·3
Wages, salaries and interest	5·8
Profit and rent	2·2
Total GDP f.c.	8·1
Tourist multiplier	0·77

The above adjustments therefore indicate that considerable reductions of the multiplier are possible at the 'margin', due to changing coefficients as hotel capacity increases. The capacity argument is a central one, since it reveals a dilemma. The concept of the multiplier is only valid in a situation where resources are idle and have no opportunity cost.[14] Yet as soon as we admit underutilisation of capacity we must admit a changing cost structure, and hence move in a world of changing coefficients.[15]

Another approach to the problem of changing input coefficients is to examine the marginal changes in inputs between two years for given changes in gross output. An attempt has been made to do this using the hotel sector accounts for Antigua in 1962 and 1963, and computing marginal coefficients. The calculations are shown in Table 9.7 below.

Table 9.7 *Antigua hotels sector – marginal inputs 1962–3 and marginal input coefficients for the hotels sector*

Receiving sector	Marginal input	Marginal coefficient
1	49·5	0·04220
2	0·0	0·00000
3	219·1	0·18677
4	7·2	0·00614
5	9·9	0·00844
6	0·0	0·00000
7	13·6	0·01159
8	0·0	0·00000
9	199·3	0·16989
10	32·9	0·02805
11	31·2	0·02660
12	610·4	0·52032
	1,173·1	1·00000

Source: Derived from O'Loughlin (1965).

14 In *sensu stricto* where the multiplier refers to real income effects.

15 Technically, the inputs are not just a function of the level of output, but also of the degree of capacity utilisation.

A comparison of these coefficients with the two previous sets of coefficients is shown in Table 9.8 below, since, in theory, the marginal coefficients ought to give some guidance as to the adjustments necessary in the average coefficients, *ceteris paribus*. In practice, the highly restrictive assumptions of this type of analysis render the utility of such comparisons rather doubtful.

Table 9.8 *Comparison of unadjusted, adjusted and marginal coefficients – Antigua hotels sector*

	1963 unadjusted	1963 with adjustment for capacity	1963 marginal
1	0·07480	0·06948	0·04220
2	0·00000	0·00000	0·00000
3	0·30511	0·26494	0·18677
4	0·01330	0·01213	0·00614
5	0·01373	0·01287	0·00844
6	0·00000	0·00000	0·00000
7	0·02826	0·02554	0·01159
8	0·00000	0·00000	0·00000
9	0·36815	0·33580	0·16989
10	0·01425	0·01650	0·02805
11	0·05767	0·05260	0·02660
12	0·12472	0·21015	0·52032

Source: Tables 9.5 and 9.7 and Appendix Table 9A.3.

While the accuracy of the marginal coefficients must be doubtful given the difficulties of measurement of the aggregates, their value does indicate that the direction of the adjustments which we had made to allow for changes in capacity utilisation were right and, if anything, underestimated. It is perhaps notable, for example, that some 52 per cent of additional purchases were payments for imports and other overseas services between 1962 and 1963.[16]

Using the marginal coefficients for the hotels sector, and proceeding as before, the tourist multiplier drops to as low as 0·58.

In order to test the effect of differing hotel input structures in the Caribbean, three other computations are carried out using the hotel input structure of other Caribbean islands with more respectable occupancy rates — notably the structure of inputs in the hotels industries of the British Virgin Islands and the Cayman Islands, again on the assumption that the agricultural sector remained static. The results are summarised in Table 9.9.

Table 9.9 *Summary of Further Computations carried out using Antigua Matrix[a] multiplier*

1	Antigua 1963 matrix with Cayman Islands hotel input structure	0·76
2	Antigua 1967 matrix with British Virgin Islands hotel input structure	0·72
3	Antigua matrix with average hotel input structure for 3 islands	0·76

Note:
[a] See also Chapter 7, Table 7.9, for the comparative input structures in the three islands.

16 But the marginal coefficients are not corrected for price change which could substantially affect the coefficients.

The principal conclusion appears to be that the variations in the hotel input structure within the smaller Caribbean islands studied have only a small effect on the size of the multiplier, but this is probably only a reflection of the very high degree of openness which is characteristic of these three economies.[17]

So far, and with the exception of the agricultural sector, constant coefficients for other sectors of the economy have been assumed. This too is unrealistic. The structure of the rest of the economy is important for the size of the multiplier — an economy with relatively weak internal relationships between sectors will have a smaller multiplier than one with relatively strong internal relationships or linkages, given a similar structure in the hotels industry and a similar pattern of tourist receipts.[18]

To illustrate the effect of the structure of the rest of the economy on the size of the tourist multiplier, the structure of two other Caribbean islands with vastly different characteristics has been analysed. Firstly, the Cayman Islands, which is perhaps the most 'open' of all Caribbean economies with extremely weak inter-sectoral linkages.[19] Secondly, Dominica, which, of the smaller islands, has probably one of the strongest economic structures. In the case of Dominica, the national accounts data contain no division for a hotels sector, this being too insignificant at the time to warrant such a distinction.[20] To overcome this we merely substitute the Antigua 1963 hotels sector input structure into the matrix. This may however be slightly unfair, since at that time the structure of the hotel industry in Dominica differed substantially from that in Antigua. The degree of local ownership was substantially greater, partly because the sector was very small, and observation suggests that very real efforts were being made by several hotels and guest houses to purchase local goods.

The tourist multipliers resulting from this exercise are:

for the Cayman Islands   0·65
for Dominica   1·195

This type of variation illustrates the danger of using the same multiplier for evaluating the impact of tourism in what are often regarded as fairly similar economies.[21]

So far we have been concerned with GDP multipliers. This takes no account of the distinction between GDP and what might be termed 'income to nationals' which, it is argued, is what government economic policy is primarily concerned with. GDP includes the following payments which do not accrue to nationals:

(a) Profits accruing to foreign owned firms or shareholders.

(b) Wages and salaries of non-nationals working in the territory concerned.

17 See also Chapter 3.

18 We ignore, for the present, the effect of tourist development itself on the structural characteristics of the economy, since we are dealing essentially with the short period of one or two years. The structural effects of tourism are discussed in Chapter 3 and Chapter 5.

19 The Cayman Islands matrix was the result of some research carried out by the author there in 1969, and is reproduced in Appendix Table 9.A4.

20 The Dominica matrix is taken from Bartell (1965), adjusted in the same way as the Antigua matrix.

21 As, for example, in the *Zinder Report*.

It is argued that these items are very significant in the hotels sector and, to a lesser extent, in other sectors. Some evidence to support this contention was presented in Chapter 7.

For the purposes of the present analysis, two separate and distinct points require discussion: first, that part of profits, wages and salaries which is remitted *directly* and therefore has no further multiplier effects within the economy; second, that part of profits, wages and salaries which accrues ultimately to non-nationals within the economy or outside it and which does not form part of the *objective function* which the government is seeking to maximise. The procedure of aggregating all wages and salaries into one 'sector' — namely households — and gross profits into another — namely profit appropriation — conceals that part which is remitted directly, which ought properly to be treated as an import by each sector, and that part which accrues to non-nationals, which ought to be identified separately for the reasons already discussed.[22] The first point — the failure to identify for each sector the direct remittances of profits, wages and salaries — leads to an overstatement of the tourist multiplier if, as it is argued is the case in the Caribbean, this feature is liable to be of greater significance in the tourist industry than in the economy as a whole.

The second point leads to an overstatement of the multiplier in so far as we are interested in income to nationals.[23] It is possible to conclude *a priori* that the ITN multiplier is, in the circumstances of the Caribbean, likely to be significantly lower — in some cases substantially lower — than the GDP multiplier.

A further source of error arises from the inclusion of the aggregate households sector within the matrix, so that induced income effects may be calculated. Defining a consumption function in this way ignores the differences in the pattern of consumption as between different income groups, the effect of income levels, even with 'neutral' changes in distribution, on the absolute volume of consumption as well as its pattern, and the possibility discussed earlier that tourism itself may have some impact on the structure of consumption either through the effect on supply or through the effect on demand in respect of different commodities.[24] Again, if the theoretical arguments and empirical evidence presented in earlier chapters are accepted, it seems likely that factors are at work which tend still further to reduce the value of the tourist multiplier at the margin.

The multiplier of hotel visitors' expenditure

The fact that visitors to hotels have a different pattern of expenditure than do other visitors was demonstrated in Chapter 6. The effect of this may be analysed by using the pattern of expenditure identified as the final demand column and tracing through the effects of this expenditure in the usual way. As might be expected, the resulting 'multipliers' are somewhat smaller than for tourist expenditure as a whole, principally because of the different consumption patterns of the various groups of tourists — in essence, categories of hotel visitors' expenditure have, in general, a higher import content than do most other visitor groups, especially those — mainly West Indians —

22 See the arguments in Chapter 5 and the evidence of Chapter 7.

23 See also Chapter 5.

24 See also Chapter 3 and Chapter 5. By excluding domestic agriculture, however, *some* account is taken of these features.

who stay with friends and relatives; the outstanding exception is cruise ship tourists whose expenditure has the highest import content of all.[25]

In order to identify the multiplier of hotel visitors' expenditure at different occupancy rates, an analysis was carried out of the actual and projected accounts of a 100-room hotel project in Antigua, which show various categories of expenditure at a range of occupancy rates. As many of these data are used for the subsequent cost–benefit analysis, the results of this analysis and the assumptions made in order to convert the categories of expenditure appearing in the financial accounts into the national accounting framework are shown in Appendix 9.B1 and Appendix 9.B2. The estimates of purchases by sector so derived are also shown in Appendix 9.B2.

The input coefficients so derived are used to replace the hotels sector coefficients in the original 13 × 13 matrix. A pattern of final demand corresponding to the pattern of hotel visitors' expenditure in Antigua (1963) was then fed into the model in the same way as before, and the 'tourist multiplier' calculated for each occupancy rate. The results may be summarised as in Table 9.10.

Table 9.10 *'Multiplier' of hotel visitors' expenditure at different occupancy rates*

Occupancy rate:	31·8%	45%	55%	65%
Tourist expenditures	1,000·00	1,000·00	1,000·00	1,000·00
Household receipts[a]	490·28	467·83	452·53	442·57
Gross profits	193·78	209·24	204·40	201·02
GDP	684·06	677·07	656·93	643·59
Imports	776·90	896·62	899·44	901·35
Multiplier	0·68406	0·67707	0·65693	0·64359

Note:
[a] Less distributed profits, otherwise double-counted.

This analysis, apart from confirming our earlier work on the effect of occupancy rates on the multiplier, confirms that the multiplier of hotel visitors' expenditure tends to be somewhat lower than for tourist expenditure by all groups of visitors.

Conclusions

This chapter has been concerned with the value of the tourist multiplier in the smaller islands of the Commonwealth Caribbean, and with identifying the empirical significance of dropping various key assumptions which underlie this type of multiplier analysis. In particular, the effects of: allowing imports to substitute for domestic agricultural product; allowing input coefficients in the hotel industry to change with utilisation of hotel capacity; making allowance directly for remittances of wages and salaries and profits and the ultimate accruals of value added to non-nationals; and distinguishing between the multiplier of hotel visitors' expenditure and the general tourist multiplier were analysed. In general, as we get closer to identifying with reality, so the value of the real income effects of tourist expenditure is reduced.

25 See also Chapter 6, Tables 6.15 and 6.16.

No doubt the analysis could be extended, were data available, to allow for changing coefficients throughout the economy resulting from capacity utilisation changes, relative price changes as a result of changing supply and demand conditions, and switching of other inputs to or from imports, depending on resource availabilities. If this were done for each sector one would in fact be coming very close to an iterative programming approach of the kind discussed in Chapter 5. As things stand at present, the multipliers derived above do not mean very much. Specifically, they give no guidance as to the merits of tourist development as compared with alternatives.

The criticisms of the multiplier approach are discussed in detail in Chapter 5. It is necessary now to move on to apply the cost—benefit approach to the problem and to see whether this offers more guidance to the policy maker, and this is the concern of Chapter 10.

Appendix Table 9.A1 *Inter-Industry Transactions Table: Antigua, 1963 ($000 EC)*

Payments to ↓ / Receipts from →	1 Export agriculture	2 Other agriculture	3 Construction and engineering	4 Manufacturing	5 Distribution	6 Transport	7 Finance and insurance	8 Hotel industry	9 Other services	10 Rent-of-dwellings	11 Households	12 Profit appropriation	13 Government	14 Savings and Investment	15 Rest of the world	1–15 Total receipts
1 Export agriculture	–	37·0	–	75·0	178·0	–	6·1	–	–	–	–	–	–	90·0	6,161·3	6,547·4
2 Other agriculture	50·0	–	3·8	3·8	692·3	6·0	–	150·0	–	–	575·7	–	30·0	–	115·0	1,626·6
3 Construction & engineering	750·0	32·0	–	12·0	85·0	520·5	19·7	450·0	25·1	200·0	129·8	–	200·0	7,959·4	–	10,383·5
4 Manufacturing	–	–	–	–	972·3	–	–	–	–	–	420·8	–	3·7	–	52·0	1,448·8
5 Distribution	1,280·6	241·6	720·1	20·0	–	375·0	72·5	1,685·5	48·7	–	16,725·6	–	641·0	16·0	3,762·7	25,589·3
6 Transport	388·5	98·0	90·2	5·0	346·2	–	46·0	80·0	10·0	–	250·8	–	60·0	–	860·0	2,234·7
7 Finance and insurance	140·0	20·0	30·2	–	340·0	86·0	–	82·6	–	135·0	247·6	–	50·2	–	220·0	1,351·6
8 Hotel industry	5·1	–	–	–	4·0	–	5·0	–	–	–	250·6	–	15·0	–	5,736·0	6,015·7
9 Other services	80·9	–	77·0	3·5	27·0	–	9·0	170·0	–	30·6	506·3	–	234·0	–	170·7	1,309·0
10 Rent-of-dwellings	–	–	–	–	–	–	40·0	–	–	–	1,819·9	–	5·7	–	250·0	2,115·6
11 Households	2,508·1	587·4	3,225·6	584·2	2,450·0	225·0	800·0	2,214·7	509·5	–	–	5,707·6	5,513·4	–	1,945·7	26,271·2
12 Profit appropriation	649·2	544·0	773·1	80·3	1,390·0	745·2	230·0	85·7	668·0	1,650·0	–	–	–	–	375·0	7,240·1
13 Government	215·0	56·6	262·0	9·3	3,345·0	260·0	30·0	346·9	32·0	100·0	2,229·9	280·0	–	–	967·1	8,134·1
14 Savings and investment	–	–	–	–	–	–	–	–	–	–	2,514·2	1,037·9	447·8	–	4,065·5	8,065·4
15 Rest of the world	480·0	10·0	–	655·7	15,759·2	17·0	43·3	750·3	15·7	–	600·0	215·0	933·3	–	–	24,681·0
1–15 Total payments	6,547·4	1,626·6	10,383·4	1,448·8	25,589·3	2,234·7	1,351·6	6,015·7	1,309·0	2,115·6	26,271·2	7,240·1	8,134·1	8,065·4	24,681·0	

Source: O'Loughlin (1965).

Appendix Table 9.A2 *Matrix of technical coefficients* **A** *Antigua 1963 13 × 13*

	1	2	3	4	5	6	7	8	9	10	11	12	13	Vector of final demand
1	0·00000	0·02275	0·00000	0·05177	0·00696	0·00000	0·00451	0·00000	0·00000	0·00000	0·00000	0·00000	0·00000	0·0
2	0·00764	0·00000	0·00037	0·00262	0·02705	0·00268	0·00000	0·02493	0·00000	0·00000	0·02191	0·00000	0·00369	0·0
3	0·11455	0·01967	0·00000	0·00828	0·00332	0·23292	0·01458	0·07480	0·01917	0·09454	0·00494	0·00000	0·02459	0·0
4	0·00000	0·00000	0·00000	0·00000	0·03800	0·00000	0·00000	0·00000	0·00000	0·00000	0·01602	0·00000	0·00045	0·0
5	0·19559	0·14853	0·06935	0·01380	0·00000	0·16781	0·05364	0·28018	0·03720	0·00000	0·63665	0·00000	0·07880	2,900·2
6	0·03934	0·06025	0·00869	0·00345	0·01353	0·00000	0·03403	0·01330	0·00764	0·00000	0·00955	0·00000	0·00738	860·0
7	0·02138	0·01230	0·00291	0·00000	0·01329	0·03848	0·00000	0·01373	0·00000	0·00000	0·00942	0·00000	0·00955	220·0
8	0·00078	0·00000	0·00000	0·00000	0·00016	0·00000	0·00370	0·00000	0·00000	0·06381	0·00952	0·00000	0·00617	5,176·1
9	0·01236	0·00000	0·00742	0·00242	0·00106	0·00000	0·00666	0·02826	0·00000	0·00000	0·01927	0·00000	0·00184	170·0
10	0·00000	0·00000	0·00000	0·00000	0·00000	0·00000	0·02959	0·00000	0·00000	0·01446	0·06927	0·00000	0·02877	230·0
11	0·38307	0·36112	0·31065	0·40323	0·09574	0·10068	0·59189	0·36815	0·38923	0·00000	0·00000	0·78833	0·00070	975·0
12	0·09915	0·33444	0·07446	0·05543	0·05432	0·33347	0·20716	0·01425	0·51031	0·77992	0·00000	0·00000	0·67781	0·0
13	0·03284	0·03480	0·02523	0·00642	0·13073	0·11635	0·02220	0·05767	0·02445	0·04727	0·08488	0·03867	0·00000	22·0
Primary input vector	0·07331	0·00615	0·50093	0·45258	0·61585	0·00761	0·03204	0·12472	0·01199	0·00000	0·02284	0·02970	0·11474	
Savings vector	0·00000	0·00000	0·00000	0·00000	0·00000	0·00000	0·00000	0·00000	0·00000	0·00000	0·09573	0·14330	0·05506	

This is the 'A' matrix. This is converted to a Leontief $(I - A)$ matrix by subtracting it from the identity matrix I.
$(I - A)$ is inverted where I is the identity matrix.
$(I - A)^{-1}$ = Leontief inverse.

Appendix Table 9.A3 A Matrix Antigua 1963: no marginal purchases from or sales to agricultural assumption

| | | | | | (i = row no.)
(j = col. no.) A matrix I | | | | | | |
col. / row	1	2	3	4	5	6	7	8	9	10	11
1	0·00000	0·00828	0·00332	0·23292	0·01458	0·07480	0·01917	0·09454	0·00494	0·00000	0·02459
2	0·00000	0·00000	0·03800	0·00000	0·00000	0·00000	0·00000	0·00000	0·01602	0·00000	0·00045
3	0·06972	0·06819	0·00000	0·17049	0·05815	0·30511	0·03720	0·00000	0·65856	0·00000	0·08249
4	0·00869	0·00345	0·01343	0·00000	0·03403	0·01330	0·00764	0·00000	0·00955	0·00000	0·00738
5	0·00291	0·00000	0·01329	0·03848	0·00000	0·01373	0·00000	0·06381	0·00942	0·00000	0·00617
6	0·00000	0·00000	0·00016	0·00000	0·00370	0·00000	0·00000	0·00000	0·00952	0·00000	0·00184
7	0·00742	0·00242	0·00106	0·00000	0·00666	0·02826	0·00000	0·01446	0·01927	0·00000	0·02877
8	0·00000	0·00000	0·00000	0·00000	0·02959	0·00000	0·00000	0·00000	0·06927	0·00000	0·00070
9	0·31065	0·40323	0·09574	0·10068	0·59189	0·36815	0·38923	0·00000	0·00000	0·78833	0·67781
10	0·07446	0·05543	0·05432	0·33347	0·20716	0·01425	0·51031	0·77992	0·00000	0·00000	0·00000
11	0·02523	0·00642	0·13073	0·11635	0·02220	0·05767	0·02445	0·04727	0·08488	0·03867	0·00000
12	0·50093	0·45258	0·64986	0·00761	0·03204	0·12472	0·01199	0·00000	0·02284	0·02970	0·11474
Primary inputs											
Final DD vector	0·0	0·0	2,900·2	860·0	220·0	5,176·1	170·7	230·0	975·0	0·0	22·0

Appendix Table 9.A4 *Cayman Islands a_{ij} matrix, 1968*

col / row	1	2	3	4	5	6	7	8	9	10	11	12	13	14
1	0·00000	0·03585	0·00826	0·05078	0·00000	0·00000	0·00000	0·00809	0·00000	0·00000	0·08445	0·00078	0·01768	0·00000
2	0·00000	0·00000	0·03976	0·03731	0·03442	0·00170	0·06517	0·03324	0·00000	0·00000	0·00204	0·02543	0·00900	0·00000
3	0·00510	0·01258	0·00000	0·00276	0·00619	0·18250	0·00988	0·13843	0·09577	0·00000	0·30768	0·00000	0·00159	0·00000
4	0·01614	0·22063	0·19029	0·00000	0·04213	0·15215	0·02172	0·12823	0·00000	0·02297	0·04100	0·02029	0·40328	0·00000
5	0·00680	0·03633	0·00619	0·00622	0·00000	0·04468	0·00326	0·06557	0·05224	0·00000	0·00000	0·00346	0·01040	0·00000
6	0·02039	0·00582	0·02949	0·00109	0·01927	0·00000	0·00380	0·00000	0·00000	0·00671	0·00027	0·01935	0·02617	0·00000
7	0·00000	0·02154	0·03306	0·00198	0·00964	0·02696	0·00000	0·00000	0·00000	0·00000	0·00000	0·01794	0·03595	0·00000
8	0·00000	0·00000	0·00054	0·00073	0·00000	0·00000	0·00109	0·00000	0·00000	0·00000	0·00000	0·05791	0·00208	0·00000
9	0·00000	0·00000	0·00000	0·00000	0·00000	0·00000	0·00000	0·00381	0·00000	0·00000	0·00000	0·01575	0·05096	0·00000
10	0·00017	0·00173	0·00118	0·00673	0·00454	0·00338	0·16944	0·00239	0·03134	0·02168	0·00000	0·02253	0·00019	0·00000
11	0·00000	0·00000	0·00000	0·00000	0·00000	0·00000	0·00000	0·00000	0·00000	0·00000	0·00000	0·32255	0·00000	0·00000
12	0·00272	0·01557	0·01681	0·14448	0·03097	0·02489	0·02031	0·04137	0·00000	0·57161	0·00000	0·00000	0·00936	0·34950
13	0·56643	0·23966	0·38337	0·41616	0·41616	0·19023	0·47105	0·25692	0·00000	0·18787	0·18959	0·39247	0·00000	0·00000
14	0·27115	0·21969	0·10001	0·06154	0·09650	0·25245	0·05485	0·04679	0·81961	0·00000	0·00000	0·00000	0·00000	0·00000
15	0·11111	0·19060	0·21517	0·61640	0·34017	0·06750	0·17943	0·27519	0·00104	0·18916	0·33179	0·10121	0·19975	0·28396
Final demand vector*	0·0	0·0	0·0	176·5	0·0	53·6	12·9	1,433·5	62·0	0·0	0·0	14·3	61·5	0·0

* Sectoral tourist expenditures, 1968 in J$000.

APPENDIX 9-B1 ANALYSIS OF ACTUAL AND PROJECTED FINANCIAL ACCOUNTS FOR A 100 ROOM HOTEL IN ANTIGUA CIRCA 1963 ($000 EC)

		(Projected)		
Occupancy rate:	*31·8% (Actual)*	*45%*	*55%*	*65%*
Sales, total	*1,029·5*	*1,554·0*	*1,819·5*	*2,079·7*
Expenses				
Payroll	226·9	233·3	255·7	279·6
Food	141·5	164·9	193·7	222·6
Drink	20·4	55·2	64·6	74·0
Other food and drink[a]	56·9	102·0[e]	111·8[e]	122·5[e]
Rooms[b]	76·3	153·2	168·1	174·1
Transport	23·1	25·0[e]	27·0[e]	29·0[e]
Advertising and promotion	44·6	76·8	90·5	102·8
Administration	73·8	75·2	81·4	87·1
Heat and power	68·3	62·4	68·6	74·7
Repairs	32·5	40·5	44·9	49·4
Property tax	22·2	4·0	4·1	4·0
Visitors' tax[c]		32·8	40·1	47·4
Insurance	15·0	15·0	15·0	15·0
Total,	*801·5*	*1,042·3*	*1,165·4*	*1,282·2*
Gross profit[d]	228·0	511·7	654·1	797·5
Total	*1,029·5*	*1,554·0*	*1,819·5*	*2,079·7*

Notes:

[a] Unspecified

[b] Includes laundry for projections

[c] Calculated at current rates on occupancy levels

[d] To cover depreciation, interest on borrowed capital and net profit. Due to concessions there was no profits tax liability.

[e] For the projections these were amalgamated, the breakdown given above is thus based roughly on the actual data given at 31·8% occupancy.

As usual with financial accounts, little guidance is given regarding the *content* of the heads of expenditure given. In order to prepare sector accounts for the different occupancy rates, therefore, some assumptions regarding the content of these categories had to be made. These are detailed below.

Hotel input-structure at different occupancy rates

Occupancy rate:	Actual	Projected		
	31·8%	45%	55%	65%
Hotel inputs from:				
Sectors:				
1 Export agriculture	0·0	0·0	0·0	0·0
2 Other agriculture [a]	0·0	0·0	0·0	0·0
3 Construction and engineering [b]	32·5	40·5	44·9	49·4
4 Manufacturing [c]	0·0	0·0	0·0	0·0
5 Distribution [d]	238·4	314·7	356·1	391·4
6 Transport [e]	23·1	25·0	27·0	29·0
7 Finance and insurance [f]	15·0	15·0	15·0	15·0
8 Hotels	0·0	0·0	0·0	0·0
9 Other services [g]	28·4	101·0	110·9	121·2
10 Rent-of-dwellings	0·0	0·0	0·0	0·0
11 Households – payroll	226·9	235·3	255·7	279·6
12 Profit appropriation [h]	0·0	0·0	0·0	0·0
13 Government [i]	90·5	99·2	112·7	126·1
14 Imports [j]	374·7	723·3	897·2	1,068·0
Total	1,029·5	1,554·0	1,819·5	2,079·7

Notes and Assumptions

[a] It is assumed that in this case no purchases are made from the domestic agriculture sector; reference to Table 7.9 will support the realism of this assumption.

[b] 'Repairs', although these may be carried out by the hotel itself the effect will be roughly the same.

[c] Assumes all 'power' expenditure is paid to government which runs the electricity service. There may be some purchases of locally produced soft drinks etc., but these will be small.

[d] This figure was arrived at by taking 70% of all 'purchases' – the remaining 30% are assumed to be imported directly. Total purchases were arrived at as follows:
Food – all
Drink – all
Other food and drink – 50%
Administration – all

[e] Again transport may be provided by the hotel itself, but we do not know this and it may be assumed that the cost profile would approximate that of the transport sector.

[f] Insurance premiums. These may well be paid directly to a foreign firm, but we have assumed that the risk is carried locally.

[g] Half of 'other food and drink' (entertainment services etc.) is assumed to accrue to this sector *plus*, for the projections, laundry expenditure at 50, 55 and 60 respectively.

[h] All gross profits assumed to be repatriated, and therefore go directly out as 'imports'.

[i] Taxes and 'power-heat', the latter assumed to mean electricity purchased from a government undertaking. Unfortunately the basic matrix does not identify a separate public utilities account.

[j] Residual item.

10   *A social cost–benefit approach to the measurement of the impact of tourism in the Caribbean*

The theoretical basis for the approach adopted in the case study presented in this chapter is outlined in Chapter 5. In essence, the 'project' consists of a hotel containing one hundred rooms, together with the public investment which is, on average, associated with this size of tourist project.[1] The costs and benefits associated with this project are identified and converted by the application of shadow pricing to a net stream of 'social benefits' for the assumed lifetime of the project which, in this case, is taken to be twenty years.[2] A number of versions of the analysis are undertaken, either to introduce more realistic – and more complex – assumptions, or to test the sensitivity of the results to the values of certain key variables. This is by now a fairly standard procedure where uncertainty regarding certain variables exists, or where the situation in different islands demands that a certain flexibility of approach is required.

The identification of costs and benefits
A project has two distinct phases, namely the construction phase and the operational phase. Construction of a project of this size would take between one and two years in the smaller islands of the Caribbean. The operational phase commences at the end of the construction phase and, for convenience, is divided into four sub-phases representing discrete increases in the utilisation of capacity at various stages in the life of the project.[3] The basic assumption here is that occupancy rates, which represent the utilisation of capacity in hotels, will increase as shown in Table 10.1.

Table 10.1 *Assumptions regarding utilisation of capacity of the hotel during the operational phase*

Operational years	Assumed occupancy rate %
1–3	31·8
4–8	45·0
9–14	55·0
15–	65·0

1   See Chapter 8.

2   This is a simplification. Many items of equipment and machinery will obviously need replacement within this period, and buildings will obviously last longer. On the other hand, it is arguable that changes in taste and technology may render the buildings obsolete in twenty years' time or sooner. On the whole, twenty years seems quite reasonable for a project of this type.

3   This is simpler, computationally, than allowing the utilisation of capacity to grow at a constant percentage rate. Version *C* of the analysis examines the effect of the assumptions regarding utilisation of capacity in the hotel industry.

The assumed rise in occupancy rates is, in the light of past experience in the Caribbean,[4] quite optimistic, and ties in with the assumptions regarding increases in government promotional expenditure which are outlined below. It will be noted that the occupancy rates chosen are those for which data are already available for the input coefficients.[5]

During the construction phase, costs are derived in terms of primary inputs required in order to satisfy the final demand which comprises the private and public investments associated with the project. These primary inputs are then revalued at shadow prices. Benefits are simply the inflow of private foreign capital and, initially, are assumed to be equal to the investment cost of the hotel. But the fact that this inflow of foreign capital is accounted as a benefit means that profits accruing to the hotel during the operational stages must be counted as a cost. No adjustment to this benefit is required as it is already in terms of foreign exchange.

During the operational phase, costs are derived in the same way as primary inputs required in order to satisfy the level and pattern of final demand which is associated with hotel visitors' expenditure at the different levels of capacity utilisation. The basic assumptions in this respect are shown in Table 10.2 below.

Table 10.2 *Tourist receipts generated by visitors to the 100 room hotel at different occupancy rates*

Recipient sector	Proportion of total[a]	Receipts at occupancy rates of:[b]			
		31·8%	45·0%	55·0%	65·0%
5 Distribution	0·26	461·5	696·6	815·6	932·3
6 Transport	0·12	213·0	321·5	376·4	430·3
7 Finance	0·02	35·5	53·6	62·7	71·7
8 Hotels	0·58	1,029·5	1,553·9	1,819·5	2,079·6
9 Services	0·02	35·5	53·6	62·7	71·7
Totals	1·00	1,775·0	2,679·2	3,136·9	3,585·6

Notes:
[a] See Chapter 7.
[b] Based on figures in Appendix 9.B1 for the receipts of hotels. Receipts of other sectors are derived by applying the proportions given above. These proportions are assumed constant.

This table gives the final demands for the operational stages of the project at different occupancy rates. The benefits in terms of foreign exchange are simply the total tourist expenditures as given in Table 10.2 at the different occupancy rates.

Government promotional expenditure

If reports on tourism are to be believed, expenditure on promotion by governments is a necessary element in achieving 'respectable' occupancy rates. The corollary of this proposition is that if we are to assume steadily increasing occupancy rates, we must assume 'adequate' increases in governmental promotion expenditure. Most reports agree that such expenditure is currently far too low in the smaller Caribbean

4   See Chapter 7.

5   See Chapter 9, Appendix 9.B2.

islands,[6] and attribute persistently low occupancy rates at least partly to this fact. Consequently, it cannot be assumed that government expenditure as calculated via the transactions matrix is an adequate measure of all expenditures necessary to achieve reasonable occupancy rates. Additional promotional expenditures of $300 per room annually have therefore been assumed, not greatly out of line with the recommendation either of the *Tripartite Economic Survey* ($10 per visitor) or of the *Zinder Report* ($1 for every $6 generated in taxes).[7] This assumption ties in with the assumptions outlined earlier regarding the rise in occupancy rates throughout the operational phase. In view of the high proportion of promotional expenditures which are direct foreign exchange costs, no adjustment has been made to this item.

Government tax receipts

It was argued in Chapter 5 that adjustments have to be made to the primary input of the Government sector to allow for direct and indirect taxes which are, after deduction of social costs of collection and assessment, a gain to society. In order to simplify the analysis, and because there are in any case good arguments to support it, the social costs of tax collection and assessment are assumed to be equal to their average money cost. In view of the small relative size of this item this assumption is unlikely to affect the results significantly in any case.

Direct taxes are almost entirely personal income tax and company profits tax; indirect taxes are very largely import or related duties.[8]

Personal income taxes are calculated by applying the average ratio of personal direct taxes to wage and salary income, and applying this ratio to all wage and salary elements, The ratio which has been used in this case is 2·71 per cent, derived from Antigua data.

Profits taxes are similarly calculated by the use of an average ratio of profits tax to gross profits, in this case 4·17 per cent. It is true that some enterprises, including practically all hotels, are normally exempted from payment of profits taxes by incentives legislation of one sort or another.[9]

Because of this it is assumed that no profits tax is paid on profits associated with foreign investment. For 'domestic' profits, it is simply assumed that the *proportion* of gross profits subject to relief in the economy remains constant.

So far as indirect taxes are concerned, these are taken to be a constant proportion of government revenues. The proportion used in this analysis is 40 per cent.[10] In a more rigorous analysis, it may be important to recognise that relief of import duties on capital investment in the hotels sector (again as a result of incentives legislation) may be a significant factor. *Average* ratios do, of course, take some cognisance of this.

6 See, for example, the *Zinder Report* (1969) and the *Tripartite Economic Survey*.

7 Zinder, however, arrives at much higher levels of promotional expenditure per room or per tourist because of exaggerated estimates of taxes generated. See also Bryden and Faber (1971) and Chapter 11 below.

8 See Chapter 3.

9 See also Chapter 8.

10 See Chapter 3, Table 3.12. We are, of course, concerned only with *local* revenues here.

The assessment and collection of taxes itself involves a cost which falls on the local economy. Although the marginal cost of tax collection may be less than the average, it will be sufficient for our purposes to use an average cost of collection figure — and a fairly rough one at that — in view of the magnitudes involved. For direct taxes, I have calculated costs of collection at 15 per cent of revenue; for indirect taxes, 10 per cent. These costs are then deducted from government receipts.

Shadow prices

Apart from government, which is discussed above, and imports of goods and services (including foreign profits), which in the present analysis present no valuation problem, two other primary inputs remain for discussion, namely labour (which receives wages and salaries) and domestic capital (which receives gross domestic profits). The treatment of domestic profits is discussed in Chapter 5. Briefly, in the absence of capital coefficients and information about the utilisation of capacity in the other sectors of the economy, it is assumed that the profit after tax can be taken as the real cost of capital used in supplying the various goods and services directly and indirectly demanded as a result of tourist expenditure. In effect it is assumed (a) that the sectors in question have no excess capacity, and (b) that the returns on the investment required to generate the given levels of output in these sectors are no higher or lower than elsewhere in the economy.

There remains, therefore, the calculation of the shadow wage rate (SWR) to be applied to the market values of wages and salaries. Since it is not possible at this stage to identify the 'marginal project' in the Little—Mirrlees sense, the formula for deriving the value of s_o, the relative valuation of savings and consumption in the base year, is redundant. All that can be done is to make a reasonable 'guess' (which may be tantamount to a value judgement) as to what the value of this variable might be in the circumstances of the smaller Caribbean islands. This guess is that the value of s_o lies between $1\frac{1}{3}$ and 2. In other words, the stream of consumption generated by the marginal project in such economies, if discounted to the present at the consumption rate of interest, is equal to between 1·33 and 2·0 times the value of consumption foregone by investing in this marginal project.

The consumption of labour in the new employment created by the project, c, is assumed to be equal to its earnings less any taxes paid. In view of the very high proportion of traded goods in the consumption budget, it is not thought necessary to make any adjustment to account for consumption goods which are non-traded. Again, in view of the low rates of domestic savings in the Caribbean, and the lack of information regarding savings behaviour in lower income groups, it is not thought necessary to make any adjustment on this account.

Letting w = the wage rate in the 'new' employment
t = the rate of direct taxes on wages
d = the rate of import duty on goods consumed by the newly employed
c = the value of consumption at 'world' prices of the newly employed.
then, $c = w - wt - d(w - wt)$.

Evidence presented earlier in this study suggests values for t and d of 2·7 per cent and 10·0 per cent respectively.[11] Thus letting $w = 100, c = 87·6$.[12]

The marginal product of labour in alternative occupations, m, may well vary considerably as a proportion of c in the smaller islands of the Caribbean. There is little evidence from the Cayman Islands and the British Virgin Islands to suggest that labour in the tourist sector is well paid by comparison to other sectors, except possibly the primary sector.[13] Elsewhere in the region the wage of unskilled male labour tends to be higher in most sectors than it is in agriculture, although comparisons are difficult because the only statutory rates tend to be agricultural rates. For unskilled female labour there are, as has been argued elsewhere, rather few alternatives, and wage rates in the tourist sector seem to be everywhere low.[14] A reasonable guess as to the value of m in relation to c for unskilled labour in the region would be somewhere between 60 and 100 per cent.

For the purposes of this analysis a value of 0·74 has been chosen for the SWR. This value is consistent with the range of values for the variables discussed above, as is demonstrated in Table 10.3 below. However, a later version of the analysis tests the effect of this assumption on the results by allowing the SWR to fall to 0·55. But, as Table 10.3 shows, this would imply a very low value for m, the marginal product of labour in alternative occupations. Even if consumption and savings were assumed to be equally valuable ($s_o = 1$), in which case SWR $= m$, a marginal product of 0·55 in alternative occupations is implied.

Table 10.3 *Values of s, c and m which are consistent with the chosen values of the* SWR *of 74 and 55*[a]

SWR	s_o	c	m
0·74	1·333	0·876	0·692
0·74	1·666	0·876	0·650
0·74	2·000	0·876	0·600
0·55	1·333	0·876	0·444
0·55	1·666	0·876	0·334
0·55	2·000	0·876	0·224

Note:
[a] $w = 100$. The values are calculated from the formula SWR $= c - (1/s_o)(c - m)$ given in Chapter 5.

It is quite probable that situations exist in the Caribbean where the chosen SWR of 0·74 is too low, especially in situations of severe manpower shortage such as exist in the Cayman Islands and the British Virgin Islands. If the results prove to be sensitive to the value of the SWR, then this would indicate a need for further research effort in individual cases.

11 The rate of import duty is slightly higher than the average rate on food imports, but lower than the average rate on all imports. See also Chapter 3.

12 $c = 100 - 2·7 - 9·7 = 87·6$ according to the above formula.

13 Median earnings of farmers in the British Virgin Islands were the lowest of those groups studied. Elkan and Morley (1971) Table 2.8. See also Chapter 7.

14 See Chapter 7.

The accounting rate of interest (ARI)

So far the appropriate ARI has not been discussed. This is because the method of analysis employed is to discover the social rate of return on the project as outlined and then to discuss whether or not this is likely to exceed the ARI in the circumstances of the region.[15] The *minimal* ARI is taken to be around 6 per cent, following Little and Mirrlees. In practice, the ARI will probably be higher than this in the smaller Caribbean islands, but not substantially higher in view of the limited range of opportunities open to small open economies of this type. In such circumstances, an ARI of 10 to 12 per cent may well be rather high.[16]

The project: Version A

In this first version of the analysis it is assumed, summarily,

(1) That the hotel is totally financed by foreign capital inflow.

(2) That investment costs in respect of the hotel are equivalent to $27,500 EC per room, so that the total hotel investment (and private capital inflow) is $2·75 m.[17]

(3) That related investment in infrastructure by the government is the equivalent of 69 per cent of direct hotel investment or $1·90 m.[18]

(4) That all construction associated with the project is completed in one year and, correspondingly, that all facilities are operational by the second year.

(5) That all 'productive' sectors of the economy will 'respond' to demand-led requirements for inputs as determined by the coefficients of the (base-year) open Leontief matrix.

(6) That all wages and salaries are 'homogeneous' and accrue to nationals, so that the SWR is applied to all wages and salaries. The purpose of this assumption is to measure the effect of employment of non-nationals on the social benefits, by dropping the assumption in later versions.

(7) That, as a result of the additional promotional expenditures by government, occupancy rates will increase as outlined in Table 10.1.

(8) That the level and structure of tourist receipts will be as given in Table 10.2.

The set of final demands for the construction and operational phases of the project derived from assumptions (2), (3) and (8) above are then applied to the inverse of the open Leontief matrix in order to discover the direct and indirect requirements for primary inputs. Initially, keeping the agricultural sectors within the matrix, a 10 × 10 basic matrix derived from the 1963 Antigua inter-industry transactions table was employed for this purpose.[19]

15 See Chapter 5.

16 Little and Mirrlees 'would hope and expect that most developing countries could achieve 10 per cent.' Little and Mirrlees (1968), p. 96.

17 See the evidence of Chapter 7.

18 See the evidence of Chapter 8.

19 The full matrix is given in Appendix Table 9.A2, Chapter 9. The MM–1A computer program employed in this analysis was kindly suggested and supplied by Mr I.J. Gillespie. This program is based loosely on the MM.1A program detailed by Lucy Joan Slater in *Fortran Programs for Economists,* University of Cambridge Department of Applied Economics Occasional Papers, No. 13. Cambridge University Press, 1967.

The resulting primary input requirements are shown in Table 10.4 below.

Table 10.4 *Primary input requirements during construction and operation of the project Version A ($000 EC)*

Primary input	Construction private and public	Operation, with occupancy rates of:			
		31·8%	45·0%	55·0%	65·0%
Wages and salaries	1,521·8	445·7	572·9	643·3	714·6
Gross profits	408·5	192·4	310·6	357·2	402·1
Government receipts	169·0	226·2	297·6	342·5	384·8
Imports c.i.f.	2,550·8	910·7	1,498·1	1,793·9	2,075·1
Total	4,647·4	1,775·0	2,679·2	3,136·9	3,576·6

Note:
Totals may differ slightly from those given in Table 10.2 above owing to rounding in the computational process.

The primary inputs given in Table 10.4 are expressed in market prices, and have to be revalued to give costs at social prices in accordance with the argument in the text. The results of this revaluation are given in Table 10.5.

Table 10.5 *Revaluation of primary inputs, Version A*

Primary input, etc.	Construction	Operation, with occupancy rates of:			
		31·8%	45·0%	55·0%	65·0%
Wages etc.[a]	1,126·1	329·8	423·9	476·0	528·8
Profits[b]	408·5	192·4	310·6	357·2	402·1
Government[c]	75·9	127·6	166·4	191·7	215·5
Imports[d]	2,550·8	910·7	1,498·1	1,793·9	2,075·5
Incremental promotion[e]	30·0	30·0	30·0	30·0	30·0
Total costs	4,191·3	1,590·5	2,429·0	2,848·8	3,251·5
Foreign exchange receipts[f]	2,750·0	1,775·0	2,679·0	3,136·9	3,576·6
Net social benefits[g]	−1,441·3	+184·5	+250·2	+288·1	+325·1

Notes:
[a] Using an SWR of 74%
[b] No adjustment; see p.175 above and Chapter 5.
[c] Less 'net' taxes; see pp. 174−75 above.
[d] At c.i.f. valuation; see Chapter 5.
[e] See argument on p. 173 above.
[f] See Table 10.4 above.
[g] Foreign exchange receipts less social costs in terms of foreign exchange; see Chapter 5.

The mean costs and benefits of the flows implied by Table 10.5 and the assumptions regarding the life of the project and the rise in occupancy rates, together with the internal rate of return of the stream of net social benefits, are shown in Appendix Table 10.A1.[20]

The social rate of return given in this version is 15·47 per cent, which is relatively high. An examination of the mean present value suggests, as might be expected, a very high sensitivity to the value of imports and of foreign exchange receipts, and a reasonably high sensitivity to the value of shadow wages, gross profits and government expenditures.

Version B

In this version an attempt has been made to make the analysis more realistic by making the following amendments:

(1) Following the argument and adjustments made in Chapter 9, the agricultural sectors are excluded; purchases from other sectors, which are in any case small, are switched to imports.

(2) The construction of the project is now assumed to take place over two years instead of one, thus delaying the operational phase for a further year.

(3) An allowance is made, following the argument of Chapter 5 and the evidence of Chapter 7, for the proportion of wages and salaries accruing to expatriates directly and indirectly in the economy. We assume, conservatively, that of direct wages in the hotel, 40 per cent accrue to expatriates, and of direct and indirect wages in other sectors, 15 per cent accrue to expatriates.[21] Since direct wages in the hotel account for a about 40–50 per cent of the total wages and salaries created during the operational phase, a reasonable figure for the proportion of wages and salaries accruing to expatriates in the smaller islands would be 25 per cent.[22]

(4) Finally, an allowance is made for the possibility that a proportion of the hotel financing is raised locally in the form of a loan from the banking sector bearing interest at 8 per cent. Although in practice there does not seem to be a great deal of this type of financing in the smaller islands, it is certainly in the interests of investors to obtain such finance as long as their expected rate of return exceeds the rate of interest and they have no access to cheaper money elsewhere.[23] One may therefore expect some pressure by interested groups on the financial institutions to provide such financing. For the purposes of the present analysis it is assumed that one quarter of the hotel investment is financed by a locally raised loan. The effect of this is to reduce the initial foreign exchange inflows

20 Again the COBE computer program used for these computations was kindly supplied by Mr I.J. Gillespie. This program was written originally by Dr Ortwin Treutler for the Overseas Development Group.

21 See also Chapter 7.

22 $(40\% \times 0\cdot40) + (60\% \times 0\cdot15) = 25\%$. This is conservative – especially if one was applying the analysis to the Cayman Islands or the British Virgin Islands.

23 Thus if the expected overall rate of return on capital is 15 per cent, if one quarter of the investment if financed by an 8 per cent loan then the rate of return on the remaining equity investment will be correspondingly increased to nearly 17·5 per cent.

for hotel construction by 25 per cent, and to reduce the outflows of hotel profits during the operational phase by the interest payments on this sum.

The first two of these amendments affect the value of the primary input requirements, and the revised requirements are shown in Table 10.6 below.

Table 10.6 *Version B: primary input requirements, $000 EC*

Primary input etc.	Construction total	Operating phases at occupancy rates of:			
		31·8%	45·0%	55·0%	65·0%
Wages etc.	776·0	433·7	555·5	623·2	692·0
Profits	202·0	183·5	297·6	342·1	385·2
Government	84·2	224·6	295·3	339·8	381·8
Imports	1,280·8	933·3	1,530·8	1,831·8	2,117·6
Total	2,325·0[a]	1,775·0	2,679·9	3,136·9	3,576·6

Note:
[a] i.e. half of the total of $4·65 m.

The second two amendments affect the revaluation of these primary inputs at shadow prices as shown in Table 10.7 below.

Table 10.7 *Version B: revaluation of primary inputs*

Primary inputs etc.	Construction phases[a]	Operation, occupancy rates of			
		31·8%	45·0%	55·0%	65·0%
Expatriate salaries[b] etc.	194·0	108·4	138·9	155·8	173·0
Wages etc. of nationals[c]	430·7	240·7	308·3	345·9	384·1
Profits[d]	202·0	183·5	297·6	342·1	385·2
Government[e]	28·8	127·2	165·6	191·0	214·7
Imports, less interest[f]	1,280·8	878·3	1,475·8	1,776·8	2,062·6
Incremental promotion[g]	30·0	30·0	30·0	30·0	30·0
Total costs	2,166·3	1,568·1	2,416·2	2,841·6	3,249·6
Benefits[h]	1,031·2	1,775·0	2,679·2	3,136·9	3,576·6
Net social benefit[i]	−1,135·1	206·9	263·0	295·3	327·0

Notes:
[a] In each of the two years.
[b] 25% of unadjusted wages and salaries.
[c] Using a shadow wage rate of 74%.
[d] No adjustment
[e] Less net direct and indirect taxes.
[f] Interest on 25% of hotel construction costs at 8% per annum deducted during operating phases
[g] As in Version *A*.
[h] No adjustment. During construction phases, 75% of hotel investment.
[i] Foreign exchange receipts less total costs in terms of foreign exchange.

The resulting computation of mean present values and the internal rate of return of the net stream of social benefits is given in Appendix Table 10.A2. The internal rate of return given in this version is now only 8·63 per cent, which, assuming a *minimal* ARI of 6 per cent, must be regarded as marginal in the light of the conservative bias in the assumptions.

Since Version *B* gives a very significantly lower internal rate of return than Version *A*. Version *C, D* and *E* respectively were run in order to test the effect of, first, the matrix change, second, the change to a two-year construction period, and third, the assumption that a quarter of hotel investment was locally financed. The effect of the subdivision of wages and salaries was found by deduction.

Version C

This variant examines the effect of the matrix change only, that is to say, it examines the effect on the outcome of amending the implicit assumption of Version *A* that production from agriculture will be forthcoming to meet demand. As Appendix Table 10.A3 shows, moving from a 10 X 10 matrix to an 8 X 8 matrix, with corresponding adjustments to the coefficients, has a relatively small effect on the outcome. The internal rate of return of the net stream of social benefits is reduced from 15·47 per cent to 14·95 per cent, or by some 0·5 percentage points. This is partly a reflection of the already low 'linkages' with agriculture in Antigua, and one might expect the impact to be larger in some of the other islands of the group.

Version D

This variant examines the effect of both the matrix change and the change to a two-year construction period, with consequent delays in the benefits. Appendix Table 10.A4 shows the results of this analysis.

The introduction of the two-year construction period leads to a reduction in the internal rate of return from 14·95 per cent to 13·38 per cent per annum — or about 1·5 percentage points; rather more significant than the matrix change. This shows one of the effects of very small size, since it is in the very small islands that this assumption becomes more realistic — the impact of a construction project of this size becomes correspondingly more disruptive.

Version E

Finally, the assumption that 25 per cent of hotel investment is locally financed is introduced. The results are shown in Appendix Table 10.A5.

The introduction of the assumption that 25 per cent of hotel investment is locally financed by loan funds bearing an 8 per cent interest rate reduces the rate of return from 13·38 per cent to 10·92 per cent, a reduction of nearly 2·5 percentage points.

By deduction, the effect of the division of wages and salaries into those accruing to expatriates and those accruing to nationals further reduces the internal rate of return from 10·92 per cent to 8·63 per cent, a reduction of some 2·3 percentage points. These latter modifications are therefore clearly the most significant in the present analysis.

We may summarise the foregoing as in Table 10.8.

Table 10.8 *Summary of results: Version A to E showing effect of changes in assumptions*

Version	Key change in assumptions of previous version	IRR %	Change % points
A	nil	15·47	nil
C	Matrix and coefficients	14·95	0·52
D	Two-year construction	13·38	1·57
E	25% local finance of hotel investment	10·92	2·46
B	Division of wages and salaries	8·63	2·29

Version F

So far we have kept the shadow wage rate constant at 74 per cent, either for total wages and salaries, as in Version *A*, or for wages and salaries of nationals, as in Version *B*. In effect, however, the division of wages and salaries into those accruing to nationals and those accruing to expatriates in Version *B* is tantamount to raising the overall shadow wage rate to about 80 per cent. One would therefore expect the rate of return to be fairly sensitive to the shadow wage rate and this, indeed, is the case.

Version *F* utilises exactly the same assumptions as Version *B* above, with the exception that a shadow wage rate of 55 per cent is used for wages and salaries of nationals. The results, which show an increase in the internal rate of return to 13·67 per cent per annum, are shown in Appendix Table 10.A6. As mentioned earlier, the actual use of a shadow wage as low as this in the Caribbean might be very difficult to justify for any period of time.

Version G. Rising occupancy rates and incremental promotion expenditure

The examples so far assume fairly rapidly rising occupancy rates, linked with the higher levels of promotional expenditure by government. In fact, the experience of the last decade would tend to make one rather sceptical of these assumptions. In Version *G*, therefore, the assumption that government will spend an additional $30,000 per annum on promotion has been omitted. As a corollary of this, the occupancy rate is held at 31·8 per cent throughout the 18-year period following construction. In all other respects this version is the same as Version *B* above, with which the results may be compared.

Appendix Table 10.A7 gives the results of this test. The internal rate of return is reduced to 7·54 per cent per annum, or about 1·1 percentage points below that given in Version *B*. If we could believe that the promotional expenditure alone would have the effect of raising occupancy rates in the manner previously assumed, clearly it would be worthwhile *ceteris paribus* to undertake such expenditure since it would raise the rate of return to 8·63 per cent. But it would be a brave man indeed who would postulate such a rigid relationship in the absence of more reliable evidence. That apart, the rate of return is obviously not particularly sensitive to the assumptions made regarding the growth in occupancy rates, or to the inclusion of the relatively small amount of incremental promotion expenditure.

Private rates of return in hotel development

For comparative purposes, the private rates of return which are implied by the figures of private costs and revenues for the hotel alone are given in Appendix 10.B. If no local financing is assumed, and the rise in occupancy rates occurs as forecast, the private rate of return lies between 15½ and 16 per cent per annum over the life of the project. If it is assumed that 25 per cent of the hotel investment is financed by a local loan bearing interest at 8 per cent, then the private rate of return increases to between 17½ and 18 per cent per annum. It can be fairly concluded that, in any likely circumstances, private rates of return to hotel development in the smaller Caribbean islands exceed the social rates of return by a substantial margin.

Conclusions

The conclusions that can be drawn from this case study are necessarily tentative, in view of the nature of the assumptions which are required without much greater study of individual islands and the alternative opportunities open to them. It is felt that, for many if not most of the smaller islands, the assumptions err, if anything, on the conservative side, so that the social rates of return will, if anything, tend to be overstated. Nevertheless, even with these conservative assumptions, the social rates of return from hotel development are sufficiently close to the minimal accounting rate of interest to suggest that a high priority be put on further research in this field. At the very least, there seems to be a clear case for controlling the growth rate of the tourist industry much more rigidly than has hitherto been the practice of Caribbean governments.

The areas of further research which, on the basis of this analysis, would appear to have high priority, are as follows:

(1) The value of the shadow wage rate. The results are highly sensitive to this value; dropping the SWR from 74 to 55 results in an increase in the social rate of return of around 5 per cent. Two key variables are likely to be of importance here, *viz*
   (a) the proportion of wages and salaries accruing to non-nationals
   (b) the treatment of female labour.
   The first of these is an empirical problem; the second poses both empirical and theoretical questions of considerable significance for this analysis.
(2) The extent to which foreign investors have access to local loan funds at relatively low rates of interest.
(3) The value of public sector investment which is associated with hotel development at the margin.
(4) For the determination of both the SWR and the ARI, much closer comparative analysis of the alternative opportunities open to these small open economies.

Appendix Table 10.A1 *Social cost–benefit analysis Version A: 100-room hotel project*

Interest rates 10, 15, 20% per annum

Mean costs and benefits $000

Year		Shadow wages	Gross profits	Government production expenditure	Incremental promotion	Imports	Foreign exchange receipts	Total
1971	Construction	−1,126·10	−408·50	−75·90	−30·00	−2,550·80	2,750·00	−1,441·30
1972	31·8%	−329·80	−192·40	−127·60	−30·00	−910·70	1,775·00	184·50
1973	occupancy	−329·80	−192·40	−127·60	−30·00	−910·70	1,775·00	184·50
1974		−329·80	−192·40	−127·60	−30·00	−910·70	1,775·00	184·50
1975		−423·90	−310·60	−166·40	−30·00	−1,498·10	2,679·20	250·20
1976	45·0%	−423·90	−310·60	−166·40	−30·00	−1,498·10	2,679·20	250·20
1977	occupancy	−423·90	−310·60	−166·40	−30·00	−1,498·10	2,679·20	250·20
1978		−423·90	−310·60	−166·40	−30·00	−1,498·10	2,679·20	250·20
1979		−423·90	−310·60	−166·40	−30·00	−1,498·10	2,679·20	250·20
1980		−476·00	−357·20	−191·70	−30·00	−1,793·90	3,136·90	288·10
1981	55·0%	−476·00	−357·20	−191·70	−30·00	−1,793·90	3,136·90	288·10
1982	occupancy	−476·00	−357·20	−191·70	−30·00	−1,793·90	3,136·90	288·10
1983		−476·00	−357·20	−191·70	−30·00	−1,793·90	3,136·90	288·10
1984		−476·00	−357·20	−191·70	−30·00	−1,793·90	3,136·90	288·10
1985		−476·00	−357·20	−191·70	−30·00	−1,793·90	3,136·90	288·10
1986		−528·80	−402·10	−215·50	−30·00	−2,075·10	3,576·60	325·10
1987		−528·80	−402·10	−215·50	−30·00	−2,075·10	3,576·60	325·10
1988	65·0%	−528·80	−402·10	−215·50	−30·00	−2,075·10	3,576·60	325·10
1989	occupancy	−528·80	−402·10	−215·50	−30·00	−2,075·10	3,576·60	325·10
1990		−528·80	−402·10	−215·50	−30·00	−2,075·10	3,576·60	325·10

Mean present values $000

Rate (%)	Shadow wages	Gross profits	Government production expenditure	Incremental promotion	Imports	Foreign exchange receipts	Net
10	−4,648·55	−2,898·72	−1,471·75	−280·95	−14,798·49	24,738·43	639·99
15	−3,652·83	−2,164·79	−1,073·26	−215·95	−11,134·51	18,283·20	41·86
20	−3,045·77	−1,721·26	−831·13	−175·30	−8,932·67	14,385·03	−321·09

Internal rate of return is 15·47% per annum

Appendix Table 10.A2 *Social cost–benefit analysis version B*

Interest rates 5, 10, 15% per annum

Mean costs and benefits $000

Year	Expatriate wages	Shadow wages	Gross profits	Government production expenditure
1971	−194·00	−430·70	−202·00	−28·80
1972	−194·00	−430·70	−202·00	−28·80
1973	−108·40	−240·70	−183·50	−127·20
1974	−108·40	−240·70	−183·50	−127·20
1975	−108·40	−240·70	−183·50	−127·20
1976	−138·90	−308·30	−297·60	−165·60
1977	−138·90	−308·30	−297·60	−165·60
1978	−138·90	−308·30	−297·60	−165·60
1979	−138·90	−308·30	−297·60	−165·60
1980	−138·90	−308·30	−297·60	−165·60
1981	−155·80	−345·90	−342·10	−191·00
1982	−155·80	−345·90	342 10	−191·00
1983	−155·80	−345·90	−342·10	−191·00
1984	−155·80	−345·90	−342·10	−191·00
1985	−155·80	−345·90	−342·10	−191·00
1986	−173·00	−384·10	−385·20	−214·70
1987	−173·00	−384·10	−385·20	−214·70
1988	−173·00	−384·10	−385·20	−214·70
1989	−173·00	−384·10	−385·20	−214·70
1990	−173·00	−384·10	−385·20	−214·70

Year	Incremental promotion	Imports	Foreign exchange receipts	Total
1971	−30·00	−1,280·80	1,031·20	−1,135·10
1972	−30·00	−1,280·80	1,031·20	−1,135·10
1973	−30·00	−878·30	1,775·00	206·90
1974	−30·00	−878·30	1,775·00	206·90
1975	−30·00	−878·30	1,775·00	206·90
1976	−30·00	−1,475·80	2,679·20	263·00
1977	−30·00	−1,475·80	2,679·20	263·00
1978	−30·00	−1,475·80	2,679·20	263·00
1979	−30·00	−1,475·80	2,679·20	263·00
1980	−30·00	−1,475·80	2,679·20	263·00
1981	−30·00	−1,776·80	3,136·90	295·30
1982	−30·00	−1,776·80	3,136·90	295·30
1983	−30·00	−1,776·80	3,136·90	295·30
1984	−30·00	−1,776·80	3,136·90	295·30
1985	−30·00	−1,776·80	3,136·90	295·30
1986	−30·00	−2,062·60	3,576·60	327·00
1987	−30·00	−2,062·60	3,576·60	327·00
1988	−30·00	−2,062·60	3,576·60	327·00
1989	−30·00	−2,062·60	3,576·60	327·00
1990	−30·00	−2,062·60	3,576·60	327·00

Mean present values $000

Rate (%)	Expatriate wages	Shadow wages	Gross profits	Government production expenditure
5	−1,967·75	−4,368·54	−3,727·36	−1,978·50
10	−1,398·23	−3,104·16	−2,505·52	−1,292·70
15	−1,074·55	−2,385·57	−1,820·83	−907·50

Rate (%)	Incremental promotion	Imports	Foreign exchange receipts	Net
5	−392·56	−19,504·12	32,735·25	796·41
10	−280·95	−13,167·33	21,531·76	−717·14
15	−215·95	−9,637·12	15,270·53	−770·99

Internal rate of return is 8·63% per annum

Appendix Table 10.A3 Version C: Effect of matrix change only

Interest rates 5, 10, 15% per annum

Mean costs and benefits $000

Year	Wage/salary	Gross profits	Government production expenditure	Incremental promotion	Imports	Foreign exchange receipts	Total
1971	−1,148·40	−404·00	−57·60	−30·00	−2,561·60	2,750·00	−1,451·60
1972	−320·90	−183·50	−127·20	−30·00	−933·30	1,775·00	180·10
1973	−320·90	−183·50	−127·20	−30·00	−933·30	1,775·00	180·10
1974	−320·90	−183·50	−127·20	−30·00	−933·30	1,775·00	180·10
1975	−411·00	−297·60	−165·60	−30·00	−1,530·80	2,679·20	244·20
1976	−411·00	−297·60	−165·60	−30·00	−1,530·80	2,679·20	244·20
1977	−411·00	−297·60	−165·60	−30·00	−1,530·80	2,679·20	244·20
1978	−411·00	−297·60	−165·60	−30·00	−1,530·80	2,679·20	244·20
1979	−411·00	−297·60	−165·60	−30·00	−1,530·80	2,679·20	244·20
1980	−461·20	−342·10	−191·00	−30·00	−1,831·80	3,136·90	280·80
1981	−461·20	−342·10	−191·00	−30·00	−1,831·80	3,136·90	280·80
1982	−461·20	−342·10	−191·00	−30·00	−1,831·80	3,136·90	280·80
1983	−461·20	−342·10	−191·00	−30·00	−1,831·80	3,136·90	280·80
1984	−461·20	−342·10	−191·00	−30·00	−1,831·80	3,136·90	280·80
1985	−461·20	−342·10	−191·00	−30·00	−2,117·60	3,576·60	317·00
1986	−512·10	−385·20	−214·70	−30·00	−2,117·60	3,576·60	317·00
1987	−512·10	−385·20	−214·70	−30·00	−2,117·60	3,576·60	317·00
1988	−512·10	−385·20	−214·70	−30·00	−2,117·60	3,576·60	317·00
1989	−512·10	−385·20	−214·70	−30·00	−2,117·60	3,576·60	317·00
1990	−512·10	−385·20	−214·70	−30·00	−2,117·60	3,576·60	317·00

Mean present values $000

Rate (%)	Wage/Salary	Gross profits	Government production expenditure	Incremental promotion	Imports	Foreign exchange receipts	Net
5	−6,263·63	−4,034·30	−2,148·98	−392·56	−21,751·88	36,201·35	1,610·00
10	−4,565·23	−2,787·51	−1,447·96	−280·95	−15,078·05	24,738·43	578·74
15	−3,600·16	−2,084·63	−1,051·04	−215·95	−11,336·01	18,283·20	−4·58

Internal rate of return is 14·95% per annum

Appendix Table 10.A4 Version D: effect of matrix change and change to two-year construction period

Interest rates 5, 10, 15% per annum

Mean costs and benefits $000

Year	Wage/salary	Gross profits	Government production expenditure	Incremental promotion	Imports	Foreign exchange receipts	Total
1971	−574·20	−202·00	−28·80	−30·00	−1,280·80	1,375·00	−740·80
1972	−574·20	−202·00	−28·80	−30·00	−1,280·80	1,375·00	−740·80
1973	−320·90	−183·50	−127·20	−30·00	−933·30	1,775·00	180·10
1974	−320·90	−183·50	−127·20	−30·00	−933·30	1,775·00	180·10
1975	−320·90	−183·50	−127·20	−30·00	−933·30	1,775·00	180·10
1976	−411·00	−297·60	−165·60	−30·00	−1,530·80	2,679·20	244·20
1977	−411·00	−297·60	−165·60	−30·00	−1,530·80	2,679·20	244·20
1978	−411·00	−297·60	−165·60	−30·00	−1,530·80	2,679·20	244·20
1979	−411·00	−297·60	−165·60	−30·00	−1,530·80	2,679·20	244·20
1980	−411·00	−297·60	−165·60	−30·00	−1,530·80	2,679·20	244·20
1981	−461·20	−342·10	−191·00	−30·00	−1,831·80	3,136·90	280·80
1982	−461·20	−342·10	−191·00	−30·00	−1,831·80	3,136·90	280·80
1983	−461·20	−342·10	−191·00	−30·00	−1,831·80	3,136·90	280·80
1984	−461·20	−342·10	−191·00	−30·00	−1,831·80	3,136·90	280·80
1985	−461·20	−342·10	−191·00	−30·00	−1,831·80	3,136·90	280·80
1986	−512·00	−385·20	−214·70	−30·00	−2,117·60	3,576·60	317·00
1987	−512·00	−385·20	−214·70	−30·00	−2,117·60	3,576·60	317·00
1988	−512·00	−385·20	−214·70	−30·00	−2,117·60	3,576·60	317·00
1989	−512·00	−385·20	−214·70	−30·00	−2,117·60	3,576·60	317·00
1990	−512·00	−385·20	−214·70	−30·00	−2,117·60	3,576·60	317·00

Mean present values $000

Rate (%)	Wage/Salary	Gross profits	Government production expenditure	Incremental promotion	Imports	Foreign exchange receipts	Net
5	−5,824·19	−3,727·36	−1,978·50	−392·56	−20,116·44	33,406·48	1,367·43
10	−4,138·48	−2,505·52	−1,292·70	−280·95	−13,577·40	22,188·11	393·06
15	−3,180·43	−1,820·83	−907·50	−215·95	−9,930·20	15,913·29	−141·61

Internal rate of return is 13·38% per annum

Appendix Table 10. A5 *Social cost–benefit analysis version E: effect of matrix change, two-year construction period, and 25% local financing of hotel investment*

Mean costs and benefits $000

Year	Shadow wages	Gross profits	Government production expenditure	Incremental promotion	Imports	Foreign exchange receipts	Total
1971	−574·20	−202·00	−28·80	−30·00	−1,280·80	1,031·20	−1,084·60
1972	−574·20	−202·00	−28·80	−30·00	−1,280·80	1,031·20	−1,084·60
1973	−320·90	−183·50	−127·20	−30·00	−878·30	1,775·00	235·10
1974	−320·90	−183·50	−127·20	−30·00	−878·30	1,775·00	235·10
1975	−320·90	−183·50	−127·20	−30·00	−878·30	1,775·00	235·10
1976	−411·00	−297·60	−165·60	−30·00	−1,475·80	2,679·20	299·20
1977	−411·00	−297·60	−165·60	−30·00	−1,475·80	2,679·20	299·20
1978	−411·00	−297·60	−165·60	−30·00	−1,475·80	2,679·20	299·20
1979	−411·00	−297·60	−165·60	−30·00	−1,475·80	2,679·20	299·20
1980	−411·00	−297·60	−165·60	−30·00	−1,475·80	2,679·20	299·20
1981	−461·20	−342·10	−191·00	−30·00	−1,776·80	3,136·90	335·80
1982	−461·20	−342·10	−191·00	−30·00	−1,776·80	3,136·90	335·80
1983	−461·20	−342·10	−191·00	−30·00	−1,776·80	3,136·90	335·80
1984	−461·20	−342·10	−191·00	−30·00	−1,776·80	3,136·90	335·80
1985	−461·20	−342·10	−191·00	−30·00	−1,776·80	3,136·90	335·80
1986	−512·10	−385·20	−214·70	−30·00	−2,062·60	3,576·60	372·00
1987	−512·10	−385·20	−214·70	−30·00	−2,062·60	3,576·60	372·00
1988	−512·10	−385·20	−214·70	−30·00	−2,062·60	3,576·60	372·00
1989	−512·10	−385·20	−214·70	−30·00	−2,062·60	3,576·60	372·00
1990	−512·10	−385·20	−214·70	−30·00	−2,062·60	3,576·60	372·00

Mean present values $000

Rate (%)	Shadow wages	Gross profits	Government production expenditure	Incremental promotion	Imports	Foreign exchange receipts	Net
5	−5,824·19	−3,727·36	−1,978·50	−392·56	−19,504·12	32,735·25	1,308·51
10	−4,138·48	−2,505·52	−1,292·70	−280·95	−13,167·33	21,531·76	146·78
15	−3,180·43	−1,820·83	−907·50	−215·95	−9,637·12	15,270·53	−491·29

Internal rate of return is 10·92% per annum

Appendix Table 10.A6 *Social cost–benefit analysis: Version F: SWR = 55% otherwise as for Version B*

Mean costs and benefits $000

Year	Expatriate wages	Shadow wages (55%)	Gross profits	Government production expenditure
1971	−194·00	−320·10	−202·00	−28·80
1972	−194·00	−320·10	−202·00	−28·80
1973	−108·40	−178·90	−183·50	−127·20
1974	−108·40	−178·90	−183·50	−127·20
1975	−108·40	−178·90	−183·50	−127·20
1976	−138·90	−229·10	−297·60	−165·60
1977	−138·90	−229·10	−297·60	−165·60
1978	−138·90	−229·10	−297·60	−165·60
1979	−138·90	−229·10	−297·60	−165·60
1980	−138·90	−229·10	−297·60	−165·60
1981	−155·80	−257·10	−342·10	−191·00
1982	−155·80	−257·10	−342·10	−191·00
1983	155·80	−257 10	−342·10	−191·00
1984	−155·80	−257·10	−342·10	−191·00
1985	−155·80	−257·10	−342·10	−191·00
1986	−173·00	−285·50	−385·20	−214·70
1987	−173·00	−285·50	−385·20	−214·70
1988	−173·00	−285·50	−385·20	−214·70
1989	−173·00	−285·50	−385·20	−214·70
1990	−173·00	−285·50	−385·20	−214·70

Year	Incremental promotion	Imports	Foreign exchange receipts	Total
1971	−30·00	−1,280·80	1,031·20	−1,024·50
1972	−30·00	−1,280·80	1,031·20	−1,024·50
1973	−30·00	−878·30	1,775·00	268·70
1974	−30·00	−878·30	1,775·00	268·70
1975	−30·00	−878·30	1,775·00	268·70
1976	−30·00	−1,475·80	2,679·20	342·20
1977	−30·00	−1,475·80	2,679·20	342·20
1978	−30·00	−1,475·80	2,679·20	342·20
1979	−30·00	−1,475·80	2,679·20	342·20
1980	−30·00	−1,475·80	2,679·20	342·20
1981	−30·00	−1,776·80	3,136·90	384·10
1982	−30·00	−1,776·80	3,136·90	384·10
1983	−30·00	−1,776·80	3,136·90	384·10
1984	−30·00	−1,776·80	3,136·90	384·10
1985	−30·00	−1,776·80	3,136·90	384·10
1986	−30·00	−2,062·60	3,576·60	425·60
1987	−30·00	−2,062·60	3,576·60	425·60
1988	−30·00	−2,062·60	3,576·60	425·60
1989	−30·00	−2,062·60	3,576·60	425·60
1990	−30·00	−2,062·60	3,576·60	425·60

Mean present values $000

Rate (%)	Expatriate wages	Shadow wages	Gross profits	Government production expenditure
5	−1,967·75	−3,246·79	−3,727·36	−1,978·50
10	−1,398·23	−2,307·05	−2,505·52	−1,292·70
15	−1,074·55	−1,772·98	−1,820·83	−907·50

Rate (%)	Incremental promotion	Imports	Foreign exchange receipts	Net
5	−392·56	−19,504·12	32,735·25	1,918·15
10	−280·95	−13,167·33	21,531·76	579·97
15	−215·95	−9,637·12	15,270·53	−158·39

Internal rate of return is 13·67% per annum

Appendix Table 10.A7 *Social cost–benefit analysis Verion G: 31·8% occupancy throughout; no incremental government expenditure on Promotion*

Interest rates 5, 10, 15% per annum
Mean costs and benefits $000

Year	Expatriate wages	Shadow wages	Gross profits	Government production expenditure	Imports	Foreign exchange receipts	Total
1971	−194·00	−430·70	−202·00	−28·80	−1,280·80	1,031·20	−1,105·10
1972	−194·00	−430·70	−202·00	−28·80	−1,280·80	1,031·20	−1,105·10
1973	−108·40	−240·70	−183·50	−127·20	−878·30	1,775·00	236·90
1974	−108·40	−240·70	−183·50	−127·20	−878·30	1,775·00	236·90
1975	−108·40	−240·70	−183·50	−127·20	−878·30	1,775·00	236·90
1976	−108·40	−240·70	−183·50	−127·20	−878·30	1,775·00	236·90
1977	−108·40	−240·70	−183·50	−127·20	−878·30	1,775·00	236·90
1978	−108·40	−240·70	−183·50	−127·20	−878·30	1,775·00	236·90
1979	−108·40	−240·70	−183·50	−127·20	−878·30	1,775·00	236·90
1980	−108·40	−240·70	−183·50	−127·20	−878·30	1,775·00	236·90
1981	−108·40	−240·70	−183·50	−127·20	−878·30	1,775·00	236·90
1982	−108·40	−240·70	−183·50	−127·20	−878·30	1,775·00	236·90
1983	−108·40	−240·70	−183·50	−127·20	−878·30	1,775·00	236·90
1984	−108·40	−240·70	−183·50	−127·20	−878·30	1,775·00	236·90
1985	−108·40	−240·70	−183·50	−127·20	−878·30	1,775·00	236·90
1986	−108·40	−240·70	−183·50	−127·20	−878·30	1,775·00	236·90
1987	−108·40	−240·70	−183·50	−127·20	−878·30	1,775·00	236·90
1988	−108·40	−240·70	−183·50	−127·20	−878·30	1,775·00	236·90
1989	−108·40	−240·70	−183·50	−127·20	−878·30	1,775·00	236·90
1990	−108·40	−240·70	−183·50	−127·20	−878·30	1,775·00	236·90

Mean present values £000

Rate (%)	Expatriate wages	Shadow wages	Gross profits	Government production expenditure	Imports	Foreign exchange receipts	Net
5	−1,585·57	−3,520·59	−2,437·28	−1,472·34	−12,278·67	21,774·26	479·82
10	−1,178·58	−2,616·86	−1,753·78	−1,003·36	−8,993·62	15,202·75	−343·45
15	−940·32	−2,087·83	−1,355·46	−731·65	−7,074·71	11,386·28	−803·70

Internal rate of return is 7·54% per annum

APPENDIX 10.B PRIVATE RATES OF RETURN IN THE HOTEL INDUSTRY

It is an easy matter to compute the private rate of return to the private foreign capital invested in hotels by extracting from the data the costs, returns and profits at different occupancy rates and finding the internal rate of return which yields a zero net present value for the stream of profits over the period.

Case 'A' All hotel investment is foreign

In this case, gross profits accrue to the investor, and the cash flow profile is as follows:

$ '000

Year	Expenses	Receipts	Net cash flow
0	−2,750·0	0·0	−2,750·0
1−3	−801·5	+1,029·5	228·0
4−8	−1,042·3	+1,554·0	551·7
9−14	−1,165·4	+1,819·5	654·1
15−19	−1,282·2	+2,079·7	797·5

The internal rate of return given by the net cash flow is about 15·9 per cent per annum.

Case 'B' 25% of hotel investment financed by a loan bearing 8% interest

In this case, the cash flows are altered as follows:

Year	Expenses as A	Interest	Receipts	Net cash flow
0	−2,750·00	0·00	+687·50	−2,062·50
1−3	−801·50	−55·00	+1,029·50	173·00
4−8	−1,042·3	−55·00	+1,554·00	456·70
9−14	−1,165·4	−55·00	+1,819·5	599·10
15−19	−1,282·2	−55·00	+2,079·7	742·50

The internal rate of return of the net cash flow has now risen to about 17·8 per cent per annum.

Appendix Table 10.B1 *Hotel–Antigua private rate of return with no residual value*

		($000 BWI)		
Year		Outgoings	Incomings	Net cash flow
0		−2,750·0	0·0	−2,750·0
1		−801·5	+1,029·5	228·0
2	31·8%	−801·5	+1,029·5	228·0
3		−801·5	+1,029·5	228·0
4		−1,042·3	+1,554·0	551·7
5		−1,042·3	+1,554·0	551·7
6	45·0%	−1,042·3	+1,554·0	551·7
7		−1,042·3	+1,554·0	551·7
8		−1,042·3	+1,554·0	551·7
9		−1,165·4	+1,819·5	654·1
10		−1,165·4	+1,819·5	654·1
11	55·0%	−1,165·4	+1,819·5	654·1
12		−1,165·4	+1,819·5	654·1
13		−1,165·4	+1,819·5	654·1
14		−1,165·4	+1,819·5	654·1
15		−1,282·2	+2,079·7	797·5
16		−1,282·2	+2,079·7	797·5
17	65·0%	−1,282·2	+2,079·7	797·5
18		−1,282·2	+2,079·7	797·5

Mean present value of net cash flow	15·5%	75
IRR	16·0%	−19

$$15·5\% < \text{IRR} < 16·0\%$$

Appendix Table 10.B2 *Private rate of return on hotel investment with 25% capital raised locally*

Interest rates 2, 5, 8% per annum

Main costs and benefits $000

Year	Outgoings	Interest	Incomings	Total
1971	−2,750·00	0·0	687·50	−2,062·50
1972	−801·50	−55·00	1,029·50	173·00
1973	−801·50	−55·00	1,029·50	173·00
1974	−801·50	−55·00	1,029·50	173·00
1975	−1,042·30	−55·00	1,554·00	456·70
1976	−1,042·30	−55·00	1,554·00	456·70
1977	−1,042·30	−55¹00	1,554·00	456·70
1978	−1,042·30	−55·00	1,554·00	456·70
1979	−1,042·30	−55·00	1,554·00	456·70
1980	−1,165·40	−55·00	1,819·50	599·10
1981	−1,165·40	−55·00	1,819·50	599·10
1982	−1,165·40	−55·00	1,819·50	599·10
1983	−1,165·40	−55·00	1,819·50	599·10
1984	−1,165·40	−55·00	1,819·50	599·10
1985	−1,165·40	−55·00	1,819·50	599·10
1986	−1,282·20	−55·00	2,079·70	742·50
1987	−1,282·20	−55·00	2,079·70	742·50
1988	−1,282·20	−55·00	2,079·70	742·50
1989	−1,282·20	−55·00	2,079·70	742·50
1990	−1,282·20	−55·00	2,079·70	742·50

Mean present values in units of units

Rate (%)	Outgoings	Interest	Incomings	Net
2	−19,842·71	−862·32	26,686·44	5,981·42
5	−15,638·26	−664·69	20,101·39	3,798·44
8	−12,772·83	−528·20	15,637·53	2,336·51

Internal rate of return is 17·77% per annum

11 An application of the cost–benefit technique to the recommendations of two reports concer with tourist development in the Caribbean

This chapter attempts an analysis — in cost–benefit terms — of the *Zinder Report* on *The Future of Tourism in the Eastern Caribbean* and the relevant sections of the *Tripartite Economic Survey of the Eastern Caribbean.*[1]

Both reports supply us with the following elements necessary for analysis using the proposed cost–benefit framework:

(1) Direct hotel investment over a period.
(2) Infrastructure and utilities investment associated with this hotel investment over the period.
(3) Additional promotional expenditures required.
(4) Additional tourist receipts forthcoming.
(5) Some idea of the sectoral breakdown of these tourist receipts.

In both cases we take as our period of analysis twenty years from the year in which all facilities are constructed.

The methodology used is fully described in Chapter 5 above. The sets of final demands given by items (1), (2), (4) and (5) above are converted, using the Antigua 8 × 8 matrix, to corresponding sets of primary inputs required directly and indirectly to satisfy these final demands.[2] These primary inputs are then revalued at 'shadow prices' to arrive at social costs,[3] to which any incremental promotion expenditure is added as before. Social benefits are then inflows of foreign private capital associated with hotel developments, together with additional tourist receipts arising from the programme.

The resulting flows of net social benefits are then discounted to find the net present value (n.p.v.), and the internal rate of return which yields an n.p.v. of zero is derived.

A The Zinder Report

The *Zinder Report* has been widely criticised elsewhere,[4] but no previous attempt has been made to subject its proposals and projections to the test of cost–benefit analysis. The report made recommendations for investments in the tourist field over the period 1969–77, and certain projections of tourist receipts were made in conjunction with the recommendations made. A summary of the proposals which concern us is given below.

1 *Zinder Report* and *Tripartite Survey.*

2 The agricultural sectors are omitted; see also Chapter 10.

3 Shadow prices are those used in Chapter 10.

4 Bryden and Faber (1971) and Levitt and Gulati (1970).

(1) *Hotel investments*

Zinder assumes a 60 per cent occupancy rate by 1972 in the Leeward and Windward Islands and 70 per cent in Barbados.[5] By 1977, this is assumed to rise to 70 per cent (75 per cent in Barbados). On the basis of this and the Report's projections of growth in tourist numbers, the number of additional rooms required is calculated and converted into capital requirements using a figure of $30, 000 EC per room.[6] This yields a requirement for hotel investment of $123.0 m by 1972 and a further $114 m by 1977. As no annual figures were given, it was necessary to convert these figures as follows:

1969–71 $41 m per annum.

1972–6 $23 m per annum.

Zinder also mentioned additional tourist facilities required in the form of golf courses, restaurants, shopping facilities, convention facilities, sound and light presentations and air-conditioned sight-seeing buses.[7] Dealing with these items poses a problem. On the whole they are new activities and thus an input—output matrix would not reflect their impact. On the other hand, one presumes that Zinder's projections of tourist expenditure take into account tourist spending on these facilities, although this is not made explicit. A large number of the facilities would be an adjunct to hotel activities, however, and so we may assume that the receipts of hotels take account of this. For convenience it is assumed that the facilities mentioned are entirely financed by foreign capital, recognising that this tends to 'favour' the project. Zinder estimated capital requirements of $40 m by 1972 and a further $50 m by 1977. Converting this to annual figures yields roughly $13.3 m annually between 1969 and 1971 and $10.0 m annually between 1972 and 1976 – a total of $89.9 m.

(2) *Infrastructure investments*

Zinder claims that infrastructure costs 'typically range between 15 per cent and 30 per cent' of hotel capital costs.[8] Further, the authors 'feel that it would be unwise to expect that infrastructure would cost any less than 20 per cent of hotel capital costs' in the Eastern Caribbean.[9]

On this basis, they calculate infrastructure requirements between 1969 and 1972 at $25 m EC and between 1972 and 1977 at $23 m EC. However, it was stated that 'this does not include relocating major roads, the cost of building new airports, or major relocation of existing airports'[10] which, from a reading of the text, might amount to some $12 m between 1969 and 1977, or some 5 per cent of hotel investment – and it could be much more than this as cost estimates are not given. For our purposes then, we may use a figure for infrastructure investments of 25 per cent of hotel capital costs and quite fairly ascribe this to the *Zinder Report*.

5 *Zinder Report* p. 98.

6 *Ibid.* p. 111.

7 *Ibid.* pp. 129 *et seq.*

8 *Ibid.* p. 112.

9 *Ibid.*

10 *Ibid.*

(3) *Additional promotion expenditures*

Zinder claims that 'resort-type areas that have successful tourism development programs... spend, at least, $1 on tourism budgets for every $6 generated by the money spent by tourists'.[11] The authors made their own calculation of government revenue generated by tourist expenditures, which have been criticised elsewhere.[12] However they evidently felt that the resulting calculations of what tourist budgets in the region *ought* to be were reasonable, claiming that 'by 1972, all of the islands can easily afford not only $200,000 EC a year, but considerably more.'[13] In their Table 6 the authors of the Report estimate the 'impact' of tourist expenditures in 1972 and 1977.[14] From their estimate of tax revenues generated, they calculate tourist budgets in the eight islands in 1972 on the basis of the '1-to-6' rule. The total for the eight islands is $12·449 m. The corresponding figures for 1977 may be derived from Table 6, while those for 1967 may be derived from Table 3 in the Report, which purports to measure the 'impact' of current tourist expenditures. For intervening years, the proposed tourist board budgets were determined by the use of logarithmic paper. 'Incremental' tourist expenditure is then derived by deducting 1968 tourism budgets of $1·158 m for the eight islands, given in Table 3 of the Report.

This method gives us the estimates shown in Table 11-1 of incremental promotion expenditure required to fulfil Zinder's recommendations.

Table 11-1 *Zinder's recommendations regarding incremental promotional expenditure by government, 1969–77*

Year	$m EC
1969	4·8
1970	6·5
1971	8·5
1972	11·3
1973	13·1
1974	15·5
1975	18·1
1976	21·1
1977 on	24.5

(4) *Projected tourist receipts*

Zinder estimates tourist receipts in the eight islands to be $65·346 m in 1967.[15] The Report's projections for 1972 and 1977 are given in Table 6 at $207·2 m and $395·3 respectively.[16] Extrapolating for 1968 and 1969 and assuming steady growth for intervening years, we may estimate *incremental* tourist receipts[17] as in Table 11-2.

11 *Ibid.* p. 142.

12 Bryden and Faber (1971).

13 *Zinder Report.* p. 143.

14 *Ibid.* p. 83.

15 *Ibid.* Table No. 3, p. 48.

16 *Ibid.* p. 83.

17 That is, those resulting from the proposals made on specific investments and promotional expenditures.

196

Table 11.2 *Zinder's estimates of incremental tourist receipts arising from their proposals*

Year	$m EC
1969	0.0
1970	28·0
1971	50·0
1972	105·2
1973	130·0
1974	164·0
1975	201·0
1976	245·0
1977 on	293·3

(5) Sectoral breakdown of tourist receipts

We are assured that 'the dominant tourist spending pattern prevailing in the Eastern Caribbean' is as follows:[18]

Food and beverages	38·5%
Accommodation	31·5%
Purchases	15·0%
Transport	15·0%
	100·0%

Zinder examines categories of expenditure rather than recipient sectors. However, it would seem a reasonable approximation to allocate expenditures on food, beverages and accommodation to hotels, purchases to distribution and transport to the transportation sector.

Projections of sectoral tourist receipts may thus be deduced as in Table 11.3.

Table 11.3 *Zinder: projections of sectoral tourist receipts*

	Hotels (0·7)	Distribution (0·15)	Transport (0·15)	Total receipts
1969	0.0	0·0	0·0	0·0
1970	19·6	4·2	4·2	28·0
1971	35·0	7·5	7·5	50·0
1972	73·6	15·8	15·8	105·2
1973	31·0	19·5	19·5	130·0
1974	114·8	24·6	24·6	164·0
1975	140·8	30·1	30·1	201·0
1976	171·4	36·8	36·8	245·0
1977 on	205·3	44·0	44·0	293·3

Capital costs associated with the proposals and their phasing may be summarised as in Table 11.4.

---

18 *Zinder Report* p. 37.

Table 11.4 *Zinder: capital costs and foreign exchange receipts*

	Infrastructure[a] $m	Hotels[b] $m	Other private[c] $m	Total[d] $m	Foreign[e] exchange receipts
1969	10·3	41·0	13·3	64·6	44·3
1970	10·3	41·0	13·3	64·6	44·3
1971	10·3	41·0	13·3	64·6	44·3
1972	5·3	23·0	10·0	38·3	27·0
1973	5·3	23·0	10·0	38·3	27·0
1974	5·3	23·0	10·0	38·3	27·0
1975	5·3	23·0	10·0	38·3	27·0
1976	5·3	23·0	10·0	38·3	27·0
	57·4	238·0	89·9	385·3	267·9

Notes:
[a] Approx. 25% of hotel capital costs − see (2) above.
[b] See (1) above.
[c] See (1) above.
[d] Received by the construction sector.
[e] 75% of hotel investment plus all 'other private'. See (1) above.

Primary input requirements of the Zinder Programme

We are now in a position to perform the necessary computations, using which will give us the primary input requirements of the Zinder proposals. The set of final demands which is derived from the above analysis of the Report is given in Table 11.5.

Table 11.5 *Zinder Report: final demands* $m

	Recipient sector:			
	Construction	Distribution	Transportation	Hotels
1969	64·6	0·0	0·0	0·0
1970	64·6	4·2	4·2	19·6
1971	64·6	7·5	7·5	35·0
1972	38·3	15·8	15·8	73·6
1973	38·3	19·5	19·5	91·0
1974	38·3	24·6	24·6	114·8
1975	38·3	30·1	30·1	140·8
1976	38·3	36·8	36·8	171·4
1977 *et seq*	0·0	44·0	44·0	705·3

Source: Tables 11.3 and 11.4 above.

As pointed out above, the Report envisaged occupancy rates of 60 per cent by 1972 in the Leewards and Windwards and 70 per cent in Barbados, rising to 70 per cent (75 per cent in Barbados) by 1977. We therefore employ the matrix which reflects cost profiles in hotels at an occupancy rate of 65 per cent, which must be very similar to the cost profiles at 70 per cent.

The primary inputs required to support these sets of final demands are given in Table 11.6.

Table 11.6 *Primary inputs required to support Zinder final demands*, $m

Year	Wages	Profits	Government	Imports	Total
1969	21·061	5·614	2·339	35·586	64·6
1970	26·366	8·479	5·310	52·446	92·6
1971	30·535	10·730	7·644	65·692	114·6
1972	32·418	14·100	12·549	84·433	143·5
1973	37·118	16·631	15·178	99·373	168·3
1974	43·560	20·110	18·785	119·845	202·3
1975	50·572	23·879	22·705	142·143	239·3
1976	58·904	28·415	27·383	168·597	283·3
1977	55·571	30·014	31·115	176·599	293·3
et seq					

These primary inputs are then adjusted as suggested in the previous chapter. Summarily, what has been done is as follows:

(1) Divide wages into those accruing to expatriates (25 per cent) and those accruing to indigenes (75 per cent). Domestic wages are then revalued at a shadow wage of 74 per cent.

(2) Estimate income tax at 2·71 per cent of gross wages and salaries, and, profits tax at 4·17 per cent of total government 'receipts'. 'Net taxes' are then calculated deducting costs of collection at 10 per cent for indirect taxes and 15 per cent for direct taxes. This sum is then deducted from 'government' inputs.

(3) Add incremental promotion expenditure as a cost in foreign exchange.

(4) Calculate interest payments at 8 per cent on the local loans made to hotels, the latter being estimated at 25 per cent of total hotel investments in any year.[19] Interest payments are then deducted from 'imports', since the gross profits of hotels are included in this category.

(5) Benefits are taken as foreign exchange receipts, firstly from funds flowing in to finance 75 per cent of hotel construction, and the 'other private' investments above; secondly from tourist receipts.

Appendix Table 11.A1 shows the results of discounting the stream of net benefits so obtained at 2, 5 and 8 per cent per annum, and gives the internal rate of return of this net stream of benefits, which turns out to be 0·89 per cent per annum. Even Zinder's own assumptions regarding infrastructure investment and the growth of tourism, which are, on the evidence presented in this study, far too optimistic, this rate of return is very far below what could be considered to be the minimal accounting rate of interest.

One of the key factors giving rise to this low internal rate of return is the recommendation regarding incremental promotion expenditure, the mean present value of which is some $439 m at a 2 per cent discount rate. The error which led to this recommendation has been fully discussed elsewhere,[20] and for this reason it is perhaps unfair to use the figures presented. The present analysis shows that direct and indirect tax receipts are at no time adequate to cover this incremental promotion expenditure.

19 One of Zinder's recommendations was for local provision of long-term low interest loans for hotel developers. *Zinder Report*, p. 119.

20 Bryden and Faber (1971).

Although the claim that the above represents a fair and reasonable attempt to analyse the *Zinder Report* in cost–benefit terms seems justified, it is worth while to consider the effect of amending the Report's recommendations regarding promotion expenditure while holding other assumptions constant. Since the authors evidently felt the level of promotion expenditure which they recommended for 1972 to be reasonable, we may fairly use the figures for 1969–72 inclusive. I have then held promotional expenditure constant at the 1972 level for the remainder of the time period.

As Appendix Table 11.A2 shows, this has a dramatic effect on the internal rate of return – raising it to 13·0 per cent per annum.

The point of this is not to suggest that 13·0 per cent per annum represents a reasonable or even likely social rate of return to tourism in the future in the Caribbean.[21] Of rather greater interest in the present context is that few of the factors which really influence the social benefit were discussed by Zinder – for example, the appropriate shadow wage rate, the effect of employment of expatriates, the measurement of the level of infrastructure investment, the logic behind the '1-to-6' rule for promotional expenditure and so on.

B The Tripartite Economic Survey

The Tripartite Economic Survey Report was published in 1967 as a result of field work by a team of economists in the Eastern Caribbean between January and April 1966. Although concerned with general economic progress towards viability in the eight islands of the Eastern Caribbean, it was clear that the development of tourism and of associated infrastructure formed a major part of the recommendations of the survey. As in the *Zinder Report*, no cost–benefit analysis was made of tourism, reliance being placed on multiplier analysis, although in this case no specific criticism attaches to the calculation of the multiplier *per se.*[22] Unlike the *Zinder Report*, infrastructure needs in conjunction with tourist development were mentioned specifically, no attempt being made to use some notional average ratio with hotel capital costs. It was however, not easy to gain accurate costings of the proposed projects, and this is reflected in the comments of Chapter 8, in which the recommendations of the *Tripartite Survey* in respect of infrastructure and utilities were analysed.

Although the *Tripartite Survey* was concerned with the whole Eastern Caribbean, in practice detailed projections of infrastructure requirements etc. were more difficult to obtain in Barbados, which in many respects is in a different position from the smaller islands. In this case, therefore, we are dealing with the Windwards and Leewards only.

(1) Hotel investments

The Survey expected 5,285 new beds (or 2,642 new rooms) to be built over the six-year period 1965–6 to 1970–1.[23] Hotel investment per room was estimated at

21 Criticism here and elsewhere of the Report will make this very clear. See also Bryden and Faber (1971). In any case, it is not possible to distinguish that part of incremental tourist expenditures the 'benefits' of which attach to the (unknown) existing investment, rather than the 'new' investment.

22 The general criticisms of the multiplier approach contained in Chapter 5 still apply, of course.

23 *Tripartite Survey*, p. 30.

200

between $25,000 and 30,000 EC,[24] and I have used an average of $27,000. This implies a total hotel investment of $72·7 m over the period or $12·1 m per annum. Of this annual sum it is assumed, in line with the previous analysis, that some $3 m per annum (25 per cent) is locally financed.

(2) Infrastructure investments

The infrastructure investments suggested in the Survey have already been analysed in Chapter 8. This analysis reveals that a more reasonable estimate of tourist infrastructure requirements would be 80 per cent of hotel capital costs. But even this is liable to be an underestimate for our purposes, since this ignores *indirect* requirements for government infrastructure. '

Given the estimates of hotel investment calculated above, the requirement for tourist infrastructure investment over the period is $58·1 m — or some $9·7 m per annum.

(3) Promotion expenditures

The Survey proposes as a 'norm' a figure of $10 per tourist as being a reasonable basis for computing the contribution of governments to tourist board expenditures.[25] Since we are concerned with *incremental* promotion expenditures, the actual promotional expenditures in the base year, 1965, have to be deducted from the totals arrived at in conjunction with the Survey's projections of visitor arrivals. According to Zinder, promotion expenditures by governments in the Leewards and Windwards were $312,000 in 1968. The 1965 figure is on this basis assumed to be $300,000. The incremental tourist board expenditures so calculated are given in Table 11.7 below.

Table 11.7 *Tripartite Survey: incremental promotional expenditures*

Year	$m EC
1965	0·70
1966	0·90
1967	1·15
1968	1·50
1969	1·93
1970	2·50
1971	3·20

(4) Tourist receipts
Incremental tourist receipts are derived from the projections given in the Survey.[26] Estimated tourist receipts in the Windwards and Leewards were given as $24·3 m in 1965 and projected at $77·6 m for 1970. Logarithmic paper was used to estimate receipts in the intervening years and for 1971, and incremental receipts calculated by subtracting the base year estimate of $24·3 m.

24 *Ibid.*, p. 67.

25 *Ibid.*, p. 29.

26 *Ibid.*, p. 30.

Table 11.8 *Incremental tourist receipts* (*$m EC*) – Tripartite Survey

	Total	Incremental
1965	24·3	0·0
1966	30·6	6·3
1967	38·5	14·2
1968	48·5	24·2
1969	61·0	36·7
1970	77·6	53·3
1971	97·5	73·2

(5) Sectoral breakdown of tourist receipts

The Survey uses O'Loughlin's breakdown of sectoral tourist receipts,[27] The resulting projections by final demand category are given in Table 11.9 below.

Table 11.9 *Tripartite Survey: projections of tourist receipts by receiving sector.*

	% Breakdown after O'Loughlin	Tourist receipts $m :					
		1966	1967	1968	1969	1970	1971
Purchases	26	1·64	3·69	6·29	9·54	13·86	19·03
Transport	12	0·76	1·70	2·90	4·40	6·40	8·78
Finance	2	0·13	0·28	0·48	0·73	1·07	1·46
Services	2	0·13	0·28	0·48	0·73	1·07	1·46
Hotels	58	3·65	8·24	14·04	21·29	30·91	42·46
Total	100	6·31	14·19	24·19	36·69	53·31	73·19

N.B. Totals may not add up due to rounding.

Primary input requirements of the Tripartite Survey Programme

As before, we are now able to deduce the table of final demands arising from the proposals in the *Tripartite Survey*, and thereby calculate the primary input coefficient this time using the matrix which reflects 45 per cent occupancy rates. This matrix was chosen because the Survey envisaged an average occupancy of about 50 per cent by 1970.[28]

Table 11.10 *Final demands – Tripartite Survey*

	1965	1966	1967	1968	1969	1970	1971
Construction	21·80	21·80	21·80	21·80	21·80	21·80	nil
Distribution	0·0	1·64	3·69	6·29	2·54	13·86	19·03
Finance	0·0	0·13	0·28	0·48	0·73	1·07	1·46
Transport	0·0	0·76	1·70	2·90	4·40	6·40	8·78
Hotels	0·0	3·65	8·24	14·04	21·29	30·91	42·46
Services	0·0	0·13	0·28	0·48	0·73	1·07	1·46
Totals	21·80	28·11	35·99	45·99	58·99	75·11	73·19

The primary input requirements which result from this set of final demands are given in Table 11.11.

27 *Ibid.*, p. 10. The percentage breakdown is also given in Chapter 6, Table 6–15.

28 *Tripartite Survey*, p. 22.

Table 11.11 *Primary inputs in $m EC – Tripartite Survey*

Year	Wages and Salaries	Profits	Government	Imports	Total
1965	7·11	1·89	0·79	12·01	21·80
1966	8·42	2·60	1·48	15·61	28·80
1967	10·05	3·47	2·35	20·12	35·99
1968	12·12	4·58	3·46	25·84	46·00
1969	14·71	5·79	4·83	32·98	58·49
1970	18·16	7·82	6·66	42·46	75·10
1971 to 1990	15·17	8·13	8·07	41·82	73·19

These primary inputs are adjusted in exactly the same way as were those derived for the Zinder programme, thus ensuring comparability. The revalued primary inputs are given below.

Table 11.12 *Revalued primary inputs in $m EC – Tripartite Survey*

Year	Domestic wages and salaries	Expatriate wages and salaries	Domestic profits	Govt. less net taxes	Incremental promotion	Imports c.i.f.
1965	−3·944	−1·780	−1·890	−0·275	−0·700	−12·010
1966	−4·684	−2·100	−2·600	−0·661	−0·900	−15·130
1967	−5·580	−2·510	−3·490	−1·150	−1·150	−19·400
1968	−6·727	−3·030	−4·580	−1·773	−1·500	−24·880
1969	−8·162	−3·680	−5·970	−2·970	−1·930	−31·780
1970	−10·079	−4·540	−7·820	−3·567	−2·500	−41·020
1971 to 1990	−8·421	−3·790	−8·130	−4·527	−3·200	−40·380

The foreign exchange receipts, which are social benefits in the present analysis, are obtained from inflows of private capital and incremental tourist receipts. The net stream of social benefits is then computed by deducting the social costs given in the previous table from the stream of benefits in terms of foreign exchange.

Table 11.13 *Foreign exchange receipts and net social benefits – Tripartite Survey, $m EC*

Year	Incremental tourist receipts	Foreign capital inflow	Total benefits	Net benefits
1965	0·0	9·1	9·1	−11·50
1966	6·3	9·1	15·4	−10·67
1967	14·2	9·1	23·3	− 9·96
1968	24·2	9·1	33·3	− 9·19
1969	36·7	9·1	45·8	− 8·26
1970	53·3	9·1	62·4	− 7·13
1971 to 1990	73·2	0·0	73·2	+ 4·75

These flows are then discounted to find mean net present values at 2, 4 and 6 per cent and the internal rate of return which gives a net present value for the net stream of social benefits of zero. The results, which are shown in Appendix Table 11.A3, show an internal rate of return of 4.17 per cent. This compares with that given for the basic Zinden programme of 0·89 per cent.

It would of course be unfair to suggest that the *Tripartite Survey* proposals were unsound on this basis alone. They made quite specific comments on the need for other sectors to grow and replace to some extent the imports required by tourism – particularly agriculture. These recommendations, if effective, would undoubtedly raise the rate of return in tourism in view of the sensitivity of the IRR in relation to imports. Nevertheless, it is true that the Survey placed great reliance on tourism as a means of achieving economic 'viability' in the Eastern Caribbean and did not give due weight to the possibility that a high rate of growth of tourism would itself make the achievement of growth in the domestic sectors an even more difficult task in view of the competition for resources involved.

Conclusions

Both the *Tripartite Survey* and the *Zinder Report* show low rates of return to their proposals for the development of tourism in the Eastern Caribbean, although the assumptions of the *Tripartitie Survey* seem to be more acceptable than those of the *Zinder Report*.[29] Nevertheless, on any reasonable assessment of the appropriate accounting rate of interest, both proposals would have to be rejected on the basis of the foregoing analysis.

29 At any rate they were not subject to the same barrage of criticism.

Appendix Table 11.A1 *Cost–benefit analysis of Zinder recommendations*

Interest rates 2, 5 8% per annum

Mean costs and benefits in units of $m EC

Year	Domestic wages	Expatriate wages	Domestic profits	Government
1969	−11·69	−5·27	−5·61	−0·84
1970	−14·63	−6·59	−8·68	−2·49
1971	−16·95	−7·63	−10·73	−3·81
1972	−17·99	−8·10	−14·10	−6·79
1973	−20·60	−9·28	−16·63	−8·27
1974	−24·18	−10·89	−20·11	−10·31
1975	−28·07	−12·64	−23·88	−12·52
1976	−32·69	−14·73	−28·42	−15·16
1977	−30·84	−13·89	−30·01	−17·57
1978	−30·84	−13·89	−30·01	−17·57
1979	−30·84	−13·89	−30·01	−17·57
1980	−30·84	−13·89	−30·01	−17·57
1981	−30·84	−13·89	−30·01	−17·57
1982	−30·84	−13·89	−30·01	−17·57
1983	−30·84	−13·89	−30·01	−17·57
1984	−30·84	−13·89	−30·01	−17·57
1985	−30·84	−13·89	−30·01	−17·57
1986	−30·84	−13·89	−30·01	−17·57
1987	−30·84	−13·89	−30·01	−17·57
1988	−30·84	−13·89	−30·01	−17·57
1989	−30·84	−13·89	−30·01	−17·57
1990	−30·84	−13·89	−30·01	−17·57
1991	−30·84	−13·89	−30·01	−17·57
1992	−30·84	−13·89	−30·01	−17·57
1993	−30·84	−13·89	−30·01	−17·57
1994	−30·84	−13·89	−30·01	−17·57
1995	−30·84	−13·89	−30·01	−17·57
1996	−30·84	−13·89	−30·01	−17·57

Year	Incremental promotion expenditure	Exports	Foreign exchange receipts	Total
1969	−4·80	−34·79	44·30	−18·69
1970	−6·50	−50·85	72·30	−17·24
1971	−8·50	−63·29	94·30	−16·61
1972	−11·30	−81·55	132·20	−7·64
1973	−13·10	−96·01	157·00	−6·89
1974	−15·50	−116·00	191·00	−5·99
1975	−18·10	−137·82	228·00	−5·03
1976	−21·10	−163·80	272·00	−3·89
1977	−24·50	−171·80	293·30	4·68
1978	−24·50	−171·80	293·30	4·68
1979	−24·50	−171·80	293·30	4·68
1980	−24·50	−171·80	293·30	4·68
1981	−24·50	−171·80	293·30	4·68
1982	−24·50	−171·80	293·30	4·68
1983	−24·50	−171·80	293·30	4·68
1984	−24·50	−171·80	293·30	4·68
1985	−24·50	−171·80	293·30	4·68
1986	−24·50	−171·80	293·30	4·68
1987	−24·50	−171·80	293·30	4·68
1988	−24·50	−171·80	293·30	4·68
1989	−24·50	−171·80	293·30	4·68

Year	Incremental promotion expenditure	Exports	Foreign exchange receipts	Total
1990	−24·50	−171·80	293·30	4·68
1991	−24·50	−171·80	293·30	4·68
1992	−24·50	−171·80	293·30	4·68
1993	−24·50	−171·80	293·30	4·68
1994	−24·50	−171·80	293·30	4·68
1995	−24·50	−171·80	293·30	4·68
1996	−24·50	−171·80	293·30	4·68

Mean present values in units of $m EC

Rate (%)	Domestic wages	Expatriate wages	Domestic profits	Government
2	−592·62	−266·95	−544·29	−304·72
5	−409·76	−184·58	−363·88	−203·13
8	−299·09	−134·73	−263·34	−142·28

Rate (%)	Incremental Promotion expenditure	Imports	Foreign Exchange receipts	Net
2	−439·33	−3126·61	5262·78	−11·75
5	−296·87	−2121·77	3552·81	−32·19
8	−211·33	−1517·07	2525·07	−42·72

Internal rate of return is 0·89% per annum

Appendix Table 11.A2 *Adjusted cost—benefit analysis of Zinder recommendations*

Interest rates 2, 5, 8% per annum

Mean costs and benefits in units of $m EC

Year	Domestic wages	Expatriate wages	Domestic profits	Government
1969	−11·69	−5·27	−5·61	−0·84
1970	−14·63	−6·59	−8·48	−2·49
1971	−16·95	−7·63	−10·73	−3·81
1972	−17·99	−8·10	−14·10	−6·79
1973	−20·60	−9·28	−16·63	−8·27
1974	−24·18	−10·89	−20·11	−10·31
1975	−28·07	−12·64	−23·88	−12·52
1976	−32·69	−14·73	−28·42	−15·16
1977	−30·84	−13·89	−30·01	−17·57
1978	−30·84	−13·89	−30·01	−17·57
1979	−30·84	−13·89	−30·01	−17·57
1980	−30·84	−13·89	−30·01	−17·57
1981	−30·84	−13·89	−30·01	−17·57
1982	−30·84	−13·89	−30·01	−17·57
1983	−30·84	−13·89	−30·01	−17·57
1984	−30·84	−13·89	−30·01	−17·57
1985	−30·84	−13·89	−30·01	−17·57
1986	−30·84	−13·89	−30·01	−17·57
1987	−30·84	−13·89	−30·01	−17·57
1988	−30·84	−13·89	−30·01	−17·57
1989	−30·84	−13·89	−30·01	−17·57
1990	−30·84	−13·89	−30·01	−17·57
1991	−30·84	−13·89	−30·01	−17·57
1992	−30·84	−13·89	−30·01	−17·57
1993	−30·84	−13·89	−30·01	−17·57
1994	−30·84	−13·89	−30·01	−17·57
1995	−30·84	−13·89	−30·01	−17·57
1996	−30·84	−13·89	−30·01	−17·57

Year	Incremental promotion expenditure	Imports	Foreign exchange receipts	Total
1969	−4·80	−34·79	44·30	−18·69
1970	−6·50	−50·85	72·30	−17·24
1971	−8·50	−63·29	94·30	−16·61
1972	−11·30	−81·55	132·20	−7·64
1973	−11·30	−96·01	157·00	−5·09
1974	−11·30	−116·00	191·00	−1·79
1975	−11·30	−137·82	228·00	1·77
1976	−11·30	−163·80	272·00	5·91
1977	−11·30	−171·80	293·30	17·88
1978	−11·30	−171·80	293·30	17·88
1979	−11·30	−171·80	293·30	17·88
1980	−11·30	−171·80	293·30	17·88
1981	−11·30	−171·80	293·30	17·88
1982	−11·30	−171·80	293·30	17·88
1983	−11·30	−171·80	293·30	17·88
1984	−11·30	−171·80	293·30	17·88
1985	−11·30	−171·80	293·30	17·88
1986	−11·30	−171·80	293·30	17·88
1987	−11·30	−171·80	293·30	17·88
1988	−11·30	−171·80	293·30	17·88
1989	−11·30	−171·80	293·30	17·88

Appendix Table 11.A2 continued.

Year	Incremental promotion expenditure	Imports	Foreign exchange receipts	Total
1990	−11·30	−171·80	293·30	17·88
1991	−11·30	−171·80	293·30	17·88
1992	−11·30	−171·80	293·30	17·88
1993	−11·30	−171·80	293·30	17·88
1994	−11·30	−171·80	293·30	17·88
1995	−11·30	−171·80	293·30	17·88
1996	−11·30	−171·80	293·30	17·88

Mean present values in units of $m EC

Rate (%)	Domestic wages	Expatriate wages	Domestic profits	Government
2	−592·62	−266·95	−544·29	−304·72
5	−409·75	−184·58	−368·88	−203·13
8	−299·09	−134·73	−263·34	−142·28

Rate (%)	Incremental promotion expenditure	Imports	Foreign exchange receipts	Net
2	−231·39	−3126·61	5262·78	196·19
5	−163·16	−2121·77	3552·81	101·53
8	−121·52	−1517·02	2525·07	47·09

Internal rate of return is 13·07% per annum

Appendix Table 11.A3 *Cost—benefit analysis of Tripartite Survey recommendations on tourism*

Interest rates 2, 4, 6% per annum

Mean costs and benefits in units of $m EC

Year	Domestic wages	Expatriate wages	Domestic profits	Government less net tax
1965	−3·94	−1·78	−1·89	−0·28
1966	−4·68	−2·10	−2·60	−0·66
1967	−5·58	−2·51	−3·47	−1·15
1968	−6·73	−3·03	−4·58	−1·77
1969	−8·16	−3·68	−5·97	−2·54
1970	−10·08	−4·54	−7·82	−3·57
1971	−8·42	−3·79	−8·13	−4·53
1972	−8·42	−3·79	−8·13	−4·53
1973	−8·42	−3·79	−8·13	−4·53
1974	−8·42	−3·79	−8·13	−4·53
1975	−8·42	−3·79	−8·13	−4·53
1976	−8·42	−3·79	−8·13	−4·53
1977	−8·42	−3·79	−8·13	−4·53
1978	−8·42	−3·79	−8·13	−4·53
1979	−8·42	−3·79	−8·13	−4·53
1980	−8·42	−3·79	−8·13	−4·53
1981	−8·42	−3·79	−8·13	−4·53
1982	−8·42	−3·79	−8·13	−4·53
1983	−8·42	−3·79	−8·13	−4·53
1984	−8·42	−3·79	−8·13	−4·53
1985	−8·42	−3·79	−8·13	−4·53
1986	−8·42	−3·79	−8·13	−4·53
1987	−8·42	−3·79	−8·13	−4·53
1988	−8·42	−3·79	−8·13	−4·53
1989	−8·42	−3·79	−8·13	−4·53
1990	−8·42	−3·79	−8·13	−4·53

Year	Incremental promotion expenditure	Imports	Foreign exchange receipts	Total
1965	−0·70	−12·01	9·10	−11·50
1966	−0·90	−15·13	15·40	−10·67
1967	−1·15	−19·40	23·30	−9·96
1968	−1·50	−24·88	33·30	−9·19
1969	−1·93	−31·78	45·80	−8·26
1970	−2·50	−41·02	62·80	−7·13
1971	−3·20	−40·38	73·20	4·75
1972	−3·20	−40·38	73·20	4·75
1973	−3·20	−40·38	73·20	4·75
1974	−3·20	−40·38	73·20	4·75
1975	−3·20	−40·38	73·20	4·75
1976	−3·20	−40·38	73·20	4·75
1977	−3·20	−40·38	73·20	4·75
1978	−3·20	−40·38	73·20	4·75
1979	−3·20	−40·38	73·20	4·75
1980	−3·20	−40·38	73·20	4·75
1981	−3·20	−40·38	73·20	4·75
1982	−3·20	−40·38	73·20	4·75
1983	−3·20	−40·38	73·20	4·75
1984	−3·20	−40·38	73·20	4·75
1985	−3·20	−40·38	73·20	4·75

Appendix Table 11.A3 continued.

Year	Incremental promotion expenditure	Imports	Foreign exchange receipts	Total
1986	−3·20	−40·38	73·20	4·75
1987	−3·20	−40·38	73·20	4·75
1988	−3·20	−40·38	73·20	4·75
1989	−3·20	−40·38	73·20	4·75
1990	−3·20	−40·38	73·20	4·75

Mean present values in units of $m EĊ

Rate (%)	Domestic wages	Expatriate wages	Domestic profits	Government less net tax
2	−161·62	−72·75	−145·09	−76·32
4	−128·91	−58·03	−114·01	−59·22
6	−105·15	−47·33	−91·53	−46·89

Rate (%)	Incremental promotion expenditure	Imports	Foreign exchange receipts	Net
2	−55·54	−733·48	1260·89	16·09
4	−43·41	−578·55	983·15	1·02
6	−34·66	−466·36	782·63	−9·29

Internal rate of return is 4·17% per annum

PART V

Conclusions

12   *Summary and conclusions:future policy choices*

In Part I of this study, recent economic changes in the smaller islands of the Commonwealth Caribbean were examined against the background of political fragmentation, geographical isolation and similarity of resource endowment. Because the small islands lack significant elements of complementarity in their resource endowments and production structures, and because, partly as a result of this, they are each nation states in their own right, each island is best considered as an individual economic and political entity. As such, the islands of the region must be considered very small indeed in terms of both population and land area. Population density is generally high, especially by reference to cultivable land, which is itself unevenly distributed among individuals. Mineral resources outside the larger islands of Trinidad and Jamaica are largely absent in commercially exploitable deposits. These features serve to explain the extreme openness of the economies, and the limited potential for development of manufacturing industry either on the basis of locally produced raw materials and/or on the basis of import substitution. Against such a background the rapid acceptance of tourism as a leading growth sector in the Caribbean, based on the relative proximity to North America and considerable natural endowments of 'basic' tourist assets of sun, sand and sea, has been a natural reaction of governments whose room for manoeuvre in economic policies and scope for expansion in alternative export or import substitution industries has been — and is — severely restricted.

All of the smaller islands have experienced fairly rapid rates of growth of population which, through the effect of this on the age-structure of the population, means a relatively low population of working age. But the evidence available suggests fairly high participation rates for men, the quite marked variations in overall participation rates between islands being mainly explained by considerable variation in female participation rates. These, in turn, reflect variations in employment opportunities for women. A large proportion of the population of working age have primary education only and, especially in the smaller islands, lack formal training, facilities for which are largely absent. There is, however, a small and highly educated elite with university education or its equivalent.

Little reliable evidence exists regarding the change in the structure and level of employment in the region during the decade under study, but some changes can be inferred from the changes in economic structure in the region and recent evidence relating to the Cayman Islands, the British Virgin Islands and the Bahamas. This suggests a declining proportion of the labour force in agriculture and, for most islands, an increase in employment in construction, services and hotels and, possibly, commerce. Since services, hotels and commerce are important sources of employment opportunities for women, it seems possible that the trend towards lower female participation rates, at least in 'formal' wage employment, noted after the 1960 Census, may have been arrested and, in some cases, reversed. But the vulnerability of the economies to male unemployment has probably increased owing to the increase significance of construction based on capital inflows.

Evidence from those islands with relatively larger tourist sectors suggests a higher requirement for trained and skilled labour. But the absence of training facilities, the low general level of formal education and the international mobility of trained and skilled labour have meant the appearance of deficit sectors in the labour market even, apparently, in the larger islands more commonly characterised as having a labour surplus. The better jobs have tended to be filled by expatriates, so that the benefits of the (in some senses) 'superior' employment structure in these tourist economies have tended to flow largely to expatriates rather than to the indigenous population.

The analysis of changes in economic structure in the region attempts to show at the 'macro' level what the effects of rapid growth of tourism in the smaller islands have been. The hypothesis advanced is that tourism has grown in competition with other sectors, principally export and domestic agriculture. This takes the form of quasi-static competition for human resources, and sometimes land, together with quasi-dynamic competition for the particular resources which would serve to change the production functions in agriculture to meet changing resource availability — in particular skilled manpower and domestic capital, especially that part which is available to government. On the demand side, there is reason to suppose that tourists and/or expatriate employees, *qua* reference groups, may well influence the consumption patterns of indigenes with whom they come into direct or indirect contact. Such an influence would almost inevitably mean a switch from locally produced to imported commodities. Such a process, operating through the supply of factors, and the demand for locally produced commodities, would explain many of the structural changes which have taken place in those islands which have experienced rapid growth in their tourist sectors during the decade, notably a tendency for the propensity to import to rise, and for both domestic agricultural production and production of agricultural commodities for export to decline. While this analysis does not by itself provide an economic case against the development of tourism in the Caribbean, it does suggest a need for rather more careful scrutiny of that case, bearing in mind the opportunity cost of resources which are used in the expansion of tourist sectors.

Part II moves from the particular context of the Caribbean to the general context of international tourism and developing countries as a whole. First, the significance of the recent rapid growth in international tourism for developing countries is examined in terms of flows of tourists and flows of foreign exchange generated by these tourist movements. In 1965, developing countries as a whole received about one quarter of all international tourist arrivals and about 30 per cent of all international tourist receipts exclusive of transportation costs. In this respect, however, the developing countries are dominated by those in Europe and the Mediterranean, with 17 per cent of all tourist arrivals. The Commonwealth Caribbean region received only about 1 per cent of arrivals and 1½ per cent of receipts by comparison.

Although developed countries as a group were in substantial deficit on their travel accounts, it is notable that most of the net flow accrued to developing countries in Europe, and in particular to Spain. Many developing countries outside Europe in fact have deficits on their travel account. Thus from the viewpoint of developing countries as a whole, tourism has not so far led to significant *net* flows of foreign exchange from developed to developing countries. And if expenditures on international transportation were included this conclusion would probably be reinforced because of the dominance of developed countries in air transportation.

Nevertheless, available statistics suggest that tourism has grown rapidly during the decade under study, with little difference in growth rates between developed and developing countries. The Commonwealth Caribbean has experienced above average growth in receipts, and about average growth in arrivals. By 1965 the region received some 9 per cent of tourist receipts of all developing countries outside Europe and the Mediterranean.

Statistics of tourist arrivals and tourist receipts, while they may tell us something about the growth of demand, tell us nothing about the economic and social impact of tourism on developing countries. Chapter 5 examines the methodological approaches of some previous studies on the economic and social impact of tourism in developing countries — of which the tourist multiplier approach is the most common. The inadequacy of these approaches to measurement of the impact of tourism is demonstrated at the theoretical level, and alternative approaches discussed, particularly the approach, based on cost–benefit techniques, used in Part IV in relation to the Caribbean. The method proposed — being partial in nature — does not cover the totality of costs and benefits associated with tourist development in developing countries, and so the most serious omissions were discussed. Viewed as a whole, the discussion of methods reveals several important areas of 'cost' which must be set against potential benefits. These costs tend to be largely ignored in previous studies of the impact of tourism on developing countries. In fact, most of the case 'against' tourist development appears to rest on its non-pecuniary or 'transcendental' impact on society, which effects are sometimes admitted, if not understood, by even the proponents of tourist development. But there has been no consistent attempt to link this type of cost to the economic costs and benefits of tourist development, and the distribution of these costs and benefits between different groups within and beyond the society. Without being accused of total economic determinism, it is possible to argue that at least some part of these 'transcendental' costs are the results of the absolute size of net social benefits, and their distribution, rather than being largely independent phenomena which can be left out of the economist's calculations.

In Part III some basic data relating to the growth and structure of the Caribbean tourist industry and the role of governments in promoting and encouraging tourism are presented and analysed. Although tourism in the Caribbean is not of very recent origin, it is only in the past decade that it has reached any significant size in most of the smaller islands of the region. Growth rates of visitor arrivals of between 15 and 20 per cent per annum, with corresponding growth in tourist receipts, were common in the smaller islands during this period. The most important source of this growth has been North America, whose tourists now constitute over half the total arrivals in all but the Windward Islands and Trinidad and Tobago. The West

Indies themselves are the next most important source of visitors, but a very high proportion of this group appear to stay with friends and relatives, though they are also important sources of custom for guest houses and the smaller, more modest hotels. Because the peak months for West Indian tourists are in the off-season, they do tend to alleviate the effects of seasonality in the main groups of other visitors. Nevertheless, occupancy rates in hotels vary very significantly between winter and summer, and are generally low over the year as a whole – quite often 50 per cent or below. Since the growth in hotel capacity has kept pace with the growth in arrivals, the utilisation of capacity has improved only slightly, as a result of a steady rise in the proportion of visitors staying in hotels.

It is hotels that receive the largest proportion of visitors and tourist receipts in the Caribbean, and subsequent concentration on the impact of hotel and guest house tourism, as opposed to cruise ship tourism or real estate type developments, is justified mainly on these grounds. It is also the case that hotel investment during the decade has been a substantial proportion of total investment, and that most of this has been foreign investment, a high proportion of new hotels being foreign owned. Although the average size of hotel tends to be small – around 30 rooms – there are signs that this is increasing, this again being indicative of the pattern of ownership insofar as most indigenous involvement is confined to the smaller hotels and guest houses.

The majority of hotel sales are to foreigners, domestic purchases from this sector tending to be insignificant in most islands for which data are available. The two most important categories of inputs in this industry are payments for commodities, a high proportion of which are imported, and payments to households in respect of wages and salaries. The input structure, however, changes in a non-linear fashion as occupancy rates change. Direct employment in hotels usually works out, on average, at about one employee per room, although substantial variation occurs according to the season. Some evidence exists to suggest that the burden of seasonal unemployment in the industry tends to fall on women, who form a much higher proportion of employees in hotels than in the economy as a whole. This female employment, however, is concentrated in the semi-skilled and unskilled categories. In the two islands studied in greater depth, a very high proportion of skilled and professional jobs in the hotel sector were held by non-nationals, and a *minimum* estimate of the proportion of wages and salaries in hotels accruing to non-national employees in the one island where data permit such an analysis is around 43 per cent. So far as semi-skilled and unskilled grades are concerned, little evidence exists to suggest that earnings are higher than elsewhere in the economy, and some evidence suggests the contrary. Since the bulk of such employees are women, this reflects the lack of female employment opportunities elsewhere in the economy, at least to some extent. The hotel industry in the Caribbean can thus be characterised as being dominated by foreign ownership, containing a high proportion of expatriates in the better paid jobs which it creates, paying a high proportion of wages and salaries to foreigners, requiring – and using – few locally produced inputs, and having underutilised capacity, especially in the summer months.

Finally, the role of the governments of the smaller Caribbean islands in promoting tourism, and the costs which are implicit in this role, ar analysed under four main headings. First, fiscal policies including incentives and special concessions offered in respect of various types of investment in tourism, where it is argued that costs exist in respect of general influences on the fiscal structure which tourism may be associated with, in respect of specific concessions granted under hotels aid legislation, and in respect of special additional concessions granted to specific developers. Second, the provision of infrastructure and utilities related to tourism the cost of which appears to have been substantial during the decade even though adverse comments occur from time to time on the adequacy of tourist infrastructure and utilities in the smaller islands of the group. In fact, in terms of monetary investment some evidence exists to suggest that governments have had to match the contribution of private investors in tourism almost on a 'dollar-for-dollar' basis. Third, the contribution of governments through training and tourist promotion activities is considered For the smaller islands at least, expenditure on training has been very small and can safely be ignored. Promotion is carried out through the medium of tourist boards and consists almost entirely of advertising expenses in Europe and North America. Such expenditures are very variable in the region, ranging from a low of $1 to over $10. Most reports on tourism in the region have, however, recommended considerable increases in this form of expenditure. Finally, physical controls and land use controls are discussed, although this area of government involvement and the associated problems remain largely untackled in the smaller islands of the region. One can safely conclude from the analysis of the role of the governments in encouraging, supporting and promoting tourism in the region that the associated costs have been very substantial. Consequently, such costs must be identified and incorporated into any analysis of the social costs and benefits of tourism.

Part IV turns to an analysis of tourist multipliers and the social costs and benefits of tourist development in the smaller islands of the region, ending with an attempt to appraise the recommendations of two reports on the future development of tourism in cost—benefit terms. In general, and following the argument of Part II, the multiplier approach is rejected as yielding no useful guidance to policy makers as regards the merits of tourism as comparted with alternatives, but some partial analysis shows how, as we attempt to make the multiplier model more realistic, so the real income effects of tourist expenditure are reduced. The social cost—benefit analysis, while retaining some disadvantages, does enable some comparison to be made with alternatives as more data become available, and, bearing in mind the 'minimal' rate of interest on government funds of around 6 or 7 per cent, permits some judgement as to the acceptability or otherwise of the social rate of return to investment in tourism over the period under study. In addition it permits analysis of the main influences on the social rate of return, and hence yields policy guidance as regards potential means of increasing that return. Even with fairly conservative assumptions, however, the present social rates of return from hotel development are sufficiently close to the 'minimal' accounting rate of interest to suggest that net social benefits from tourism are rather small in the Caribbean. These results are highly sensitive to the value of the 'shadow' wage rate, which depends on alternative opportunities for employment and consumption in that employment, as well as the relative valuation of savings and consumption, on the extent of foreign ownership in the industry and the availability of local loan funds to these foreign investors, on the extent of employment of non-nationals whose income does not form part of the social welfare function which governments seek to maximise, and on the value of public sector investment which is associated with the particular form of tourist development. Finally, the recommendations as regards future tourist development in the Windward and Leeward islands contained in the *Tripartite Survey* and the *Zinder Report* would, on the basis of a social cost benefit analysis, and on any reasonable assessment of the appropriate accounting rate of interest, require to be rejected.

To state that this study has provided a definitive economic case against the further development of tourism in the Caribbean would be going too far. Nevertheless, the consistency between the findings of the micro-analysis contained in Part IV and of the macro-analysis contained in Part I does raise some very serious doubts about the viability of tourist development *in its present form,* at least for the smaller islands of the Caribbean, and suggests that under certain circumstances a perfectly recognisable 'economic' case can be made against tourist development without necessarily calling upon the various kinds of external diseconomy or on 'transcendental' costs which may be associated with tourism in developing countries. Since the circumstances identified are obviously not unique to the Caribbean this conclusion would seem to be of some significance, for the economic case *for* tourism in developing countries seems to have been largely taken for granted, most of the arguments 'against' being framed in largely 'transcendental' terms. Indeed, it is possible that the explanation of at least part of those costs which are normally thought of as being within such a category lies in the low net social benefits and in the distribution of costs and benefits within the society itself.

The circumstances which appear to be important for the main conclusion of this study are first, the degree of foreign ownership in the industry, which means that the surplus either accrues to third countries or to individuals whose welfare does not form part of the 'welfare function' which governments seek to maximise; second, for similar reasons, the employment of non-nationals in skilled and professional positions in the industry; third, the extent of government involvement through the provision of infrastructure, the granting of incentives and in other ways which involve a real resource cost to the nation. By comparison, the effect of the failure of the hotel industry to purchase a higher proportion of its food require-locally, while not unimportant, may be rather small. The effect of tourism on agriculture achieves its significance mainly in the competition for resources which the past growth of tourism has involved in the region, and possibly also through the effect of tourists and/or non-national employees, *qua* reference groups, on the pattern of demand.

The low social rate of return is consistent with a net gain accruing to some groups in the society, while others are net losers from the process of change involved. Although it has not been possible to incorporate distributional objectives within the analysis to any significant extent, both because of data inadequacies and because one often lacks a clear idea of these objectives in the case of Caribbean governments, it is possible to make a few qualitative observations on the distributional effects of tourist development in the region. In the circumstances prevailing during the decade the most likely group of losers are the small peasant farmers, whether they own or rent their land. For while plantation owners may lose their labour force, or at least face a rise in the supply price of labour, they are in a better position to substitute capital for labour where such substitution is permitted and, because they have clear title in law and own large blocks of land, usually in the more fertile areas closer to, or even bounded by, coastal areas, can look forward to rising land prices associated with tourist development. Small farmers, on the other hand, often lack clear title even where they own their land, are unable to substitute capital for labour, tend to be situated in areas which do not benefit from rising land prices, lose their family and hired labour and, in proportion to their numbers, tend to lack political power. For them the alternatives are to retreat into semi-subsistence or to join the labour force as unskilled labour. Other groups will also suffer if forced to purchase imported foods, often processed, in place of local foods when the supply of local foods declines. Insofar as it is the lower income groups who tend to purchase a high proportion of domestically produced food, it will be the less well-off who tend to suffer from this change. Still other groups will suffer because with rising land prices near to the growing centres of employment they find themselves no longer able to purchase a plot of land to build a house on. Moreover, the building regulations introduced with the intention of controlling residential development and hotels tend to affect lower income groups adversely both because of their complexity and also because the traditional way of building houses, perhaps over a period of time with the help of family and friends, is not catered for by such legislation. Finally there is the fiscal structure itself with its heavy reliance on import duties on necessities, which suggests that a relatively large part of the burden of financing the contribution of government to tourist development falls on the lower income groups.

The low rates of social return to tourist development, taken together with the tentative suggestions regarding distributional effects which have not been satisfactorily included in the analysis, can explain why hostility or animosity towards tourists and towards those connected with the tourist business arises in certain circumstances. One does not need to be an economic reductionist to suggest such a connection. On the other hand, it may be going too far to suggest that such animosity would disappear if the rate of social return on tourist investments were raised and if the benefits were distributed more equitably; there may be good reasons in the realm of social psychology to suggest why this would not necessarily be the case. But one may fairly conclude that, on the basis of the findings of this study, the campaigns launched by the Bahamas and Jamaica, to name but two, to 'enlighten' the people about the benefits which they derive from tourism, in an attempt to counter such animosity, rest on a misunderstanding on the part of those responsible of the effects of tourism on the lower income groups in society.

Future policy choices

It is convenient to analyse the future policy choices open to the small Caribbean islands under two main headings. First, within tourism itself there are measures which could be taken to raise the net social benefits arising from this industry. Second, the alternatives in other industries, whether or not these supply inputs to the tourist sectors, must be examined. Within tourism itself, the analysis suggests at least four major areas of policy which could significantly alter the social benefits arising from future tourist development. First, policies as to the structure and ownership of the industry would appear to be of some importance. So long as growth in the industry is based on large luxury hotels, then it seems almost inevitable that ownership will remain in foreign hands. One alternative here would be public ownership, though the smaller islands would find it difficult to raise funds for this type of investment, and might also find themselves forced to employ foreign managers or even sign contracts with foreign firms who specialise in management of hotels of this kind. This could be both politically awkward and economically costly. Nevertheless, there would seem to be room for rather more experimentation in public ownership than has been the case to date, though this need not be in large luxury hotels. Further development of the more 'indigenous' smaller hotels and guest houses, possibly within the range of a broader band of indigenous private investors as well as government, would seem to be worthy of closer examination, since experience in large bureaucratically organised business would be less important, and the distributional implications might be more acceptable. At present, the hotel developments in the region seem to be predicated on the assumption that the only market worth exploiting is that represented by upper income groups in North America and Europe. While this may be true from the point of view of the private investor, and possibly also from the point of view of tour operators and airlines, it is quite probable that different conclusions would emerge from a consideration of social costs and benefits.

Secondly, the structure of employment opportunities and related policies regarding the employment of non-nationals in skilled and professional positions would seem to be worthy of close scrutiny. An allied point concerns the failure of the hotel industry to train indigenes to fill positions currently filled by expatriates. Again, casual observation would suggest that guest houses and smaller hotels require a somewhat different structure of employment, catering as they do for simpler tastes and being less orientated towards the highly sophisticated standards of cuisine, accommodation and management thought to be required by the tourist market currently being tapped by the larger hotels in the region. But if large hotels remain, as seems likely, then work permits should only be granted for limited duration and on condition that the period involved should be used to train indigenes to fill the posts at the end of the period. Obviously such work permits should be granted for well defined skilled jobs only if indigenes are not available. Although in theory such a restriction operates in some territories, in practice the operation of work permit regulations usually leaves a great deal to be desired.

Thirdly, the future needs in respect of infrastructure and utilities would seem to be worthy of close analysis with a view both to their minimisation and possibly also to shifting the burden of their provision on to the private investor. With both 'priced' utilities and 'unpriced' general infrastructure an adequate social return must be assured. In some cases this will no doubt require changes in pricing policies. A related point concerns promotional expenditures through tourist boards which can all too easily reach large proportions without very clear ideas of the responsibilities of these organisations, or the objectives of such expenditures.

Fourthly, as regards fiscal policies and incentives, it is almost certain that the specially negotiated concessions in the smaller islands, of which examples were given in Chapter 8, yield very low rates of social benefit, and very likely that the general incentives offered also yield low social benefits. If any incentives are to be given, a case could be made for arguing that these should be to encourage indigenous participation in guest houses and smaller hotels, at present largely excluded from incentives legislation through the criteria relating to minimum size. In general, the fiscal system must be designed, so far as possible, to ensure that losers from the inevitable structural changes are compensated by beneficiaries. The systems already discussed, which relieve taxes on imported luxuries on the grounds that this increases tourist expenditures, are unlikely to be consistent with this objective.

The analysis contained in this study suggests that policy action in these four areas could somewhat increase the benefits to nationals from tourist development. If implemented, a corollary would almost certainly be a lower rate of growth of tourism in the region, since the attempt to raise social benefits would sometimes raise private costs in the industry. On the evidence presented, however, this may not be a bad thing, though existing hotel proprietors, tour operators, travel agents and airlines are not likely to agree. It makes little sense from the point of view of national policy to base the rate of growth of the industry on the expected rate of growth of demand, which is the approach adopted by the *Zinder Report.*

Apart from the tourist industry itself, alternative opportunities need to be assessed on comparable terms. Given the size and population of the smaller Caribbean territories, and their endowments of natural resources, it is difficult to see socially profitable opportunities of any size arising in the field of manufacturing industry, even within a common market which embraced these smaller islands. And within a regional common market which embraced large and small islands, the fear is that all such industry would migrate to the larger islands. Two areas where socially profitable opportunities for the small islands are most likely to exist are in export and domestic agricultural production, including livestock and fisheries within these sectors.

But there is little hope of achieving growth in these sectors until the competitive demands of tourism, discussed earlier, are reduced. Thus to predicate, as the *Zinder Report* does, increased benefits from tourism largely on the basis of increased domestic production of foodstuffs, while at the same time predicting the growth of tourism solely on the basis of demand factors is, in the view of this study, to misunderstand the whole process of economic change in the smaller islands of the Caribbean during the past decade or so.

But when all the alternatives have been carefully explored, it is likely that tourism in some form will be almost inevitable for at least some of the smaller islands of the region, with or without a wider political union than at present seems likely. If this is so, then the findings of this study would suggest that progress towards higher real incomes for the bulk of the population is likely to be slow, much slower than is suggested by most previous studies in the region, and that to achieve such progress considerable change will be required in the structure of the tourist industry, as well as elsewhere in the economy.

BIBLIOGRAPHY

This bibliography is arranged alphabetically by Author. Where no author is given, the work is listed under the sponsoring organisation or publisher.

Adams, N.A. (1968), An Analysis of Food Consumption and Food Import Trends in Jamaica 1950–53', *Social and Economic Studies,* Vol. 17, No. 1, March 1968.

'Analyst', 'Currency and Banking in Jamaica', *Social and Economic Studies,* 1953.

Anderla, G., *Trends and Prospects of Latin American Tourism,* International Institute of Scientific Travel Research, Geneva. 92.

Andic, F.M. (1968), 'Fiscal Incentives: A Brief Survey', *Social and Economic Studies,* Vol. 17, No. 1, March 1968.

Antigua, *Estimates of Revenue and Expenditure of Antigua,* 1966, 1967, 1968, 1969, Government Printing Office, St. John's, Antigua.

Arrow, K.J. and Scitovsky, T. (1969), *'Readings in Welfare Economics',* American Economic Association Series, Vol. XII, Allen and Unwin, 1969.

Aspinall, Sir Algernon (1907), *A Pocket Guide to the West Indies,* 1907.

Aspinall, Sir Algernon (1930), *A Wayfarer in the West Indies,* 1930.

Bahamas, Ministry of Tourism, *Annual Report on Tourism in the Commonwealth of the Bahamas Islands,* 1969.

Bahamas, Ministry of Tourism, *1969 Visitor Statistics,*

Barbados, Government Statistical Service, *Digest of Tourism Statistics 1964,* Special Studies No. 9.

Barsotti, F. (1966). 'The Prospects for Export Crops', paper presented to the First West Indian Agricultural Economics Conference, University of the West Indies, Trinidad, 1966.

Bartell, Ernest (1965), *National Income Statistics: Dominica 1961–64,* University of the West Indies, Institute of Social and Economic Research (Eastern Caribbean) Statistical Series No. 2, July 1965.

Beckford, G. (1967), 'The West Indian Banana Industry', *Studies in Regional Economic Integration,* Vol. 2, No. 3, Institute of Social and Economic Research, University of the West Indies, Jamaica, 1967.

Benedict B, (Ed.)(1967), *Problems of Smaller Territories,* Athlone, 1967.

Bergson, A. (1938), 'A Reformulation of Certain Aspects of Welfare Economics', *Quarterly Journal of Economics,* 1938. Reprinted in Arrow and Scitovsky (1969).

BNEC (British National Export Council), *Britain's Invisible Earnings! Report of the Committee on Invisible Exports,* 1967.

British Development Division in the Caribbean, *Economic Surveys and Projections.* A series of surveys relating to the Windwards, Leewards and the Northern Group published between 1967 and 1970. The following are referred to:
Economic Survery and Projections – Grenada.
Economic Surveys and Projections – St Vincent.
Economic Surveys and Projections – St Lucia.
Economic Surveys and Projections – Dominica.
Economic Surveys and Projections – Antigua.
Economic Surveys and Projections – Montserrat.
Economic Surveys and Projections – St. Kitts.
Economic Surveys and Projections – British Virgin Islands.
Economic Surveys and Projections – Turks and Caicos.
Economic Surveys and Projections – Cayman Islands.

British Development Division in the Caribbean, *West Indies Census of Agriculture, 1961: The Eastern Caribbean Territories,* Barbados Government Printing Office, 1968.

British Virgin Islands, *Hotels Aid Ordinance No. 1 of 1953.*

British Virgin Islands, *National Accounts 1967/68, Working Paper,* 1969.

Bryden, J.M. (1967), 'Agriculture and Economic Growth in the West Indies 1955–65', unpublished Departmental Paper submitted to the Department of Agricultural Economics and Farm Management, University of the West Indies, Trinidad, 1967.

Bryden, J.M. (1970), *Economic Surveys and Projections: A Methodology for the Associated States and Dependencies of the Caribbean,* British Development Division in the Caribbean, 1970.

Bryden J.M. and Faber, M.L.O. (1971), 'Multiplying the Tourist Multiplier', *Social and Economic Studies,* March 1971.

Bryne, Joycelin (1969), 'Population Growth in St. Vincent'.*Social and Economic Studies,* Vol. 18, No. 2, June 1969.

CADEC (Caribbean Ecumenical Consultation for Development), *The Role of Tourism in Caribbean Development,* Barbados, 1971.

Campbell, L.G. and Edwards, D.T. (1960), *Agriculture in Antigua's Economy: Possibilities and Problems of Adjustment,* Agricultural Series No. 1, University of West Indies, Institute of Social and Economic Research (Eastern Caribbean) July 1965.

Cayman Islands, *Hotels Aid Ordinance Law 1 of 1955.*

Cayman Islands, *Hotels Aid Amendment Ordinance No. 5 of 1960.*

Cayman Islands, *Hotels Aid Amendment Ordinance No. 46 of 1966.*

Cayman Islands, *Hotels Aid Amendment Ordinance No. 24 of 1967.*

Cayman Islands, *National Accounts 1967–69. Working Papers,* Ministry of Finance and Development 1969.

Checchi and Co. (1961), *The Future of tourism in the Far East,* 1961.

Chenery, H.B. and Clark, P.G. (1959), *Interindustry Economics,* Wiley, New York, 1959.

CODECA *Caribbean Statistical Yearbook,* 1967, Puerto Rico.

Cozier, T. (1971), in the *Financial Times,* 15 July 1971.

Cumper, G.E. (1959), 'Tourist Expenditure in Jamaica, 1958' *Social and Economic Studies,* Vol. 8, No. 3, 1959.

Cumper, G.E. (Ed.)(1960), *The Economy of the West Indies,* Institute of Social and Economic Research, University of the West Indies, Jamaica, 1960.

Cumper, G.E. (1960B), 'Employment and Unemployment in the West Indies' in Cumper (Ed.) *The Economy of the West Indies,* 1960.

Cumper, G.E. (1960C) 'Personal Consumption in the West Indies' in Cumper (Ed.) *The Economy of the West Indies.*

Cumper, G.E. (1960D), 'The Development of the West Indies, in Cumper (Ed.) *The Economy of the West Indies.*

Cumper, G.E. (1964), 'A Comparison of Statistical Data on the Jamaican Labour Force 1953–61', *Social and Economic Studies,* Vol. 13, No. 4, 1964.

Cumper, G.E. (1970), 'Two Notes on the Multiplier', *Social and Economic Studies,* September 1970.

Dag Hammerskjold, Seminar (1969), 'The Development and Promotion of Tourism in Africa', *Report,* 1969.

De Castro, S. (1967), 'Problems of the Caribbean Air Transport Industry', *Studies in Regional Economic Integration,* Vol. 2, No. 6, University of the West Indies, ISER, 1967.

Demas, W. (1965), *The Economics of Development in Small Countries with Special Reference to the Caribbean,* McGill, 1965.

Demas, W. (1970), 'The Prospects for Developing Agriculture in the Small Commonwealth Territories: The Role of the Small-Scale Farmer' in *Proceedings of the Fifth West Indian Agricultural Economics Conference,* University of the West Indies, St Augustine, Trinidad, 1970.

Department of Employment (UK), *Manpower Studies No. 10: Hotels,* HMSO 1971.

Dosser, D. (1962), 'General Investment Criteria for Less Developed Countries: A Post Mortem', *Scottish Journal of Political Economy,* Vol. IX, No. 2, June 1962.

Economic Surveys and Projections, British Development Division in the Caribbean, Barbados. A series published for individual islands of the Windwards, Leewards and Northern Group between 1967 and 1970. See British Development Division.

Economist, The London, 5 June 1971.

Edwards, D.T. and Campbell, L.G. (1965), *Agriculture in Antigua's Economy: Possibilities and Problems of Adjustment,* Agricultural Series No. 1, University of the West Indies, Institute of Social and Economic Research (Eastern Caribbean), July 1965.

Elkan, W. and Morley, R. (1971), *Employment in a Tourist Economy: British Virgin Islands,* University of Durham, Department of Economics, July 1971.

Faber, M.L.O. and Bryden, J.M. (1971), 'Multiplying the Tourist Multiplier', *Social and Economic Studies,* March 1971.

Feldstein, M.S. (1964), *Net Social Benefit Calculations and the Public Investment Decision,* Oxford Economic Papers, 1964.

Feldstein, M.S. (1964), 'The Social Time Preferance Discount Rate', *Economic Journal,* 1964.

Financial Times, London

Forbes, Urias (1970), 'The West Indies Associated States: Some Aspects of the Constitutional Arrangements', *Social and Economic Studies,* March 1970.

Foster, C.D. in Lawrence (Ed.) Operational Research and the Social Sciences, 1966.

Grenada *Hotels Aid Ordinance No. 12 of 1953.*

Grenada *(Amendment) Ordinance No. 19 of 1956.*

Grenada *(Amendment) Ordinance No. 14 of 1958.*

Grenada *(Amendment) Ordinance No. 16 of 1965.*

Griffin, K. (1969), *Underdevelopment in Spanish America,* Allen and Unwin, 1969.

Gulhati, I. and Levitt, K. 'Income Effect of Tourist Spending', *Social and Economic Studies,* 1970.

Harewood, J. (1963), 'Employment in Trinidad and Tobago, 1960', 1960 Population Census Research Programme No. 5, University of the West Indies, Jamaica, 1963.

Harewood, J. (1966), 'Employment in Grenada, 1960', *Social and Economic Studies,* Vol. 15, No. 2, 1966.

Hart, K. and Hart, M.N. (1971), 'Manpower Survey of the Cayman Islands', 1971, Government of the Cayman Islands (unpublished report).

Hasan, P. (1960), 'The Investment Multiplier in an Underdeveloped Economy', *Economic Policy for Development,* Penguin, 1971.

Hawkins, Irene (1971), 'Caribbean Transport' in *Financial Times,* 25 May 1971.

Hicks, J.R. (1959), 'The Foundations of Welfare Economics', *Economic Journal,* 1939.

HMSO, *Annual Statements of the Trade of the United Kingdom.*

HMSO, *Constitutional Proposals for Antigua, St Kitts-Nevis, Anguilla, Dominica, St Lucia, St Vincent and Grenada,* Cmnd. 2865, 1965. Later embodied in the West Indies Act of 1967, and the various Constitution orders.

HMSO, *Proposals for an Eastern Caribbean Federation,* Cmnd. 1746, 1962.

Howard, H. (1971), 'The Problem of Tourism', *Financial Times,* 1 July 1971.

IATA (International Air Transport Association), *World Air Transport Statistics,* No. 13, 1968.

Institute of Social and Economic Research (ISER) of the University of the West Indies, *Statistical Digests.*

IUOTO (International Union of Official Travel Organisations), *Economic Review of World Tourism,* Geneva, 1970.

IUTO, *International Travel Statistics,* published annually since 1953.

IUOTO, *Study on the Economic Impact of Tourism on National Economics and International Trade,* special issue of *Travel Research Journal,* 1966, Geneva.

IUOTO, *Tourist Bibliography Series.*

IUOTO, *Tourist Legislation* Documentation Service.

IUOTO, *World Travel* (Magazine of IUOTO).

Jefferson, O. (1970), 'Economic Situation of the Commonwealth Caribbean', paper presented to the Human Resources Seminar, University of the West Indies, August 1970.

Johnson, H.G. (1967), *Economic Policies Towards the Less Developed Countries,* Brookings Institute, 1967.

Joshi, V. (1972), 'Rationale and Relevance of the Little–Mirrlees Criterion', *Bulletin of the Oxford Institute of Economics and Statistics,* February 1972.

Kaldor, N. (1939), 'Welfare Propositions of Economics and Interpersonal Comparisons of Utility', *Economic Journal,* 1939. Reprinted in Arrow and Scitovsky (1969).

Leibenstein, H. (1957), *Economic Backwardness and Economic Growth,* John Wiley, 1957.

Levitt, K. and Gulhati, I. (1970), 'Income Effect of Tourist Spending: Mystification Multiplied: A Critical Comment on the Zinder Report', *Social and Economic Studies,* September 1970.

Lewis, G.K. (1968), *The Growth of the Modern West Indies,* MacGibbon and Kee, 1968.

Lewis, W.A. (1965), *The Agony of the Eight,* Advocate Press, Barbados, 1965.

Lewis, W.A. *Eastern Caribbean Federation.*

Little, I.M.D. and Mirrlees, J.A. (1968), *Manual of Industrial Project Analysis: Volume II Social Benefit: Cost Analysis,* OECD Development Centre, 1968.

Little, I.M.D., Scitovsky, T. and Scott, M. (1970) *Industry and Trade in Some Developing Countries. A Comparative Study,* OEC Development Centre, Paris, 1970.

Little, I.M.D. and Tipping, D.G. (1970), *Social Cost: Benefit Analysis of the Kulai Palm Oil Estate, West Malaysia,* Mimeo, Nuffield College, July 1970.

Little, I.M.D. 'A reply to some Criticisms', *Bulletin of the Oxford Institute of Economics and Statistics,* February 1972.

Lowenthal, David (1960), 'Physical Resources' in Cumper (Ed.) *The Economy of the West Indies,* University of the West Indies (ISER), 1960.

Luce and Raffia (1957), *Games and Decisions,* John Wiley, 1957.

Mamalakis, M. and Reynolds, C.W. (1965), *Essays on the Chilean Economy,* Yale University, Irwin, 1965.

McFarlane, Carmen (1970), 'The Employment Situation in Over-Populated Territories in the Commonwealth Caribbean', paper to the Human Resources Seminar, University of the West Indies, Jamaica, August 1970.

Mackintosh, A.S. *et al* (1967), 'Fiscal Survey of St Vincent', unpublished Report to the Government of St Vincent, 1967.

Marglin, S.A. (1963), 'The Social Rate of Discount and the Optimal Rate of Investment', *Quarterly Journal of Economics,* Vol. 7, 1963.

Maynard, G. (1970), 'The Economic Irrelevance of Monetary Independence: The Case of Liberia', *Journal of Development Studies,* Vol. 6, January 1970.

Meier, G.M. (1958), International Trade and International Inequality, *Oxford Economic Papers,* Vol. 10, No. 3, October 1958.

Mills, D. (1970B), 'Employment Situation of the Commonwealth Caribbean', paper for the Human Resources Seminar, University of the West Indies, Jamaica, 1970.

Mills, G.E. (1970A), 'Public Adminstration in the Commonwealth Caribbean: Evolution, Conflicts and Challenges', *Social and Economic Studies,* March 1970.

Mirrlees, J.A. and Little, I.M.D. (1968), *Manual of Industrial Project Analysis: Volume II Social Benefit: Cost Analysis,* OECD Development Centre, 1968.

Mishan, E.J. (1971), *Cost Benefit Analysis,* Allen and Unwin, London, 1971.

Mitchell, E. (1968A), *The Costs and Benefits of Tourism in Kenya.* Report prepared for the Kenya Tourist Development Corporation, Institute for Development Studies, University College, Nairobi, 30 November 1968.

Mitchell, F. (1969B), 'The Impact of Tourism on National Income'. Institute for Development Studies Staff Paper No. 30, January 1968, Nairobi.

Mitchell, F. (1969), 'The Value of Tourism in East Africa', Institute for Development Studies, University College Nairobi, Discussion Paper No. 82, July 1969.

Mordecai, Sir John (1968), *The West Indies: The Federal Negotiations,* Allen and Unwin, 1968.

Myint, H. (1954–5), 'The Gains from International Trade and the Backward Countries', Review of Economic Studies, Vol. XXII (2), No. 58 (1954–5) pp. 129–42.

Naipaul, V.S. (1962), *The Middle Passage,* 1962, Andre Deutsch, The references to page numbers refer to the Penguin edition 1969.

Nelson, R. (1956), 'A Theory of the Low Level Equilibrium Trap', *American Economic Review,* December 1956.

Norris, K. (1962), *Jamaica – The Search for an Identity,* Institute of Race Relations, Oxford, 1962.

Nurkse, R. (1953), *Problems of Capital Formation of Underdeveloped Countries,* first published 1953. References from the 1962 Blackwell edition.

Nurkse, R. (1959), *Patterns of Trade and Development,* First Wicksell Lecture, Stockholm, 1959.

Nyerere, President, Essay in the house magazine of the National Development Corporation, Tanzania (circa 1968).

Ogilvie, F.W. (1933), *The Tourist Movement,* Staples Press, 1933.

O'Loughlin, Carleen (1963), *A Survey of Economic Potential and Capital Needs of the Leeward Islands, Windward Islands and Barbados,* HMSO, London, 1963.

O'Loughlin, Carleen (1965), *National Income Statistics of Antigua 1954–64,* University of the West Indies, Institute of Social and Economic Research, Barbados, 1965.

O'Loughlin, Carleen (1966), *Methods and Sources of the National Income Statistics of the Leeward and Windward Islands,* University of the West Indies, Institute of Social and Economic Research, (Eastern Caribbean) December 1966.

O'Loughlin, Carleen (1968), *Economic and Political Change in the Leeward and Windward Islands,* Yale, 1968.

Padmore, Keith (1966), *National Income Statistics, St Kitts-Nevis-Anguilla, 1953–64,* University of the West indies, Institute of Social and Economic Research (Eastern Caribbean) Statistical Series No. 2, May 1966.

Pearce, D.W. (1971), *Cost:Benefit Analysis,* Macmillan, 1971.

Peters, Michael (1969), *International Tourism,* Hutchinson, 1969.

Philips, W.T. (1966), *A Report on the British Virgin Islands,* Government of the British Virgin Islands, May 1966.

Pope Pius XII, Speech to Directors of Italian Tourist Organisations, 30 March 1952.

Prebisch, R. (1963), 'Development Problems of the Peripheral Countries and the Terms of Trade', in *Towards a Dynamic Development Policy for Latin America,* Ch. 1, UN, 1963.

Prest, A.R. *Fiscal Survey of the British Caribbean,* 1957.

Reynolds, Lloyd G. (1969), 'Economic Development with Surplus Labour: Some Complications', *Oxford Economic Papers* Vol. 21, No. 1, March 1969.

Reynolds, Lloyd G. (1971), *The Three Worlds of Economics,* Yale, 1971.

Rosenstein, Rodan (1943), Problems of Industrialisation of Eastern and South-Eastern Europe, *Economic Journal,* Vol. LIII, 1943. Reprinted in Agarwala and Singh (Ed.) *The Economics of Underdevelopment,* Oxford, 1958,

Runciman, W.G. (1969), 'The three Dimensions of Social Inequality' in Bétaille, A. *Social Inequality,* Penguin Modern Sociology Readings, 1969.

Runciman, W.G. (1972), *Relative Deprivation and Social Justice,* Routledge and Kegan Paul, 1966. Pelican edition 1972.

Rutter, Owen (1933), *If Crab No Walk,* Hutchinson, 1933.

Scitovsky, T. (1941), 'A Note on Welfare Propositions in Economics', *Review of Economic Studies,* 1941. Reprinted in Arrow and Scitovsky (1969).

Scitovsky, T. (1954), 'Two Concepts of External Economies', *Journal of Political Economy,* Vol. 17, 1954. Reprinted in Arrow and Scitosky (1969).

Seers, D. (1964A), *Cuba: The Economic and Social Revolution,* University of North Carolina Press, 1964.

Seers, D. (1964B), 'The Mechanism of an Open Petroleum Economy', *Social and Economic Studies,* 1964. Reprinted by the Economic Growth Center, Yale.

Seers, D. (1969), 'A Step Towards a Political Economy of Development', *Social and Economic Studies,* Vol. 18, 1969.

Sessa, Alberto (1970)., 'Dominant Economics' in *World Travel* April/May 1970 (IUOTO).

Singer, H. (1971), 'Rural Unemployment as a Background to Rural–Urban Migration in Africa', Paper presented to the Conference on Urban Unemployment in Africa, Institute of Development Studies, Sussex, September 1971.

Singer H.W. (1950), 'The Distribution of Gains between Investing and Borrowing Countries', *A.E.R. Papers and Proceedings,* May 1950.

Smith, T.E. (1967), 'Demographic Aspects of Smallness' in Benedict (Ed.) *Problems of Smaller Territories,* Athlone, 1967.

Stewart, F. and Streeten, P. (1972), 'Little–Mirrlees Methods and Project Appraisal', *Bulletin of the Oxford Institute of Economics and Statistics,* February 1972.

Strauss, J., 'Pilot Project examining the Structure of Food Demand in Hotels in Grenada', currently in draft.

Strauss, J., 'Tourism, Agriculture and Economic Growth in the Windwards and Leewards' (mimco.), Department of Agricultural Economics and Farm Management, University of the West Indies, St Augustine, Trinidad.

St Lucia, *Hotels Aid Ordinance No. 25 of 1959.*

St Lucia, *Hotels Aid Amendment Ordinance No. 22 of 1961.*

St Vincent, *Hotels Aid Ordinance, 1954.*

St Vincent, *Hotels Aid Amendment Ordinance, 1958.*

St Vincent, *Hotels Aid Amendment Ordinance, 1963.*

Taylor, W. (1970), in 'A Scotsman's Log', *The Scotsman,* 7 April 1970.

Thoburn, J. (1971), 'Exports in the Economic Development of West Malaysia', 1971, Ph.D. Thesis submitted to the University of Alberta, Canada.

Thomas, C.Y. (1963), 'The Balance of Payments and Money Supplies of a Colonial Monetary Economy', *Social and Economic Studies,* March 1963.

Tripartite Economic Survey, Report of the HMSO, 1967. (Referred to as the *Tripartite Survey*)

UN, *Statistical Yearbook 1968.*

UN, *Yearbook of National Income Statistics.*

UN, *Yearbook of Trade Statistics.*

University of the West Indies, ISER, Barbados, *Abstract of Statistics,* 1964.

University of the West Indies, Proceedings of the Fifth West Indian Agricultural Conference, St Augustine, Trinidad, 1970.

Watkins, M.H. (1963), 'A Staple Theory of Economic Growth', *The Canadian Journal of of Economics and Political Science,* Vol. XXIX, No. 2, May 1963.

Watty, F. (1970), 'Alien Land Ownership and Agricultural Development: Issues, Problems and Policy Framework' in *Proceedings* of the Fifth West Indian Agricultural Economics Conference, University of the West Indies, Trinidad, 1970.

Weeks, John (1971), 'The Problem of Urban Imbalance', Paper to the September 1971 Conference on Urban Unemployment in Africa, Institute of Development Studies, Sussex.

World Council of Churches, 'Leisure — Tourism: Threat and Promise', Geneva, 1970.

Yankey, J.B. and Watty, W.R.F. (1969), 'A Small Agricultural Economy in CARIFTA: A Case Study of Dominica' in *Proceedings of the Fourth West Indian Agricultural Economics Conference,* University of the West Indies, Trinidad, 1969.

Zinder, H. and Associates, Inc. (1969), *The Future of Tourism in the Eastern Caribbean,* May 1969 (otherwise known as the *Zinder Report*)

230

96; applied to *Tripartite Survey*, 5–6, 200–4, 209–10, and to *Zinder Report*, 5–6, 194–200, 205–8; conclusions from, 215, 217–18; method used for, 82–8; for 'project' of 100-room hotel, 172–83

cotton: in Antigua, 26; export of, 25, 27, 47

cruise ships, 100–1, 107, 117; expenditure on harbour for, 142; expenditure by tourists from, 112, 114

debt, servicing of, 46, 143

Declaration of Grenada (1971), 11

deprivation, relative: concept of, 92, 93, 96

developed and developing countries: international tourist arrivals and receipts for, 60; net balance of tourist receipts and expenditures for, 64–5, 215; regional sources of tourist arrivals in, 61

'diseconomies', in cost–benefit analysis, 82, 89

discount rate, in cost–benefit analysis, 79, 81–2

distribution and finance sector, 38–40; contribution to GDP from, 32, 49, 50, 51, 52; in national accounts, 157; tourist receipts in, 156; use of transport by, 41; *see also* finance and insurance sector

domestic sectors, contributions to GDP from, 32, 47

Dominica, 10, 11n, 12
    capital formation in, 30; sources of capital revenue in, 46
    domestic sectors in: agriculture, 33, 34, 47; distribution and finance, 38, 40; manufacturing, 37; public utilities, 45
    employment in, 16
    GDP by sectors in, 49, 51, 52
    government expenditure in: on infrastructure, 140, 141, 142; promotional, 145
    hotels in: capital in, 120; concessions to investors in, 148; contribution to GDP from, 28; revenues of, 123, 124; statistics for, 117, 118
    hydroelectric power in, 37n
    population and land of, 12, 13
    tourist multiplier for, 162
    tourists in: expenditure of, 109, 110, 111; statistics for, 100, 104

Eastern Caribbean Currency Authority, 39,, 134

economic growth, long-term: tourist development and, 146

economies of scale, in cost–benefit analysis, 88

education, 14n, 19, 21, 213; *see also* training, vocational

elections: Federal (1958), 9; Grenada (1962), 10

electricity undertakings, 44, 45; in calculation of GDP by sectors, 37, 50

emigration, British restrictions on, 11, 18

employment: in domestic agriculture, 33; of expatriates, *see* expatriates; in hotel industry, 126–32, 135, 147, 148; per hotel room, 73, 126–7, 216; percentage of population in, 15, 17, 213; ratio of capital to, in hotel industry, 73n, 132; tourism as creator of opportunities in, 72–3

Europe, in international tourist business, 59, 60, 62

excise duty, in revenue, 43, 134

expatriate employees: as crew on yachts, 115n; future policy on, 220; in higher occupational grades, 20, 22, 128, 214, 216, 217, 218; incomes of, 28, 130, 131 131–2, 216; incomes of, in cost–benefit analysis, 79, 80, 85, 179–81, and in multiplier analysis, 75; not considered in *Zinder Report*, 200

exports: developers exempt from duties on, 150; duties on, in revenue, 43, 134; in GDP, 3, 24; marketing difficulties for, 4

farmers: loans to, 39–40; peasant, probable losers from tourism, 218–19; percentage of population as, 19; subsistence, not counted in census as economically active, 15n

farms: percentage of land in, 13; sizes of, 13–14

finance and insurance sector: in calculation of tourist multiplier, 156; tourist receipts in, 156; *see also* distribution and finance sector

fiscal policies: proposals for, 220–1; and tourism, 31, 133, 134–9, 216–17, 219

fisheries: expenditure on development of (Antigua), 53; opportunities in, 221

Florida, competitive with Caribbean, 134

food: estimated extent of self-sufficiency in, 34; total supply of, as percentage of GDP, 33; value and growth rate of imports of, 32–3, 34, 42

foreign exchange: inputs and outputs valued in terms of, in cost–benefit analysis, 83; receipts of, from tourism, 1, 5, 71, 179

forestry, 13

France, tourist development scheme in, 144n

Geest Industries, Ltd, 34

government sector, 41–6; in calculation of tourist multiplier, 156; contribution to GDP from, 32, 49, 51; growth rate of, 52; tourist receipts in, 156

governments: and agriculture, 26, 36, 53; bargaining strength of, 139; and growth of tourism, 133–47; and infrastructure for tourism, *see* infrastructure; revenues of, 43, 84–5

Grenada, 10, 11n
    capital formation in, 30; sources of

tourists in: expenditure of, 110, 111;
statistics for, 100, 104
white plantocracy in, 122n
St Lucia, 10, 11n, 12
capital formation in, 30; sources of capital
revenue in, 46
domestic sectors in: agriculture, 33, 34;
distribution and finance, 40; manufacturing, 37; public utilities, 45
education in, 19
employment in, 16
GDP by sectors in, 49, 51, 52
government expenditure in: on infrastructure, 140, 141, 142; promotional, 145
hotels in: capital and revenues of, 120,
122, 123, 124; concessions to investors
in, 147; contribution to GDP from,
28; statistics for, 117, 118, 119
population and land of, 12, 13
tourists in: density of, 93; dependence on,
91; expenditure of, 110, 111; statistics
for, 100, 101, 103, 104, 106; yachts
chartered by, 107, 114
St Vincent, 10, 11n
capital formation in, 30; sources of capital
revenue in, 46
domestic sectors in: agriculture, 33, 34;
distribution and finance, 40; government, 42; public utilities, 45
employment in, 16, 17
GDP by sectors for, 49, 51, 52
government expenditure in: on infrastructure, 140, 141, 142; promotional, 145
hotels in: capital and revenues of, 120,
123; concessions to investors in, 138,
148; contribution to GDP from, 28;
statistics for, 117, 118
population and land of, 12, 13
tourists in: density of, 93; dependence on,
91; expenditure of, 109, 110, 111;
statistics for, 100, 103, 104; yachts
chartered by, 107
savings, 30, 39–40; effect of tourism on, 36;
net capital inflows in, 156; shortage of
domestic, 81, 121
savings-investment sector, in estimation of
tourist multiplier, 155–6
schooner trade, between islands, 41, 115
season: distribution of tourist arrivals by,
103; and occupancy rate for hotels, 119
sectors: GDP by, 49, 51, 52; matrix of transactions between, 74, 76–7, 166; tourist
receipts by, for different occupancy rates,
173
services, numbers employed in, 17, 18
services sector (other than hotels): in calculation of tourist multiplier, 156; tourist
receipts in, 27–8; see also hotels and
services sector
sewage disposal, 89, 146, 151
sharing mechanism, in employment of unskilled
labour from agriculture, 86

ships, owned and subsidised jointly by islands,
41, 107
small country: definition of, 21n; diseconomies
of scale in government of, 42
social benefits from tourism, 5, 72, 78, 91,
215
cost–benefit calculation of, 87–8, 215,
217, 218; for hotel project, (Version
A) 178–9, (Versions B to G) 179–83;
from Tripartite Survey figures, 203;
from Zinder Report figures, 199, 200
social costs of tourism, 1, 2, 6, 91–6
social welfare function, in cost–benefit analysis of tourism, 79, 80
Spain, tourist expenditure in, 64, 215
spices, export of, 25, 27
sterling, devaluation of (1967), 107
sugar: in Antigua, 26, 139, 142; export of,
24–5, 27, 47; price of, 26
Switzerland, price of land in, 94

tax havens, 20, 38, 44
taxes: in cost–benefit analysis, 84, 86,
174–5; cost of collection of, 84, 175;
exemption of developers from, 31, 42,
134, 136, 147, 148, 150, 151, 152, 174;
not adequate to meet promotional expenditure suggested in Zinder Report, 199;
in operating costs of hotels, 125; in
revenue, 43; tourist expenditure on,
109, 111, 112, 113
telephones, 45
time preference rate (social), 81
Tortola Island (Antigua), 151
tourist, definition of, 99–100
tourist boards, 99, 144, 145, 217
tourist expenditure (1), in Caribbean, 28,
40, 41, 47, 107–15; estimated future
amounts of, (Tripartite Survey) 201–2,
(Zinder Report) 196–7; growth rate of,
66, 67, 107, 109; per hotel bed, 123;
net receipts from, in financing of trade
deficit, 24, 46; by sectors, 111, 156
tourist expenditure (2), international: growth
rate of, 57–8; net balance of, by regions,
63, 64; per head, by regions, 63; percentage of, on foreign travel, 58; as percentage of total consumer expenditure, 57;
receipts from, as percentage of national
income and of visible exports for different
countries, 91; totals for, 59, 60, 63, 214
tourist tax, 134
tourists (1), to Caribbean: length of stay of,
104–5, 114; numbers of, 99–101; regions
of origin of, 102; season and arrivals of,
103; social impact of, 91–6, 219; social
origins of, 35–6; statistics of, 57, 66
tourists (2), international: density of, per
1000 population and per square mile of
land, 93; legislation favouring, 58; numbers
of, 59, 60, 61, 63; rate of growth of numbers of, 66, 67; supposed benefits to

235